The Slaw
and the Slow Cooked

The Slaw and the Slow Cooked

Culture and Barbecue in the Mid-South

Edited by James R. Veteto
and Edward M. Maclin

Foreword by
Gary Paul Nabhan

Vanderbilt University Press
NASHVILLE

© 2011 by Vanderbilt University Press
Foreword © 2011 by Gary Paul Nabhan
Published by Vanderbilt University Press
Nashville, Tennessee 37235
All rights reserved
First printing 2011

This book is printed on acid-free paper.

Library of Congress Cataloging-in-Publication Data

The slaw and the slow cooked : culture and barbecue in the mid-south / edited by James R. Veteto and Edward M. Maclin ; foreword by Gary Paul Nabhan.
  p. cm.
Includes bibliographical references and index.
ISBN 978-0-8265-1801-9 (cloth edition : alk. paper)
ISBN 978-0-8265-1802-6 (pbk. edition : alk. paper)
1. Food habits—Southern States. 2. Barbecuing—Southern States. 3. Cooking, American—Southern style. 4. Southern States—Social life and customs.
I. Veteto, James R. II. Maclin, Edward M.
GT2853.U5S57 2011
394.1′20975—dc22
2011003011

CONTENTS

Foreword:
From Coa to Barbacoa to Barbecue   vii
Gary Paul Nabhan

Acknowledgments   xi

1 Smoked Meat and the Anthropology
of Food: An Introduction   1
James R. Veteto and Edward M. Maclin

**Part I.
Traditional and Contemporary Landscapes
of Mid-South Barbecue**

2 A History of Barbecue
in the Mid-South Region   25
Robert F. Moss

3 Patronage and the Pits: A Portrait,
in Black and White, of Jones Bar-B-Q
Diner in Marianna, Arkansas   43
John T. Edge

4 Piney Woods Traditions at the Crossroads:
Barbecue and Regional Identity
in South Arkansas and North Louisiana   51
Justin M. Nolan

5 Priests, Pork Shoulders, and
   Chicken Halves: Barbecue for a Cause
   at St. Patrick's Irish Picnic   65
   Kristen Bradley-Shurtz

6 Identity, Authenticity, Persistence,
   and Loss in the West Tennessee
   Whole-Hog Barbecue Tradition   83
   Rien T. Fertel

Part II. Old/New Barbecue Moving Forward

7 The Changing Landscape
   of Mid-South Barbecue   107
   Edward M. Maclin

8 Swine by Design: Inside
   a Competition Barbecue Team   117
   Jonathan Deutsch

9 Barbecue as Slow Food   151
   Angela Knipple and Paul Knipple

10 Southern Barbecue Sauce
   and Heirloom Tomatoes   167
   James R. Veteto

11 Mid-South Barbecue in the Digital Age
   and Sustainable Future Directions   181
   Edward M. Maclin and James R. Veteto

   Contributors   199

   Index   203

FOREWORD

From Coa to Barbacoa to Barbecue

Gary Paul Nabhan

Start with a *coa*, a sharpened, skinned stick that may be used for digging and planting seeds or for skewering and smoking mammalian meats, fish, or fowl. *Coa* may indeed be one of the oldest and most widespread words in the Americas—including the Caribbean. It may also be embedded in one of the oldest and most ubiquitous means of slowly smoking meats and making them savory and storable, rather than leaving them raw and perishable: the *babricot* of the Taino and Carib, the *barbacoa* of the Hispanicized natives and immigrants, and the *barbecue* of the Anglicized natives and immigrants of the New World.

When meat, fish, or fowl is crucified on coa skewers and placed over red-hot coals, the flesh does not perish but is made immortal and eminently memorable by both fire and smoke. The coas may be set vertically as the barbecue racks in Argentina are, or woven into a horizontal grate as they are in northern Mexico, or leaned at 60-degree angles as they are at salmon bakes in the Pacific Northwest. Of course, the quality of the meat itself matters most—whether it is from pig or peccary, Criollo cattle or Churro sheep—but whatever meat is chosen will be transmogrified by the kind of wood used to roast or grill it: hickory, oak, pecan, alder, or mesquite. Each wood offers a certain intensity and duration of heat which reshapes the muscle and fat cells in the meat, but it also infuses the meat with antioxidants from the smoke passing through it. Sweet smoke, savory smoke, dark smoke or light—they waft up from the fire as wisps of vaporized carbon and secondary chemicals, then linger.

But meat, fire, and smoke are not enough to make *barbecue* as many recognize it—by taste, smell, and sight—today. The term *barbecue* has, in many hills and hollers, become synonymous with a savory sauce, although that was not always its meaning. The savory sauces and dry rubs of the Taino and Carib first encountered by the Spanish may have had several different red, green, yellow, and orange peppers among their ingredients—*aji, chilli, chilpotli,* or *habanero*—but they likely included a distant kin of black peppers as well: allspice, *pimienta gorda,* or *pimienta de Tabasco*. The original American *chilmollis* or *moles* may have also included cacao, vanilla, wild oreganos, wild sages, or epazotes. Old World immigrants and refugees—not just blue-blooded Spaniards but also Moors and Jews escaping the Inquisition—introduced to these sauces cumin, cinnamon, coriander, cane sugar, black pepper, mustard, onion, and garlic.

The immigrants and refugees—Europeans, Africans, and Asians—also introduced another ingredient for flavoring and saving meats from spoilage: vinegar. The "cooking" of meat, fish, and fowl in vinegar, as well as sour orange and sweet lime juice, in the manner of *ceviches* and *escabeches* go back to ancient times, and these culinary techniques were perfected by the Persians, Arabs, and Berbers. They arrived in the Americas along with swine, sheep, cattle, and goats that were so large they could not be consumed in a single meal—hence the need for additional preservation techniques so that the meats could be "put up." The vinegar transforms the very cells of flesh, fish, and fowl very much like smoke does.

Of course, concentrated sugars and salts, through their osmotic processes, may do the same. And so, sorghum cane syrup, maple syrup, fruit syrup, and prickly pear cactus syrup were added to the sauces. In some cases, so was alcohol in the form of mescal, whiskey, or various and sundry other "moonshines." The more illegal the fermented or distilled juice used to marinate or baste the meat, the more memorable the meal.

When mixed in particular proportions, these ingredients—fire, smoke, spices, vinegars, sweets, and meats—are so iconic that entire cultural communities link their identities to them. The rituals of preparing for a barbecue in each American culture are tightly scripted, with gesture, vocal tone, and social behavior being learned at an early age and viscerally maintained for decades—until death do the barbecue master and his (or her) barbecue pit part. Most of the current masters have had no book to guide them; their training has been as rigorous as that of Zen masters, guided by elders who both encourage and critique every move.

Indeed, barbecue is not merely the process or the paraphernalia of grilling, or the meaty burnt ends that result, but a choreographed dance, from woodlot to smokehouse to mixing bowl to platter to picnic table, bar, roadside diner, or juke joint. Prospective barbecue aficionados are selected early by their fathers, mothers, aunts, or uncles and nurtured for many years, until their predilection for a certain balance of smoke, sour, sweet, and meat is finely honed. They may not be able to verbally describe how to reach that perfect balance, but they definitely know when it has been achieved or when some gargantuan effort seems to have missed the mark. Satisfaction with barbecue is a lot like pregnancy—either you are or you aren't.

Someone recently wondered aloud to me, "Why in the world would anthropologists and historians, linguists and ethnozoologists, theologians and evolutionary biologists be consumed by the topic of barbecue?" What other American food and its preparation are so strongly linked to the distinctive identities of so many American cultures? We are *what* and *where* we eat, but we are also *how we prepare* our most beloved foods. And who we prepare it with. And who we eat it with. And who we leave out beyond the smokehouse, who longingly wishes they were in there with us, no matter how stifling hot and claustrophobically congested it may be. No other American food is imbued with such symbolism, such smoke, such *spirit*.

Not far from my rustic office on Tumamoc Hill in downtown Tucson, Arizona, there is a barbecue joint and African American history museum that are joined at the hip, sharing the same rundown building in a neighborhood filled with indigents, derelicts, and others that mainstream society consider "lowlifes." And yet on any day of the week, politicians, police officers, and college professors congregate there with construction workers, surveyors, truck drivers, and street musicians. The owner-chef—who was born in Texarkana, not far from the Arkansas line—had an incredibly successful professional career before he returned to his true love, barbecue. The folks who flock to his tables may be from Texas, Arkansas, Georgia, Mississippi, Tennessee, Kansas City, or Chicago, but when they come there for lunch, dinner, or to cure a hangover, they know they are coming for communion, to reaffirm their perceived (and felt) roots. If food rituals are the last cultural practices that many cultures abandon when they become refugees or immigrants in a strange land, then barbecue is the glue that holds America together, bringing our past into some fleeting moment of flowering, giving us hope for a sweeter, if hotter and smokier, future. Barbecue is to America what bread and wine are to Italy. It is our sacrament.

ACKNOWLEDGMENTS

James R. Veteto would first of all like to thank his father, Benny Veteto, who introduced him to the pleasures of proper Mid-South barbecue at an early age with endless hours of side trips, mom and brother in tow, through the countryside to find the perfect barbecue sandwich. He would also like to thank his late grandfather, Jim Neff, who took the time to teach him the art of smoking meat, and his late grandmother, Fletch Neff, who—along with being an excellent host and creator of countless side dishes—helped Grandpa Neff come up with the family barbecue sauce known as "Colonel Neff's Sauce." He would also like to thank all the other family members and friends whom he has shared barbecue camaraderie and cheer with over the years: you are too numerous to mention here but this book is for all of you. Special mention goes to Robert Rhoades, who co-created the venue (the Southern Seed Legacy Project's Old Timey Seed Swap at Agrarian Connections Farm) with his wife, Virginia Nazarea, at which the barbecue collaboration between Edward and James was first born. Eli Bortz at Vanderbilt University Press deserves much credit for suggesting the volume and for his gracious support throughout. Finally James would like to thank his wife, Alena—without whose loving support none of this was possible—and his young son, Ian, for giving him hope that the family barbecue tradition has indeed survived another generation.

Edward Maclin would like to thank his wife, Ellie, for her support and assistance throughout the brainstorming and editing processes. Thanks to his daughter, Evie, for her seemingly endless patience and occasional "help" at the keyboard. A little bit of exuberant banging goes a long way toward reorganizing one's thoughts. Thanks also to his family for their support and assistance, and for introducing him to barbecue at a young age; to the Society for Applied Anthropology, whose annual meeting planted the seeds for this work; to the contributors, whose enthusiasm and diligence brought this volume together so rapidly; and to the many friends and colleagues who have shared in the barbecue adventure, for indulging him in this productive and delicious effort.

The Slaw and the Slow Cooked

1

Smoked Meat and the Anthropology of Food
An Introduction

JAMES R. VETETO AND EDWARD M. MACLIN

It seems only fitting that anthropology would have an interest in the slow cooking of meat on a spit over an open pit of coals, as it is one of the most ancient ways of food preparation known to human beings. Yet it is also a contemporary foodway in many parts of the world, so its persistence spans nearly the whole trajectory, as we currently know it, of human cultural experience. Many would perhaps not be surprised then that the much discussed and maligned etymology of the word *barbecue* can be traced to the Spanish word *barbacoa*, a bastardization of an American Indian term, used by the pioneering nineteenth-century anthropologist E. B. Tylor to describe "a framework of sticks set upon posts" (used by the Arawak of Hispaniola to smoke animals over a hot coals) in his work *Researches into the Early History of Mankind and the Development of Civilization* (cited in Warnes 2008). Of course, Andrew Warnes has argued that Tylor's term was significantly lacking in accuracy and infused with Eurocentrism. Nonetheless, it is striking that one of the founding fathers of anthropology has been so influential in the origin and spread of the word that we now know, in English, simply as "barbecue" (so much so that the *Oxford English Dictionary* cites Tylor, apparently inaccurately, as the original authority on the term).

Nearly all anthropologists, and perhaps a smattering of other anthropologically savvy readers, will recognize that our title is a play on the book *The Raw and the Cooked*, by the great French structural anthropologist Claude Lévi-Strauss (1969). Lévi-Strauss saw these two categories of food as representing a pair of binary opposites that denoted a deeper level of structural organization universally common to

1

all human beings. Ours is not quite such a broad claim. By denoting "Slaw" and "Slow Cooked," we have pointed out two components of a barbecue meal that are ubiquitously present in all subregions of the American South. However, that is where our modest structural analysis will end, not the least of reasons being that the human culinary variation laid upon those two basic categories of food is so dazzlingly diverse and particular that it prompted barbecue scholar John Shelton Reed to famously make the observation that "Southern barbecue is the closest thing we have in the U.S. to Europe's wines or cheeses; drive a hundred miles and the barbecue changes" (2004, 78).

Situated among a wide diversity of world barbecue traditions are those of the American South, where intraregional variations of slow-cooked, smoked meat have an almost cultlike following. It is an oft-repeated saying in the South that there are three subjects that must either be avoided in casual conversation or be defended to the death, and those are, in no particular order, religion, politics, and barbecue (with college football not far behind as a fourth contentious topic). This book is a collection of essays that articulate a kaleidoscopic look at one of the major barbecue regions within the U.S. South, that of the Mid-South. West Tennessee/Memphis is the best known, and arguably the hub, of the Mid-South barbecue tradition and as such receives the bulk of our attention. Yet the spokes of this hub reach out into neighboring subregions and states. This collection investigates snapshots of Mid-South barbecue from middle Tennessee and Mississippi to central and southern Arkansas, and even into the Piney Woods of northernmost Louisiana.

Our delineation of the Mid-South is, of course, to a large extent arbitrary, but has also been borne out through the life experiences and ethnographic work of the authors. Veteto came of age eating barbecue at family gatherings and roadside joints between Lexington, Tennessee, and Hot Springs, Arkansas, every summer, and Maclin grew up firmly in the West Tennessee barbecue tradition from the vantage point of his family's historic farmstead near Stanton, Tennessee. Though Veteto noticed differences between the barbecue served in Lexington and Hot Springs, he also observed that they were a lot more similar to each other than to the barbecue of North Carolina, Georgia, or Texas. Other scholars have likewise noticed continuity in the barbecue of the Mid-South, but have defined the region in slightly different geographic terms. For instance, Southern food writer John Egerton sees Mid-South barbecue as existing in the section of Tennessee "that includes the area north of

Jackson and around Dyersburg. It extends into parts of Arkansas and Kentucky. There are, of course, exceptions to the rule, but that's barbecue country to me" (qtd. in Kelly 2007, 112). In this book we will attempt to define our interpretation of Mid-South barbecue as we go along. We are confident that readers will get a better understanding of the variety and commonalities of barbecue served within the region as they read through the case studies presented in this volume. We will also challenge the boundaries of our delineated region by presenting case studies from border areas such as the Timberlands of southern Arkansas and northernmost Louisiana, where barbecue enthusiasts are torn between two competing traditions: the Delta-style Mid-South pork barbecue and vinegar-based sauces found in the eastern portion of the Timberlands, and the Texas-style beef brisket and sweeter sauces found in its more westerly locations (see Nolan, Chapter 4, this volume).

Unfortunately, Southern barbecue has received scant attention in the vast literature of the anthropology of food. Warnes (2008) argues that this is because of a bias by famous anthropological food scholars such as Sidney Mintz, who dismiss the assumed-to-be completely invented, commercialized, and unhealthy nature of Southern barbecue in favor of the more organic and traditional lifeways of regions such as Mediterranean Europe. Warnes also argues that Southern barbecue revels in disdain toward such elitist notions, upholding its grease, paper towels, plastic plates and cutlery, and drive-through windows in an almost punklike contempt for the conventions of an effete Western civilization, and that such competing attitudes are to some extent a carryover from the relegation of native ways of cooking meat to a barbaric and "savage slot" by the very first European explorers to visit the New World. Whatever the reasons for the absence of serious anthropological scholarship on Southern barbecue, the resulting silence is one that we hope to, at least in part, begin to rectify with the publication of this volume.

In fact, the barbecue tradition of the Mid-South touches on many of the themes current in the anthropology of food and culture, and we will highlight several of the most salient here. To start, it is a culturally constructed phenomenon that is both traditional in many regards and at the same time undergoing constant change and reformulation. Warnes (2008) traces the construction of barbecue to Spanish conquistadors who characterized the cooking of various meats over fire and coal as a savage and barbaric act. The early essentialisms of the conquistadors continued wherever waves of European colonists cast their gaze upon the native "savages" of the New World and their "primitive" cooking techniques. This historical revision, using his own interpretation and expansion of the theoretical framework set forth in Eric Hobsbawm and Terence Ranger's classic *The Invention of Tradition* (1983), has led Warnes to draw the following conclusion: "We need to grasp that this most contentious food is necessarily transatlantic—that European ideas of the primitive have shaped it from Day One, and that its native credentials have been somewhat overstated. We need to grasp, in other words, that barbecue is an invented tradition" (2008, 4). After making a complex historical argument about the Eurocentric and racist origins of Southern barbecue, Warnes also notes that the dubious history of barbecue has helped influence, but has maintained a degree of separation from, a "pit" barbecue tradition that has quite often served to help bridge deep racial divides. It is with this pit tradition that this volume is primarily engaged. Although Warnes's observation that Southern barbecue is an invented tradition is a point well taken and undoubtedly an important contribution to the history of the evolution of the cuisine, his assertion that barbecue was essentialized as savage by an all-embracing and seemingly homogeneous European gaze is probably somewhat overstated.

John Shelton Reed and Dale Volberg Reed (2008), for example, have traced Southern barbecue in the North Carolina Piedmont tradition back to its predecessors in German-speaking and other regions of Europe and found that the barbecuing of meat slowly over hot coals has been an acceptable form of cooking since at least the Middle Ages. Smoked pork shoulder, or *Schäufele*, is a specialty in the Franconia region of southern Germany, where pork is the traditional meat of the peasant classes. Tracing the lineages of the founding purveyors of barbecue restaurants in and around Lexington, North Carolina, Reed and Reed show that they all come from significantly German heritages, and it is more than likely that their ancestors sprang from a large German peasantry who immigrated to America in the eighteenth and nineteenth centuries. They conclude that slow-smoked pork, flavored with vinegar and other spices, was not in fact a taste that was alien and "savage" to German American immigrants, but a time-honored tradition they brought with them from the Old World that changed and evolved as they met with then-exotic New World ingredients such as tomatoes and peppers. The tensions between the constructed and well-researched histories provided by Warnes and by Reed and Reed are symptomatic of larger issues pertaining to the push-and-pull or hybridizing tendencies of cultural forces such as tradition, change, invention and reinvention, modernity, revitalization, and essentialism that are present in almost all contemporary studies of food and culture in anthropology (e.g., Counihan and Van Esterik 1997) and other disciplines.

Identity formation is also a central theme in food and culture studies, and "like all culturally defined material substances used in the creation and maintenance of social relationships, food serves to both solidify group membership and set groups apart. . . . Ethnicity is born of acknowledged difference and works through contrast. . . . Once imagined, such cuisines provide added concreteness to the idea of national or ethnic identity" (Mintz and Dubois 2002, 109). Southern barbecue is a tradition and cuisine that has been used both to promote in-group regional solidarity and (by outsiders) to denigrate those who participate in eating it. No other foodstuff has contributed more to the formation and delineation of diverse Southern identities: "Of all the signature foods of the South, none unites and divides the region like barbecue. When it comes to barbecue, southerners cannot agree on meat, sauce, technique, side dishes, or even how to spell the word. What they can agree on is that barbecue in all its variety is one of the fond traditions that makes the South the South. It drifts across class and racial distinctions like the sweet vapors over hickory embers" (Auchmutey 2007, 22–23).

In other words, to be a Southerner is to love barbecue with very few exceptions. And to be a North Carolinian is to love either Eastern or Piedmont styles of barbecue, to be from West Tennessee is to love to order particular cuts of meat from the whole hog, to be from Memphis is to prefer shoulder sandwiches and wet or dry ribs, and to be from most of Texas is to expect nothing but smoked beef brisket the moment the word *barbecue* has been uttered. And these are not just rhetorical and stylistic arguments—they are fundamental to the identity formation of each situated Southerner who claims them. In North Carolina, defenders of Eastern-style whole-hog barbecue served with a sauce consisting of little more than "God's own apple cider vinegar, salt and pepper" (Dennis Rogers, qtd. in Reed and Reed 2008, 38) insist that they are preparing barbecue in the old, traditional, orthodox manner, as opposed to the Piedmont-based "upstarts" who prepare their barbecue shoulders "Lexington style" and serve it with a "dip" that sinfully includes miniscule amounts of tomato. The Piedmont purveyors of Lexington-style barbecue, by contrast, insist that there are parts of the whole hog that you just do not want to eat and that they have vastly improved on methods that began in the eastern part of the state but have remained locked in a pattern of semi-arrested infancy there (Reed and Reed 2008).

John Shelton Reed has even gone so far as to suggest that Southerners replace that long-standing and controversial symbol of pan-Southern regional identity, the rebel flag, with a more fitting representation of their cultural unity:

> I once suggested half-seriously that if the South needs a new flag—as it surely does—we could do no worse than to use a dancing pig with a knife and fork. You want to talk about heritage, not hate. . . . That represents a heritage we all share and can take pride in. Barbecue both symbolizes and contributes to community. And that's without even mentioning its noncommercial manifestations—for instance, in matters like fund-raising for volunteer fire departments. But there's another side to this coin. It's often the case, and it is in this one, too, that community is reinforced by emphasizing its differences from and with outsiders. (2004, 81)

He goes on to elaborate on how barbecue helps to create and maintain diversity among unique and localized Southern identities:

> As I wrote once, barbecue is not like grits—in more ways than just the obvious. Grits (if you'll excuse the image) glue the South together. Barbecue, on the other hand—well, you could say that it pits community against community. This rivalry, this competitive aspect of barbecue, has been institutionalized in the formal contests that seem to have become a permanent feature of the Southern landscape.
> . . . And those traditions reflect and reinforce the fierce localism that has always been a Southern characteristic, the "sense of place" that literary folk claim to find in Southern fiction, the devotion to states' rights and local autonomy that was an establishment characteristic of Southern politics long before it became a major headache for the Confederate States of America. (2004, 82)

Across much of the South and the Mid-South, ethnicity, for better or worse, is often cast in terms of a binary distinction between black and white. This is despite considerable ethnic and racial diversity within the region. In one sense, such a dualistic distinction makes life seemingly simpler, but it also washes over a great deal of underlying cultural variation. And the barbecue tradition of the Mid-South is not immune from this tendency, often being cast solely in terms of black and white by those who participate in eating and discussing it. The racial politics and identities associated with barbecue are touched on from various angles in many of the essays in this collection and are instructive in the complexity that they reveal. We refrain from commenting much more on this controversial subject here, preferring instead to let our readers form their own interpretations of the empirical fieldwork presented in the case studies that follow. We will say that it is clear that large numbers of people from various ethnic backgrounds are involved in and knowledgeable experts at preparing and celebrating the countless delicious variations of unique local barbecues. The importance of barbecue to the identity (in all of its complex forms) of Southerners across the Mid-South is a theme that continually interweaves itself throughout most of the essays in this volume.

The ritual aspects of eating have been identified by anthropologists as another central theme in food and culture studies (Sutton 2001; Mintz and Dubois 2002). This theme is not lost on food writers engaging Southern barbecue; William Schmidt, for example, has described barbecue as "a cultural ritual, practiced with a kind of religious fervor among various barbecue sects, each of whom believes their particular concoction of smoke and sauce and spices is the only true way to culinary salvation" (qtd. in Reed and Reed 2008, 7). John Egerton has also couched his observations about Southern barbecue in overtly religious terms: "There are more barbecue factions and smoked-meat sects around here, each with its own hair-splitting distinctions, than there are denominations in the far-flung Judeo-Christian establishment" (1990, 67).

To elaborate on the theme touched on by Egerton, such distinctions can run along several lines. The smoking of the hog is where it all starts. Hogs are smoked whole or divided into any number of sections to be slow cooked over hot coals: shoulder (subdivided into "Boston butt" and "picnic" cuts), middlin, tenderloin, catfish, ham, or ribs. Each of these sections of the pig is considered desirable for their different eating qualities. Next you have the matter of whether or not to smoke the meat directly over coals or to use indirect heat by cooking the meat slightly to the side of the coals or by way of a side-box smoker. While cooking the meat, it further has to be determined whether to moisturize the meat while cooking it, by spraying it with water or basting it with a special concoction, or to dry-smoke it and add the sauce later. Once you have finished smoking the meat (time varies according to what portion of the hog you use: up to twenty-four hours for whole hog, eight hours for shoulders, and four hours for ribs), the highly contentious subject of how to remove it from the bone and serve it is approached in one of several ways: pulled, shaven, sliced, chopped, minced, chipped, shredded, or ground. In most of West Tennessee and Memphis, for example, barbecue is not considered barbecue unless it is pulled straight off the cut or whole hog by human hands. The entire act of preparing barbecue is typically ritualized from the moment the fire is started and is often done in the company of friends, family, and beer or whiskey. During overnight sessions lasting as long as twenty-four hours, a lot of fun is to be had and life's deepest insights, fears, aspirations, and secrets are oftentimes shared. Topics of a more overtly religious and pious nature are discussed with increased frequency (sans alcohol) when the barbecue is being prepared, as it often is, for a gathering or fund-raiser at a local church (see Bradley-Shurtz, Chapter 5, this volume).

Once you have actually placed the smoked meat onto a plate or between a bun, several more options become readily apparent, not the least of which is what side dish should accompany your barbecue. (In West Tennessee and eastern Arkansas you do not even have to ask to have coleslaw put on top of your pulled or coarse-chopped sandwich meat—it is just assumed.) But we will leave those aside for the moment to focus on the most controversial of all the options—sauce. In the Mid-South you can encounter a variety of sauces, from mustard to vinegar to tomato based, from sweeter to spicier to tangier, and anything else in between. In North Carolina you will encounter a sauce called "dip" that is vinegar combined with a few pepper flakes and a dash of tomato, in parts of Texas and Kansas City you mostly get a thick and sweet sauce the consistency of ketchup, in parts of South Carolina and Georgia you get mustard-based sauces, and in Alabama you can procure barbecue sauce that is mayonnaise based. However, we would argue that a good Mid-South barbecue sauce is usually an attempt at blending four key variables—tomato, vinegar, pepper, and sweetener of choice—with tendencies toward one or the other depending on the tastes of its creator (see Veteto, Chapter 10, this volume).

Despite all this variation, most Southerners who engage in the act of cooking or consuming barbecue think the way they are used to having their barbecue prepared is the only way God intended it to be done. Sitting down to a meal of barbecue excites Southern sensibilities like no other foodstuff; it can only be properly understood as a ritual act of cultural continuity and identity formation. Barbecue has been the central component of meals in many areas of the American South at important family, political, and religious gatherings for the past three hundred years (Reed and Reed 2008; Moss, Chapter 2, this volume). Stephen Smith sums up the ritual aspects of Southern barbecue in metaphorical terms:

> In many ways, the Barbecue Eucharist serves as the perfect metaphor for understanding contemporary Southern society. The catechism contains a reverence for tradition and heritage of the past, the vestiges of rural camp meetings, a chorus of regional chauvinism, a pulpit for oratory, and opportunity for community participation, appreciation for the vernacular, equality of opportunity, and subtle interracial respect. . . .
> The community values represented by the high priest cooks and the dedication of their congregations suggest that the rhetorical ritual of barbecue, characterized by hyperbole and boastful humor among friends, may also serve to further human understanding and humanitarian values among the faithful. As such, it is a regional community ritual worthy of our academic analysis as well as our voracious appetites. (2004, 68)

Since the 1980s, food scholars and anthropologists have increasingly identified gender as an important topic of scholarly inquiry. As Carole Counihan and Penny Van Esterik have noted, "Across history and cultures, women have a special relationship to food and a particularly vivid experience of their bodies" (1997, 3). In the preparation, performance, and consumption of Southern barbecue, however, the participation of women has often been understated and invisible. Men dominate the official stories. Eric Lolis Elie has provided some insight into why that may be the case:

> First of all, barbecue requires the taming of fire, and it was this act of taming that first lighted man's path out of the cold drafts and raw-meat dinners of cave life. Any prehistorian worth his weight in testosterone can tell you with certainty that it was a man, not a woman, who first bent fire to human will. Women are perfectly capable of cooking in controlled environments, of starting fires with pilot lights and adjusting the heat with knobs, the logic goes, but from the beginning of human time, men have lighted fires from sparks and beaten

small flames into blazes. It is this image of themselves that men cling to. . . . Women barbecue cookers are not rare, but neither are they common. . . . To an extent women *don't* barbecue because men *do* barbecue. (1996, 68–70)

Elie's half tongue-in-cheek account seems linked to Warnes's contention that Southern barbecue is entrenched in an essentialized performance of the "savage." And there is certainly an element of that entrenchment in barbecue preparation, particularly in its more modern formulation in events such as barbecue competitions (see Deutsch, Chapter 8, this volume). But there are also more benign reasons why women are not as visible in Southern barbecue traditions. As Elie goes on to write, men have taken over certain American culinary "events" such as making pancakes on Sunday morning, while women have been generally responsible for the day-to-day cooking. Such is often the case with noncommercial Southern barbecue, as the smoker is only lit up on the Fourth of July, Memorial Day, or other special occasions when the man of the house labors a full day over hot coals. Women, however, are not absent from the occasion, as they are usually responsible for preparing side dishes and making sure that the overall timing and preparation of the event go smoothly (see Bradley-Shurtz, Chapter 5, this volume). Elie notes that if women had to cook the barbecue too, it would be too much work. However, men receive the majority of the praise for the event, even though the role of women is just as important to its success.

In the commercial barbecue business, despite the overall dominance of men again, there are also examples of successful female smokers. Amy Evans (2009), oral historian at the Southern Foodways Alliance, has documented case studies in which two of Memphis's most famous barbecue restaurants, Payne's Bar-B-Q and Cozy Corner, were taken over, and have since been run successfully, by the widows of the men they cofounded the businesses with. Elie (1996) has also documented three prominent women in the Texas barbecue trade: Mrs. Softa, Soul Sister, and Sis Ward. Our book, like most on the topic of Southern barbecue, is male dominated in its subject matter, and this reflects the reality of barbecue as a Southern social institution. However, we fully recognize the need for more scholarship on women and gendered spaces in Mid-South barbecue, and several of the chapters in this book address these subjects in varying degrees.

The anthropology of food and memory is another current research theme (Holtzman 2006; Counihan 2004; Sutton 2001; Serematakis

1996) that has particular relevance to the study of Southern barbecue. The smelling, preparing, eating, and sharing of barbecue engages the memories and histories of Southerners in unique ways that parallel those that have been described among other cultures, such as the flood of sensory memories that Serematakis (1996) experiences when biting into a certain old and delicious variety of Greek peach. We are certainly not the only Southerners who, when confronted by even the faintest hint of hickory smoke wafting off the skin of properly smoked pork, experience an immediate flood of fond personal memories. For Veteto, such memories consist mostly of past family gatherings hosted by his late grandparents on the shores of Lake Hamilton in Hot Springs, Arkansas, featuring his grandpa's mouthwatering smoked ribs slathered in the family sauce. Or of watching his grandpa's forehead bead up in sweat as he struggled to finish off a pork sandwich doused in the irresistibly spicy sauce at McClard's Bar-B-Q while his dad cracked jokes about it. In fact, McClard's sauce and restaurant has a primary role in Hot Springs lore, its story known to practically any locals worth their weight in barbecue. According to the official story, as articulated

McClard's Bar-B-Q building.

by the restaurant on their website and every menu in the store, in the 1920s, Alex and Gladys McClard owned Westside Tourist Court in Hot Springs. "When a down-and-out traveler could not come up with the $10 he owed for his two-month stay, he asked the couple to accept instead a recipe for 'the world's greatest bar-b-que sauce.' Since something was better than nothing, the couple accepted the recipe. To their great surprise and delight, they tasted the truth in the traveler's claim. In 1928, the Westside Tourist Court became Westside Bar-B-Q." Much has changed at the restaurant since then, but the kitchen is still manned by second-, third-, and fourth-generation McClards, and the main ingredient is still that "priceless sauce," the recipe for which resides in a safe-deposit box (McClard's Bar-B-Q 2009).

Aside from the actual food, even the location, architecture, and furnishings in barbecue restaurants can contain significant historical memories (both accurate and mythologized). Take, for instance, the origins of a wooden bar that is located inside Papa KayJoe's Bar-B-Que in West Tennessee, according to Devin Pickard, the restaurant's owner:

> Supposedly, when my grandfather passed away—he was 95 years old, so he was a real packrat, never kept house, never kept the house clean. His wife, my grandmother, passed away in the middle 70s, so he was pretty much single for the last like 25 years of his life. He said, his opinion was, if someone wants to come look at my house, I'd just as soon them not come. If they want to come visit me, I want 'em to come. You know, he was into [harvesting wild] ginseng, hunting, growing a garden, and all that. So anyhow, when he died, we were out back kind of cleaning up, and this bar was out underneath a little shed that he had. It had a bunch of wood and old stuff on it. And dad recognized it, and he said, "Hey, that'd be a pretty neat deal to put in your restaurant." So we did. Evidently, it came out of a grocery store. The name of it was Walt Thompson's Grocery, probably back in the 40s, 50s, 60s. It was the type of grocery store like in a lot of small towns. Walt, the owner, would allow folks to run up really large bills, and then when the crops came in, they'd come in and pay it all off at one time. My dad worked there, his brother, lots of kids worked there during the summer, would deliver groceries on a bicycle and all that. So, he said that this was the bar—I don't know if it was maybe the meat-cutting bar or just the bar that kind of sat there with the register on it. Supposedly, and I don't know how true this is, Davy Crockett—now this may be an urban legend—but he supposedly danced on

this bar. I don't know if he got drunk or what. But it was in a, I don't know if it was actually, if he actually did it in the grocery store, and this may have been in a bar, more of a saloon, previous to that. Now I don't have any proof of that. But that's one thing someone told me one time, that Davy Crockett danced on this bar. So, you know, that's something good to tell, whether it's true or not. (Qtd. in Southern Foodways Alliance 2009)

The lot on which the restaurant is built and the name of the joint are also infused with memories, both past and current, linking the generations:

In 1999, my grandfather passed away. He owned all this property. And if you could see, there's a—well, you can see it at some point—there's a hill behind us. There's a house up on that hill. When he passed away, this was all growed up land. So we decided, you know, we had done it for a good long while [cooked barbecue], thought we sort of knew what we were doing, and decided we would give it a shot. We cleaned all this off, built this little building, and so the "Papa" in the Papa KayJoe's name is my grandfather, Papa. [Points to a photo on the wall] That's him with the overalls and all that. The "Kay" is for our daughter. Her name is Kaylee—we call her Kay. And the Joe is for Jordan, our son. We call him Joe. So "Papa KayJoe's." (Ibid.)

Clearly, rather than simply thrown-together shacks of wood and steel located in a commercially desirable location—with a bunch of old flea-market knickknacks thrown around haphazardly to decorate—barbecue restaurants are often historical sites wrapped up in deeply meaningful intergenerational familial and local memories.

The subject matter of this volume is far from being the cheap and greasy bastion of an overly commercialized American culture that many scholars think of when considering (or not considering) fare such as Southern barbecue. We would argue instead that the Southern barbecue tradition, its participants, and it methods—even its seemingly quaint or meaningless commercial artifacts—are often aspects of a localized and particular Southern culture that is deeply infused with history, identity, ritual, memory, gender, and sense of place and belonging. Furthermore, it is currently at the crossroads between tradition and modernity, community cookouts and corporatization, hickory-smoked pits and modern electric cookers. In other words, like other subjects of anthropological inquiry, it is situated in the present postmodern moment, "liquid and prone to incessant reinvention" (Warnes 2008, 91), and is threatened in its more traditional localized forms by homogenous commercialization. As such it is a fascinating topic of inquiry that has much to add to the contemporary study of food and culture.

Despite a decidedly anthropological focus, the contributions to this volume are highly interdisciplinary. Most of the essays come from authors situated in diverse disciplines in the humanities and social sciences, but important and illuminating essays have also been submitted by popular food writers, journalists, and community food activists. We realized very early in our editorial process that anthropologists who have made a study of Southern barbecue are few and far between. Yet the popular literature and culinary scholarship on Southern barbecue is, at this point in its trajectory, perhaps more voluminous than that of any other American food. With this edited volume we hope to bring the unique cultural phenomenon that is Mid-South barbecue to the attention of other scholars working in the anthropology of food and culture, but to do so we have had to seek expertise from writers working outside of our discipline. Following previous studies and methodological recommendations by other researchers (e.g., Brown and Mussell 1984), we agree that the only way to gain an understanding of a subject as complex as food traditions and their relation to culture is to engage an interdisciplinary lens. As editors we have joyfully gleaned insight from all the fine contributions to this volume and have come to realize that any anthropology of Southern barbecue will necessarily borrow insight from and engage a wide variety of expertise from other disciplines, from food writers for popular magazines and journalistic outlets, and particularly from the purveyors of barbecue traditions themselves.

Despite the diverse academic and professional backgrounds of the authors in this volume, ethnography is perhaps the theoretical and methodological approach that stands out as uniting us all. The following chapters contain a strong ethnographic and ethnohistoric presence, suggesting that to truly gain an understanding of regional and ethnic foodways, it is necessary to sit down and get firsthand information from local participants and experts through intensive participant observation and the documentation and analyzing of oral history and interviews. To engage in ethnography is to use one of the most time-honored methodologies of anthropology and helps to make this collection recognizable as "an anthropology," but it is also important to remember that "anthropology is not ethnography" (Ingold 2008) and that ethnography is also a robust fieldwork methodology in current use among many other disciplines as well (Marshall and Rossman 2006). The extensive presence of ethnography as a fieldwork and literary methodology herein also serves to distinguish this book from almost every other work that has been written about Southern barbecue, save a few (e.g., Engelhardt 2009; Elie 1996).

An additional benefit of having among us some of the most established and upcoming food writers working on Southern barbecue from both outside and inside the academy is that it lends readability to many of the chapters that will have appeal beyond academic audiences. Our intent is to create an academically rigorous book with the flexibility of being enjoyed by casual readers on the topic of Southern barbecue. We as coeditors both have family roots in Mid-South barbecue traditions and have learned most of what we know of the subject through oral tradition, down-in-the-pits hog smoking, gatherings of family and friends, and feasting at the tables of the region's many barbecue joints, and we want to be able to receive feedback on our work from the true local experts. We are curious to see how this hybrid collection is received along both sides of the academic-popular divide and sincerely hope it goes down as easily as a plate of smoked ribs slathered with Mid-South-style barbecue sauce and washed down with a big glass of sweet tea. (But then again, the subject *is* barbecue, so we would be mildly disappointed if we didn't at least step on a few toes and start a controversy or two!)

Our argument is that this type of collection should be attempted more often and has the promise of at least two worthwhile opportunities: (1) making academic work more relevant by appealing to a more popular audience, and (2) making popular work more rigorous by situating it, to an extent, within the contemporary theoretical concerns of the academy. This follows efforts by others to develop a more public anthropology through collaboration with individuals outside the discipline (Lamphere 2004; Scheper-Hughes 2009). While the chapters in this volume function independently, together they serve as an attempt to mediate multiple perspectives and engage food enthusiasts, folklorists, historians, anthropologists, and others in a conversation about how Mid-Southern barbecue has developed and how it should develop in the future. As such, our multidisciplinary, dual-audience approach brings a reflexivity common to many ethnographic works since James Clifford and George E. Marcus's *Writing Culture* (1986), combined with a range of writing styles, from the academic to the journalistic. A more public anthropology of food may also be a step toward preserving local food traditions.

The remainder of this introduction will provide an overview of each of the chapters in the book, identifying themes that hold the collection together as a unified, yet diverse, undertaking and situating—but not limiting—it within the range of topics current in the study of food and culture that we have identified above. For the sake of internal structure, we have divided the book into two sections—though the divide is admittedly rough and somewhat arbitrary. The first section, "Traditional and Contemporary Landscapes of Mid-South Barbecue," looks at the creators and purveyors of a rich and varied barbecue tradition in the Mid-South. The second section, "Old/New Barbecue Moving Forward," looks at shifting trends in barbecue, with an eye toward both preserving diversity and recognizing change.

In Chapter 2, Robert F. Moss introduces readers to the origins and evolution of what can be recognized as the barbecue tradition of the Mid-South, placing the region's barbecue in the context of the historical development of other subregions in the South as well. The chapter begins by tracing the development of barbecue in Virginia and the Carolinas and its migration across the Appalachian Mountains into the Mid-South. Moss provides historical vignettes of political rallies featuring barbecue from pioneer times, of how barbecue was experienced by plantation slaves in the antebellum period, and of send-off and welcome-home barbecues for soldiers in times of war. Arguing that American barbecue was relatively uniform up until the late nineteenth and early twentieth centuries, Moss identifies the rise of the barbecue restaurant business as the primary causal agent in the differentiation, development, and continuation of regional Southern styles. He documents the histories of famous Mid-South barbecue restaurants such as Leonard's Pit Barbecue and Charlie Vergos's Rendezvous in Memphis, Tennessee, and McClard's Bar-B-Q in Hot Springs, Arkansas, and of regional specialties such as the Memphis barbecue sandwich. Moss also shows why commercial fast-food barbecue has traditionally been less successful than local mom-and-pop joints in the Mid-South.

In Chapter 3, John T. Edge narrates a personal and ethnographic story about his visits with the family that operates Jones Bar-B-Q Diner in Marianna, Arkansas. He documents the complex historical and contemporary circumstances surrounding the restaurant and delights in its production of excellent barbecue. The chapter touches on the differences between black and white barbecue experiences in the American South and offers insight into why African Americans are overrepresented among barbecue pitmasters in the Arkansas Delta. Edge relates his recent conceptualization of barbecue as something of a "booty call" for Southern whites patronizing black-owned restaurants, allowing whites to receive the benefits of indulgence without suffering the often oppressive socioeconomic circumstances that surround barbecue production in African American communities.

Justin M. Nolan, in Chapter 4, presents an introduction and analysis of the complexity of the barbecue tradition in the Timberlands region of southern Arkansas and northern Louisiana, a crossroads between the Mid-South and Texas styles of preparing barbecue. A native of the region, Nolan visits old friends and pitmasters and locates other local experts through snowball sampling, providing results from fourteen oral history interviews using methods largely drawn from cognitive anthropology. His statistical analysis is complemented by a personal narrative and textual analysis that provide the benefit of triangulating qualitative and quantitative research methods. In a fascinating discovery using correspondence analysis, Nolan found that the barbecue styles of pitmasters could be identified geographically.

In Chapter 5, Kristen Bradley-Shurtz documents the history and contemporary scene of the St. Patrick's Irish Picnic in McEwen, Tennessee, a fund-raiser for the St. Patrick's Church and School that has been ongoing since 1854. Bradley's extensive ethnographic fieldwork, grounded in her personal experience as a former student of the school, reveals an annual barbecue event that has grown to be recognized as one of the major tourist attractions in Tennessee—hailed by the *Guinness Book of World Records* in 1988 as "The World's Largest Outdoor Barbecue"—while also remaining true to its humble roots. Pork and chicken are smoked by intergenerational barbecue teams and feature two secret sauces, the oldest of which is rumored variously to have originated in Ireland or to have developed locally in the 1920s. Along the way, Bradley-Shurtz also challenges assumptions regarding gender roles in traditional barbecue scholarship and shows that work crews at the Irish Picnic are more often divided along familial rather than gender lines these days.

Rien T. Fertel, in Chapter 6, engages the complexity of identity, authenticity, persistence, and loss in the West Tennessee whole-hog barbecue tradition. Fertel's analysis of oral history interviews with ten individuals from eight of the most well-known barbecue establishments in the region traces whole-hog barbecue back to its origins on the farms and homesteads of an older generation. Fertel finds whole-hog barbecue to be not just a method of preparing meat but also a whole way of life and a cultural practice that is of foremost importance to the identity of local people. Fertel also finds controversy—where there was once unity—regarding the corporatization of hog farming, and the topic of traditional smoke pits versus modern electric smokers. Staunch traditionalists like Ricky Parker think that anyone who would convert to an electric smoker is "lazy" and doomed to the production of inferior swine. Other pitmasters like Billy Frank Latham have been converted by the convenience, efficiency, and safety of modern electric smokers. In the final analysis, Fertel finds traditional West Tennessee whole-hog barbecue to be an important, yet endangered, culinary tradition.

Maclin focuses on large-scale change in barbecue and the pork industry in Chapter 7. Drawing from both personal experience and literature on food, history, agriculture, marketing, and economics, he paints a picture of the dynamic tension inherent in the current Mid-South barbecue landscape. He contrasts the popularity of landmark barbecue institutions such as Craig's in De Valls Bluff, Arkansas, with that of barbecue chains like Corky's in Memphis. The juxtaposition of these restaurants, each a success in their own right, acts as a lens for viewing political and economic currents that underpin today's commercial barbecue industry. The glossy photographs and polished delivery that surround the newest wave of barbecue can be seen as a type of food pornography—luring in consumers and justifying the industrialization of pork—while historic barbecue restaurants continue to operate much as they always have.

Jonathan Deutsch, in Chapter 8, continues the theme of old and new barbecue in his ethnography of a competition barbecue team. This is not your typical competition barbecue team, however; it is a group of white-collar professionals who did not grow up within a barbecue tradition of their own. As the team moves through competitions, ongoing narratives reflect what counts as "traditional," what roles are to be played by men versus women, and how new technological innovations are incorporated within the group. Many of these narratives are revealed in moments of tension—physical, mental, and culinary—when team members must decide on a course of action.

Chapter 9 looks at barbecue from a different perspective: that of the Slow Food Movement. Angela and Paul Knipple are food writers and former members of the board of Slow Food Memphis. In this chapter, they explore the history of Slow Food and the place of barbecue within the movement. They look at how barbecue can be conceived in relation to the Slow Food standards of good, clean, and fair. They also place emphasis on threats to barbecue's status as a Slow Food and assert that not all slow-cooked food is Slow Food. The impact of barbecue on the environment and the fairness of labor practices in the hog industry are explored, along with the impact of confined animal feed operations (CAFOs) on hog production. Using the guiding philosophy of the international movement as scaffolding, they describe two very different modes of barbecue production along traditional and modern lines.

Veteto, in Chapter 10, looks at variations in sauce across the region. While pitmasters may be open to visitors looking at their cooking gear or even helping with the smoking process, their sauce recipes are often guarded secrets. Veteto uses examples from the professional barbecue community as well as his own family's sauce to illustrate the unity and diversity of Mid-South sauces, identifying tomato, vinegar, spice, and sweetener as the "Big Four" elements common to most Mid-South barbecue sauces. In conclusion, Veteto ties barbecue sauce to his ongoing research into Southern heirloom tomato varieties, providing descriptions of several heirlooms that would stand up well in the sauce-making process in addition to preserving regional history and agricultural diversity in delicious acts of "eater-based conservation."

We conclude, in Chapter 11, with a view of barbecue in the digital age and an eye toward the future. What do online ordering, social networking groups, and other digital-age technologies mean for barbecue lovers? How does technology shape experience, and culture shape behavior? What does the future of barbecue hold? And as barbecue, culture, and technology continue to coevolve, will those changes lead toward local sustainability and diversity? We identify the incorporation of Southern heritage hogs back into regional barbecue traditions as one particularly promising trend.

Together, the chapters in this volume paint Mid-South barbecue as a tradition that is simultaneously invented, historic, dynamic, and multifaceted. As a subject for study, barbecue contains many of the issues seen with other foods—questions about representations and categorizations, links to health and obesity, the organic movement, and the impacts of increasing globalization (Watson and Caldwell 2005). The cultural politics of barbecue present vast potential for both academic and journalistic research. To paraphrase anthropologist Claude Lévi-

Strauss, barbecue is not only good to eat—it is also "good to think." As anthropological researchers and barbecue aficionados, we have a stake in understanding the full spectrum of barbecue production—especially given that barbecue is such an important part of multiple Southern identities. It is our hope that the chapters in the current volume will contribute to an ongoing dialogue—not only within anthropology but also among multidisciplinary groups of both academic and casual readers.

References

Auchmutey, Jim. 2007. "Barbecue." In *Foodways: The New Encyclopedia of Southern Culture*, vol. 7, edited by John T. Edge, 22–26. Chapel Hill: University of North Carolina Press.

Brown, Linda Keller, and Kay Mussell, eds. 1984. *Ethnic and Regional Foodways in the United States: The Performance of Group Identity*. Knoxville: University of Tennessee Press.

Clifford, James, and George E. Marcus, eds. 1986. *Writing Culture: The Poetics and Politics of Ethnography*. Berkeley: University of California Press.

Counihan, Carole. 2004. *Around the Tuscan Table: Food, Family, and Gender in Twentieth-Century Florence*. London: Routledge.

Counihan, Carole, and Penny Van Esterik, eds. 1997. *Food and Culture: A Reader*. New York: Routledge.

Egerton, John. 1990. *Side Orders: Small Helpings of Southern Cookery and Culture*. Atlanta: Peachtree.

Elie, Lolis Eric. 1996. *Smokestack Lightning: Adventures in the Heart of Barbecue Country*. Berkeley: Ten Speed Press.

Engelhardt, Elizabeth S. D. 2009. *Republic of Barbecue: Stories beyond the Brisket*. Austin: University of Texas Press.

Evans, Amy. 2009. Personal communication. October.

Hobsbawm, Eric, and Terence Ranger, eds. 1983. *The Invention of Tradition*. Cambridge: Cambridge University Press.

Holtzman, Jon D. 2006. "Food and Memory." *Annual Reviews in Anthropology* 35:361–78.

Ingold, Tim. 2008. "Anthropology Is *Not* Ethnography." *Proceedings of the British Academy* 154:69–92.

Kelly, Leslie. 2007. "Barbecue, Memphis, and Tennessee." In *Foodways: The New Encyclopedia of Southern Culture*, vol. 7, edited by John T. Edge, 112–15. Chapel Hill: University of North Carolina Press.

Lamphere, Louise. 2004. "The Convergence of Applied, Practicing, and Public Anthropology in the 21st Century." *Human Organization* 63, no. 4: 431–43.

Lévi-Strauss, Claude. 1969. *The Raw and the Cooked: Introduction to a Science of Mythology*, vol. 1. New York: Harper and Row.
Marshall, Catherine, and Gretchen B. Rossman. 2006. *Designing Qualitative Research*, 4th ed. Thousand Oaks, CA: Sage.
McClard's Bar-B-Q. 2009. "Our History." McClard's Bar-B-Q website. *www.mcclards.com/mcclards-bbq-history.htm* (accessed October 1, 2009).
Mintz, Sidney W., and Christine M. Dubois. 2002. "The Anthropology of Food and Eating." *Annual Reviews in Anthropology* 31:99–119.
Reed, John Shelton. 2004. "Barbecue Sociology: The Meat of the Matter." In *Cornbread Nation 2: The United States of Barbecue*, edited by Lolis Eric Elie, 78–87. Chapel Hill: University of North Carolina Press.
Reed, John Shelton, and Dale Volberg Reed. 2008. *Holy Smoke: The Big Book of North Carolina Barbecue*. Chapel Hill: University of North Carolina Press.
Scheper-Hughes, Nancy. 2009. "Making Anthropology Public." *Anthropology Today* 25, no. 4: 1–3.
Serematakis, C. Nadia, ed. 1996. *The Senses Still: Perception and Memory as Material Culture and Modernity*. Chicago: University of Chicago Press.
Smith, Stephen. 2004. "The Rhetoric of Barbecue: A Southern Rite and Ritual." In *Cornbread Nation 2: The United States of Barbecue*, edited by Lolis Eric Elie, 61–68. Chapel Hill: University of North Carolina Press.
Southern Foodways Alliance. 2009. "Papa KayJoe's Bar-B-Que." Southern Foodways Alliance Rural Tennessee Oral History Project. *www.southernfoodways.com/documentary/oh/tnbbq/rural/papa_kayjoes.shtml* (accessed October 1, 2009).
Sutton, David E. 2001. *Remembrance of Repasts: An Anthropology of Food and Memory*. New York: Berg.
Warnes, Andrew. 2008. *Savage Barbecue: Race, Culture, and the Invention of America's First Food*. Athens: University of Georgia Press.
Watson, James L., and Melissa L. Caldwell, eds. 2005. *The Cultural Politics of Food and Eating*. Malden, MA: Blackwell.

PART I

Traditional and Contemporary Landscapes of Mid-South Barbecue

2

A History of Barbecue in the Mid-South Region

Robert F. Moss

From Memphis-style dry ribs to pork sandwiches topped with coleslaw and even such novelties as tamales and barbecue spaghetti, the Mid-South region today has a vibrant and distinctive barbecue tradition. This tradition has its roots in the earliest days of settlement, but it was very different in the beginning than it is now. The Mid-South style evolved considerably over the years, reflecting the key shifts going on in Southern American society at large. In fact, the region's barbecue is best looked at not just as something to eat but as a social institution. It has long had a remarkable power to bring people together from diverse walks of life, helping them celebrate important events, debate contentious issues, and have a good time. This power has made it an inseparable part of life in the Mid-South.

By the time barbecue reached the region it was already a 150-year-old American tradition. The word itself originated with the Taino Indians in the Caribbean, whose name for a frame of green sticks on which meat was roasted was adopted as *barbacoa* by the Spanish and *barbecue* by the English. The technique of cooking meat on a frame of sticks over coals was used widely by Native Americans along the eastern coast of North America. Both the name and the technique were borrowed by English settlers, and by the early eighteenth century barbecues could be found in a region stretching from the Carolinas to New England (Reed and Reed 2008, 12–20).

It was in the colony of Virginia that barbecue first took root not only as a cooking technique but as a social institution. Tidewater Virginians, who immigrated to the New World primarily from southern and western England, brought with them a culture of roasting and broiling and a love of feasting. The colony also had lots of pigs, which thrived on the acorns and chestnuts in Tidewater forests (Kiple and Ornelas 2000). This combination made barbecues a natural fit for the colony, and by the 1750s, they were one of the chief forms of entertainment in Virginia. Pork was generally the preferred meat, and it was roasted whole over a pit of coals. A "barbecue day" in Virginia could last from the morning until late in the evening, with the feast accompanied by dancing and heavy drinking.

Barbecue spread southward from Virginia following the main pattern of Southern settlement. As Virginians migrated down the eastern edge of the Appalachian Mountains, they carried their barbecue tradition with them into the Carolinas and Georgia and across the Appalachians into eastern Tennessee and Kentucky. Barbecues were common features of militia musters, which brought together the white men from all over a county for a day of drilling and socializing, and they early on became the standard way to celebrate American Independence on the Fourth of July. By most accounts, these early barbecues were pretty crude affairs. They took place in clearings in the woods or in dusty open fields, with improvised tables and furnishings and whatever dishes and utensils the settlers had on hand. The meat might be pork, beef, or mutton, depending on what was available, and accounts of stifling heat, undercooked meat, and other unappetizing conditions are common.

It was from this background that barbecue arrived in the Mid-South region, being brought by migrants who moved across the Appalachians from Virginia and the Carolinas in the early nineteenth century. The first settlers of Madison County, Tennessee, for example, arrived around 1810, drawn from middle Tennessee by the rich farmlands to the west. The city of Jackson was created by an act of the General Assembly in 1821, and the first lots went on sale in 1822 (*A History* 1886). Just two years later, the town held its first Independence Day celebration on July 3rd (since the 4th fell on a Sunday). The festivities kicked off at noon with a reading of the Declaration of Independence by a Mr. Bigelow, after which John F. Wyatt delivered a one-hour oration on "the characters of some departed Heroes." The "Hickory Guards" Light Infantry Company paraded around the public square, then led "a numerous assembly of both sexes" in a procession to Samuel Shannon's spring where "a very excellent Barbacue" was enjoyed. Following the meal, a series of thirteen "regular" toasts were drunk, each punctuated with salutes from the guns of the Hickory Guards. These toasts were presented by a preselected committee of four men, who presumably had carefully composed the content well in advance. The subjects of the toasts ranged from patriotic figures such as George Washington, Thomas Jefferson, and James Madison to political issues of the day such as "Grecian Emancipation," "Internal Improvements," and "The Western District of Tennessee." The toast for James Monroe, then the sitting president, captures the general tenor of the expressions: "James Monroe, President of the U.S.—The voice of an independent people will award him an escutcheon worthy of his services." As was standard at Independence Day celebrations throughout all the Southern states, the thirteenth and final toast was to American women. Twenty-nine "volunteer" toasts then followed from members of the crowd (all of them men), and the text of them was transcribed and printed for posterity by the editor of the *Jackson Gazette* (1824).

As in Tennessee, barbecues arrived in Arkansas and Mississippi with the very first settlers too. In 1821, just a year after it was created and fifteen years before Arkansas was admitted to statehood, Phillips County, Arkansas, held its first Fourth of July celebration, where "several beeves were roasted whole and served in barbecue style." The description of Josiah H. Shinn, who chronicled the event in his 1908 history of Arkansas, suggests that a little whiskey might have been present as well: "The Phillips County barbecue was held near a spring in the neighborhood, where a fine quality of Kentucky mint had taken hold, though why the mint patch should be immortalized I cannot say. There must have been some beverage of very strong parts, though of this the record is silent." The address was made by W. B. R. Horner, one of the first settlers of the region. Horner was born in Falmouth, Virginia, in 1785 and arrived in the St. Francis settlement in 1811 when Arkansas was still part of the Louisiana Territory, and he served several terms in the territorial legislature. Following Horner's speech, a series of toasts were drunk, each concluded by a salute of between three and nine guns. Horner presided over the Phillips County barbecue regularly until his death in 1838 (Shinn 1908, 120–23).

It didn't take long for politicians to recognize that community barbecues, with their unparalleled power to pull people together from all over a county, were ideal platforms for electioneering. Campaign barbecues became commonplace in the 1830s, and as they grew larger and became more frequent they were increasingly put on not by the candidates themselves, but by groups of supporters, who arranged the venue, purchased the food and drink, and advertised the events in local newspapers. Such activities were part of the early formation of political parties in Southern states, and barbecues became an important forum for political discourse in the region.

By the presidential election of 1840, the political barbecue was fully mature. After suffering a stinging loss four years before, the Whigs united behind war hero William Henry Harrison, famous for his victory over the Shawnee at the Battle of Tippecanoe in 1811, and his running mate John Tyler. Harrison had little to campaign on except his military record. Samuel Eliot Morison characterized the election as "the jolliest and most idiotic presidential contest in our history. . . . The Whigs beat the Democrats by their own methods. They adopted no platform, nominated a military hero, ignored real issues, and appealed to the emotions rather than the brains of voters" (Morison 1965, 456). All across the country, the Whigs staged massive parades and campaign barbecues, which were accompanied by popular campaign songs and catchy slogans such as "Tippecanoe and Tyler, Too." Much of this activity took place in the Mid-South region. In 1840, the Tippecanoe Club of Little Rock adopted a resolution to give "a free Barbecue to the people of Pulaski county, and as many others from the adjoining counties as can conveniently attend" (*Arkansas Star*, May 14, 1840). Campaign barbecues remained a fundamental feature of the region's political life well into the twentieth century.

Mid-South barbecues in the antebellum period were typically held outdoors in a wooded grove near a running spring, which provided much-needed shade and drinking water. Preparations began days in advance, as animals were brought to the site and slaughtered. In most of the Mid-South region today, pork dominates barbecue restaurant menus, but in the early days pitmasters would cook whatever the members of the community had on hand to donate. At the 1846 Independence Day barbecue near Frog Bayou in northwest Arkansas, a reporter for the *Arkansas Intelligencer* (1846) noted, "The noble steer was immolated at this sacrifice—lambs, shoats, and poultry sent up their quotas to this patriotic feast." Beef, hogs, sheep, goats, and chickens were par for the course at such events, and game such as deer, wild turkeys, and squirrels were often donated too.

The barbecue pit was usually a long, shallow trench dug in the earth. It was four to six feet wide and, depending on the event's expected attendance, might run up to two or three hundred feet in length. Hardwood logs—generally oak and hickory—were burned until reduced to coals and then spread in the trench. Once the coals were ready, the pit attendants would run the whole animal carcasses through with either green sticks or iron bars and lay them across the pit. Slaves frequently performed the hard work of tending the pits at Mid-South barbecues, sometimes supervised by white men but just as frequently by an older slave who was recognized as the local barbecue master. The sauce used at these nineteenth-century gatherings was quite different from the tomato-based recipes common in the Mid-South today. In those days, it was essentially the same as that used throughout the rest of the country: melted butter, vinegar, and perhaps a little water, along with salt and pepper. This basting liquid was kept in pots along the sides of the pit, and the cooks moved up and down either side, daubing the meat with long-handled brushes. The attendants periodically turned the meat and refreshed the coals from a small pit of hardwood kept burning off to the side. The cooking began early in the morning or even the night before to allow plenty of time for the meat to be ready to serve to the crowds by early afternoon.

At a typical barbecue, the shady grove served as both an outdoor auditorium and a banquet hall. The politicians and orators spoke from an improvised platform at one end of the grove, and the diners ate at temporary tables made of long boards supported by crosspieces on stakes driven into the ground. Puncheons, which were large logs cut in half, served as benches. The gatherings tended to be boisterous, and whiskey flowed freely alongside the barbecued meat. After the feasting was finished, the crowds engaged in round after round of toasts, and gatherings generally lasted through the afternoon and sometimes into the early evening.

As the sheer number of toasts suggest, early Mid-South barbecues could be pretty rough and tumble affairs. Arguments and fistfights were par for the course, and even duels were not uncommon. Before long, though, social reformers turned their sights on taming the barbecue. An 1833 act of the Tennessee legislature declared that anyone preparing a barbecue within one mile of a worshipping church assembly "shall be dealt with as rioters at common law, and shall be fined in a sum not less than five dollars" (*American Annual Register* 1835, 310). The temperance movement had a particularly strong effect on civilizing barbecues. During the 1840s and 1850s it became more and more common to see "cold water" or "temperance" barbecues, where the same rituals of pit-cooked meat, speeches, and toasts were maintained, but the whiskey was replaced with cold water from a spring. As the drinking and fighting were toned down, more women and children began to attend, and barbecues became a much more respectable part of the region's civic life.

Barbecue played a central role in the lives of slaves on Mid-South cotton plantations as well. They were frequently the pitmasters for the barbecues at which whites were the diners, but they often cooked barbecue for themselves as well. Back east in Virginia in the early decades of the nineteenth century, slaves had a relative amount of latitude in their movements, and gatherings were allowed during nonwork times, usually on Sundays. Slaves in the Tidewater state often raised their own livestock, and they would frequently barbecue one of their pigs for their own entertainment. These privileges were greatly curtailed and then put to an end altogether as a result of two notable slave revolts—Gabriel's Rebellion in Henrico County in 1800 and Nat Turner's Rebellion in Southampton County in 1831—both of which involved slave barbecues used as a cover for planning the uprisings (Rose 1999, 107–10; Higginson 1861, 173).

Slaveholders in the Mid-South states, cautioned by the events that had unfolded in Virginia, greatly restricted freedom of movement and assembly. Apart from an occasional clandestine pig roast with a stolen animal, slaves on the cotton plantations of western Tennessee, Arkansas, and northern Mississippi seldom were able to stage unsupervised barbecues. However, plantation owners did use officially sanctioned barbecues as a means of both rewarding and controlling slaves. Such events formed the centerpiece of Christmas celebrations and either the Fourth of July or a more general late-summer holiday held once the crops were "laid by." The owner usually provided a pig, a sheep, or even a whole cow, and the slaves were given an entire day free from work. Often they would be allowed to invite friends and family members from other plantations to join them. The barbecue was cooked by the standard pit method, and the slaves prepared plenty of side items such as sweet potato pies, corn bread, ginger cake, and peach cobbler. Fiddle music and dancing was almost always part of the celebration, and depending on the strictness of the plantation owner, alcohol sometimes was as well.

Louis Hughes, who was raised a slave on a cotton plantation near Pontotoc, Mississippi, recalled a plantation Fourth of July barbecue as follows:

> The children who were large enough were engaged in bringing wood and bark to the spot where the barbecue was to take place. They

worked eagerly, all day long; and, by the time the sun was setting, a huge pile of fuel was beside the trench, ready for use in the morning. At an early hour of the great day, the servants were up, and the men whom Boss had appointed to look after the killing of the hogs and sheep were quickly at their work, and, by the time they had the meat dressed and ready, most of the slaves had arrived at the center of attraction. They gathered in groups, talking, laughing, telling tales that they had from their grandfather, or relating practical jokes that they had played or seen played by others. These tales were received with peals of laughter. But however much they seemed to enjoy these stories and social interchanges, they never lost sight of the trench or the spot where the sweetmeats were to be cooked. (1897, 47–48)

Ironically, and perhaps deliberately, Hughes's account of the Fourth of July barbecue immediately follows a section on "Methods of Punishment" that enumerates many of the barbarous ways in which slaves on Mississippi plantations were bound, whipped, and humiliated. The delights of the barbecue stand in sharp contrast to such treatment, and Hughes recalls, "It mattered not what trouble or hardship the year had brought, this feast and its attendant pleasure would dissipate all gloom. Some, probably, would be punished on the morning of the 4th, but this did not matter; the men thought of the good things in store for them, and that made them forget that they had been punished" (47). Hughes himself recalls being so excited on barbecue days that he could barely do his housework, calling the events a "ray of sunlight in their darkened lives" (51).

As life in the Mid-South evolved in the decades just before the Civil War, the barbecue was adapted for new forms of public gathering and celebration. Barbecue played a supporting role in the Mexican-American War, which was declared in May 1846 after a decade of simmering tensions between the United States and Mexico over the territory of Texas. The standing U.S. army was too small for the war, so tens of thousands of volunteers were raised according to state militia laws. Volunteers enlisted for twelve months of service and assembled at a central rendezvous point in each state. There they were organized into regiments, elected their officers, and were accepted into service by the federal mustering officer (Bauer 1992, 69–70).

The Mid-South states, being close to Texas, contributed many of the volunteers for the war, and barbecues were routinely used both for recruiting soldiers and for sending them off to battle. The volunteer company raised from Washington County in western Arkansas numbered seventy soldiers, and they assembled at Major Billingsly's farm in Mountain Township on June 10, 1847. The people of Washington and Crawford counties gathered and prepared "an extensive barbecue" for the volunteers at which, in the words of one of the soldiers, "we were all most agreeably entertained, and after a cordial exchange of sentiment, we were billeted, in small parties, among the different householders in the neighborhood" ("To the Editor" 1847). Such festivities were repeated in county after county throughout the region as each community sent off its volunteers to fight in Mexico. The brief twelve-month term of service encouraged a lot of volunteers, but, with training and transport time taken into account, it also meant a high turnover of troops after only a few months of active combat duty. As a result, communities frequently staged grand barbecues to welcome volunteers home in the same style used to send them off just a year earlier.

During the 1850s, the barbecue started being enlisted for a very different cause: the building of the region's first railroads. Railroad promoters used barbecues to draw crowds to giant rallies, where they would be encouraged to subscribe for shares in the railroad companies. These subscriptions provided the financial capital needed to build the expensive lines. The Mississippi, Ouachita, and Red River Railroad was the first railroad to be incorporated in the state of Arkansas, and the citizens of Camden—a town on the Ouachita River—were active proponents of the undertaking. When the surveying party for the railroad arrived in Camden in 1854, the town's citizens welcomed them with a "great barbecue" and "people came from near and far to hear the speakers eulogize the advantages of the proposed railroad." Despite the enthusiasm of Camden's citizens, the railroad struggled to raise sufficient capital. After four years, with only a few miles of track laid and one handcar to run on it, the building of the Mississippi, Ouachita, and Red River Railroad was ended by the onset of the Civil War (Herndon 1922, 525). Railroad building resumed in earnest after the war was over, and barbecues remained a key means of raising funds. In November 1868, for instance, the citizens of Caledonia, Mississippi, held a barbecue to raise subscriptions for completing the Mississippi division of the Memphis and Selma Railroad, for which the town was slated to be a border station. Through their subscription of "three thousand acres of land and a considerable amount of money," the *Memphis Daily Avalanche* (1868c) declared, "the citizens proclaimed their willingness to go to the utmost limit of their means whenever the line should be run, establishing their town as a station."

As they had during the Mexican-American War, the residents of the Mid-South used barbecues both to send local troops off to the Civil War and, on occasion, to welcome them home when they returned. The economic and social impact of that conflict was so great, however, that large public gatherings effectively ceased for the duration of the war. The barbecue returned to prominence in the region's political life after the war and served as an important device in Reconstruction political battles as white Southerners struggled to regain political power and federal military occupation ended. In Haywood County, Tennessee, in July 1867, the local Democrats staged a free barbecue to which all citizens, white and black, were invited, and both white and black speakers made orations. The event was promoted as "A Grand Rally to Bury Brownlowism," a reference to Unionist-editor-turned-politician W. G. Brownlow, who served as the Republican governor of Tennessee from 1865 to 1869 (*Memphis Daily Avalanche* 1868a). Democrats in Yalobusha County, Mississippi, where black voters outnumbered whites by a small majority, tried similar tactics. They hosted a grand barbecue outside the town of Grenada in June 1868, "designed more particularly for the colored population, whose minds it was sought to enlighten with the gospel of Democracy" (*Memphis Daily Avalanche* 1868b). The orators condemned the Republican-controlled legislature and the recently enacted state constitution, which had instituted universal suffrage. The radical Republicans, the speakers insisted, were just exploiting Southern blacks for profit; the Democrats were actually the ones most concerned with the welfare of black Southerners. Predictably, barbecue pork and big promises did little to win African American votes. In Tennessee, despite the Democrats' exhaustive courting of freedmen's votes, Brownlow was reelected by an overwhelming majority, and Democrats made little headway with African American voters in Arkansas or Mississippi. Conservative whites soon adopted harsher means of ensuring their political power, including intimidation and the systematic disenfranchisement of black voters.

Outside of politics, barbecue remained an important part of the social lives of both white and black residents of the rural Mid-South, and as they started moving into towns and cities in the late nineteenth century they took that barbecue tradition with them. In the process, barbecue took on a broader role in all aspects of Mid-South life. County fairs, church gatherings, school reunions, and Confederate veterans' reunions were just a few of the many events at which barbecue was typically served. In the African American community, Emancipation Day celebrations, which commemorated Lincoln's Emancipation Proclamation, became a standard occasion for a barbecue, and the Fourth of July remained one as well, although most Southern whites refused to celebrate the holiday until the Spanish-American War rekindled national patriotic sentiments.

Today, barbecue fans have gone to great detail documenting the multitudinous variations in barbecue styles in different regions of the country. Up until the early twentieth century, though, there seems to have been little difference in the way barbecue was cooked in different parts of the country. Whether in North Carolina, Texas, or California, a barbecue usually involved multiple types of meats (everything from beef and pork to mutton and game) cooked over wood coals in a shallow dirt pit and basted with a salty, spicy vinegar sauce. The single greatest influence on the regionalization of barbecue styles seems to have been the rise of barbecue restaurants. As they transformed what were once large-scale, occasional public gatherings into smaller, more regular businesses, barbecue restaurateurs standardized the meat they served, creating new and different methods of cooking and their own signature sauces. These styles and techniques were passed from one local pitmaster to another through an informal apprentice system, in the process creating distinct styles in different regions of the country.

Most regional barbecue styles are categorized by a state or a portion of a state. Memphis, Tennessee, is one of just two American cities (the other being Kansas City, Missouri) that have earned the distinction of having their own barbecue style. This style was developed by the city's restaurant pioneers in the early twentieth century, when smoked ribs and pork sandwiches became both a lunch staple and, because of Memphis's lively nightlife scene, a late-night delicacy. The city during this period was an economic magnet that attracted people—particularly African Americans—from all over the rural Mid-South. Between 1865 and 1900, Memphis's black population grew from 3,800 to over 50,000, and African Americans accounted for more than half of the city's total residents. Memphis had the world's largest timber market at the time, fed by hundreds of lumber and turpentine camps in the bottomlands of Mississippi. On weekends, workers from these camps flooded into the city with their week's wages, joining thousands of waiters, porters, railyard workers, and deckhands from Mississippi riverboats looking for entertainment.

Beale Street was the heart of African American commerce in the city. Its black-owned banks, stores, and restaurants kept the sidewalks busy during the day, and at night it was transformed into a hopping entertainment district. Beale Street's theaters, bars, and music halls were the birthplace of the Memphis blues, and the district was also home to many late-night barbecue joints. The most famous of these was operated by Johnny Mills on 4th Street between Beale Street and Gayoso Avenue in the 1920s. Mills cooked his barbecue in a large pit in the alley behind his restaurant and served it in two dining rooms, one reserved for white patrons and one for black. Frank Sinatra always visited Johnny Mills's restaurant when he played the Peabody Hotel, and Bing Crosby is said to have regularly had Mills's ribs flown out to him in Hollywood (Keogh 2004, 10; Elie 1996, 9).

In 1922, Leonard Heuberger bartered his Model-T Ford for a sevenstool sandwich stand and opened Leonard's Barbecue on the corner of Trigg and Latham, four blocks south of McLemore Avenue. A decade later he moved to the corner of McLemore and South Bellevue and converted his restaurant into a drive-in. Heuberger was a white man of German-Jewish ancestry, and while the neighborhood was largely African American and Leonard's cooks were all black, the restaurant served only white patrons until the end of segregation in the 1960s. Leonard's specialties were barbecue pork shoulders and ribs, which were cooked overnight on a brick pit fired by hickory charcoal. According to James Willis, who started as a "tray picker" in 1938 at the age of fifteen and worked his way up to pitmaster, working the pits at Leonard's was a long, hot job. He cooked up to thirty-two pork shoulders at a time, replenishing the charcoal and turning the meat every hour and a half. Between turns, he would "open that pit every five or six minutes and see whether it's caught a fire or not. You cooking it on an open pit. That grease gets hot and starts a fire" (qtd. in Fisher 2002a). The shoulders cooked a total of seven hours before being removed from the pits and prepared for serving to the next day's crowd.

Leonard's claims to have invented one of the city's distinctive specialties: the Memphis-style barbecue pork sandwich. This delicacy consists of pulled or chopped pork shoulder served on a hamburger bun and topped with coleslaw and an often-spicy tomato-based sauce (Ferris 2004). Leonard's sold them two for a quarter in the 1930s, and at its peak in the 1950s it was one of the largest drive-in restaurants in the country. The Bellevue restaurant closed in 1991, but Leonard's is still in operation today at locations on Fox Plaza and downtown on Main Street.

Leonard's chief competitors were the Pig n' Whistle, which was located on Union Avenue from 1929 to 1966, as well as Miss Culpepper's, Willie King's, Jeff's, Joe's After Hours, and Jim's Rib Shack, which now exist only in the memories of old Memphis residents (Johnson and Staten 1988, 93; Elie 1996, 9). Many other early barbecue businesses were more late-night beer and dancing joints than restaurants. Their owners cooked a dozen slabs of ribs during the day and sold them to the crowds at night. The rib sandwich was one of the most popular items at these nightspots, providing hungry revelers with a couple of pork ribs served still on the bone between slices of bread and topped with coleslaw and barbecue sauce. The bread was more a platform than anything else, since the sandwich was usually pulled apart with the fingers and eaten.

As in Memphis, barbecue stands started cropping up on street corners in towns across the Mid-South during the first two decades of the twentieth century. As Americans took to the road in newly affordable automobiles like the Model-T, barbecue started appearing along the side of Mid-South highways as well. Up until the 1920s, restaurants and hotels could be found only in downtown business districts. Early motorists camped out overnight along the roadside, sleeping in tents and cooking their meals over campfires. Soon, tourist campgrounds appeared, offering amenities such as running water, electricity, and bathhouses to cater to this new trade. Entrepreneurs saw a chance to sell food to motorists as well. They set up roadside food stands—often just flimsy wooden structures—and sold the same kind of food found at county fairs: hamburgers, hot dogs, ice cream, sandwiches, and, most popular of all, barbecue.

Barbecue was perfect for roadside stands. All the operator needed was some hickory wood and a pit dug in the ground. The cooked meat was simply wrapped in brown paper or placed between slices of bread, so it was cheap and easy to serve. At first, most roadside barbecue stands were seasonal operations and sold food for take-away only. Often, proprietors of other roadside businesses like gas stations or general stores started selling barbecue as a sideline, and some found the sideline pursuit more profitable than the original enterprise. McClard's, the legendary barbecue joint in Hot Springs, Arkansas, is a classic example.

Alex and Gladys McClard owned the Westside Tourist Court near Hot Springs National Park in Hot Springs, Arkansas. In 1928, they added a barbecue pit so they could sell slow-cooked goat, beef, and pork to their guests. According to the McClard family, the fourth generation of which still operates the restaurant today, Alex and Gladys acquired a secret barbecue sauce recipe from a tourist court resident who couldn't pay the ten dollars he owed for two months' lodging. Fueled by that distinctive red sauce, which has a tomato-paste base and plenty of fiery pepper, barbecue sales took off, and before long the McClards were selling to nonlodgers as well. It was the era of Prohibition, and their barbecue attracted the business of some of the country's most notorious gangsters, including Lucky Luciano, Meyer Lansky, and Al Capone, who ran bootlegging operations out of Hot Springs. In 1942, Mc-Clard's Bar-B-Q moved into a whitewashed stucco building. For many years, it operated as a drive-in, complete with carhops and a jukebox that broadcast over an AM band so diners could listen to music in their cars. The carhops are now gone, and goat is no longer on the menu. But McClard's sliced beef, sliced pork, and pork ribs are favorites of both local residents and visiting celebrities, including former president Bill Clinton, who lived just down the road as a boy in the 1950s (Johnson and Staten 1988, 32–33).

Several other classic Mid-South barbecue restaurants also evolved from other businesses. In Blytheville, Arkansas, Ernest Halsell opened the Rustic Inn in a log cabin in 1923, later moving the restaurant to a rock building, and finally to its current location on Sixth Street in the 1950s. Like McClard's, it operated as a drive-in with curb service during the 1950s and 1960s but later scaled back to just a regular family-style restaurant. Abraham Davis, an immigrant from Lebanon, opened a snack stand in Clarksdale, Mississippi, in 1924. During the early years of his business, Davis learned to cook barbecue, and his snack stand evolved into Abe's Barbecue with its own distinctive style of chopped-pork sandwiches. Davis started by cooking Boston butt over pecan wood, which he allowed to cool overnight and then sliced. When a customer ordered a sandwich, he would heat a few slices on a griddle and put them on a bun with a thick red barbecue sauce. It was common at the time to find street vendors selling tamales in small towns throughout Mississippi, and Abe adopted that local specialty too. Abe's is still in business today at the corner of Highways 61 and 49, where his son Pat serves the same style pork sandwiches and tamales (Evans 2005).

Restaurants like these helped establish barbecue as one of the most popular restaurant foods in the Mid-South by the Second World War, and it could soon be found at many more places than just barbecue stands. Full-service restaurants added brick pits for cooking pork, ribs, and chicken, and many of the region's restaurants with tablecloths and silverware had signs that advertised "Steaks—Chops—Barbecue." More and more drive-in restaurants added barbecue sandwiches alongside their hamburgers, hot dogs, and fried chicken.

By this point, the Mid-South region already had its own distinctive barbecue style, but that style would continue to evolve as new restaurateurs came into the business in the postwar years. Memphis's Charlie Vergos was perhaps the most influential of these new restaurateurs. Vergos's family emigrated from Greece to the United States in the early 1900s. His father, John, sold hot dogs in Memphis, and Charlie followed him into the restaurant business. He ran a meat-and-three restaurant called Wimpy's with his brother-in-law during the 1940s, then opened his own snack bar in the basement of the same building. Vergos found an old unused elevator shaft in the corner of the basement and converted it into a smoker, which he used to cook hams. His plan was to keep things simple and sell just ham and cheese sandwiches on rye bread along with beer. The idea was to target men who were downtown with their families, drawing them in for a sandwich and beer while their wives did the shopping. The sandwiches were sold almost at cost so Vergos could make money off of the beer.

Over time Vergos started experimenting with smoking other items like salami, chicken, and oysters. In the late 1950s his meat distributor suggested he try pork ribs. Vergos had never cooked ribs before, but one of his employees, a man named Little John, was an experienced barbecue man. Unlike restaurants in Texas and Kansas City, which slow-smoke ribs for hours on end, the Rendezvous cooked their ribs eighteen inches over a hot fire for only an hour and fifteen minutes. To keep the meat moist, Little John suggested they baste it in water and vinegar. Vergos invented his own spice rub based on a combination his father used for chili—salt, pepper, bay leaf, cumin, chili powder, and oregano—with a little paprika added to give color. The result was the dry-rib style for which Memphis is famous today (Fisher 2002b; Raichlen 2003, 36).

The city of Memphis had already helped revolutionize the grocery industry thanks to locally based Piggly Wiggly, which pioneered the concept of the self-service grocery store. Another local enterprise, Little Pigs of America, tried to do the same for the barbecue business. The corporation began selling barbecue restaurant franchises in the early

1960s. Franchisees needed no prior barbecue experience. In exchange for a $6,000 initial investment, Little Pigs trained franchisees at their Memphis headquarters, helped them select a restaurant location, and provided designs for their brick barbecue pit. The resulting businesses, the company promised franchisees, would deliver a net return of $18,000 per year. Little Pigs announced a lofty goal of opening at least one thousand restaurants nationwide, and by 1965 they were a fifth of the way there with over two hundred franchised units in operation (*Daily Times News* 1965; *Time* 1963). Rapid growth was one thing; turning a profit was another. Little Pigs quickly became America's largest barbecue chain, but it ran in the red every year except 1963 and filed for bankruptcy before the end of the decade (Securities and Exchange Commission 1966, 1).

As the fate of the short-lived Little Pigs empire suggests, barbecue was not well suited for the fast-food restaurant market. Barbecue dominated the industry through the 1960s, but then it began to falter. National hamburger chains like McDonald's and Burger King grew rapidly with an operating model based on speed of service, standardization, and inexpensive, low-skilled labor. Barbecue could not compete on any of these fronts. Most of the full-service restaurants that once served barbecue began phasing out their inefficient, labor-intensive pits, and one drive-in after another retired barbecue sandwiches in favor of hamburgers. Many of those pitmasters who stayed in the business stopped cooking over hardwood, which was growing increasingly expensive and difficult to obtain, and began using automatic gas or electric cookers that could be left to cook unattended overnight.

By the middle of the 1970s, barbecue had begun to disappear from the national scene. Roadside barbecue stands had once sprouted like mushrooms across the Midwest and in the sunny states of California and Florida, but they faded out almost as quickly against the rise of the paper-wrapped cheeseburger. Today, barbecue has all but vanished in the state of Virginia, the birthplace of the American tradition, where if it is to be found at all it is often labeled "North Carolina" style. The tradition, however, remained much stronger in the Mid-South region, particularly in the city of Memphis. "In Memphis," Lolis Eric Elie wrote in 1996, "particularly in the black sections of the city, barbecue pits are more common than lawn furniture. Many stores also have an old drum smoker chained to a telephone pole out front to advertise that in addition to grits and groceries, they sell barbecue" (10).

This endurance of the slow-smoke tradition has made the city of

Memphis synonymous with barbecue. The Memphis in May World Championship Barbecue Cooking Contest, the largest barbecue competition in the United States, has furthered this association. In the inaugural event in 1978, Bessie Louise Cathey's ribs, smoked in a ramshackle backyard barrel cooker, beat out twenty-seven other contestants for the five-hundred-dollar grand champion prize (*Memphis Commercial Appeal* 2005). The next year, the contest moved to Tom Lee Park along the Mississippi River, where it is still held today, and within a few years hundreds of teams were lining up to compete, forcing the competition to impose an invitational format (Trillin 1985, 56). The Memphis in May event not only helped establish the national competitive barbecue circuit but also contributed to the city's reputation as a capital of American barbecue. In recent years, the city's signature pulled-pork sandwiches and dry-rub ribs have gained fans from well outside the Mid-South region and inspired a host of imitators. Sticky Fingers, a barbecue chain based in Charleston, South Carolina, decorates its walls with pictures of Delta bluesmen and serves "the best authentic Memphis-style ribs and barbecue in the South" with "a flavor so good you'll think you're walking down Beale Street with B. B. King!" Most of the chain's eighteen restaurants are in the Carolinas, and the closest to Memphis are two outlets in Chattanooga. From New York to Los Angeles, numerous restaurants offer "Memphis-style" barbecue—a testament to the success of the region's distinctive style.

Barbecue is as essential to the history and culture of the Mid-South as the blues, cotton, and the Mississippi River. From the very beginning it played a central role in the region's institutions and social traditions, evolving along with local culture to remain relevant to and reflective of the people as a whole. While barbecue itself is a national American institution, within the Mid-South region it has taken on its own unique and, increasingly, world-famous style. And if history is any indication, that style will continue to flourish and evolve for years to come.

References

The American Annual Register for the Year 1832–33. 1835. New York: William Jackson.
Arkansas Intelligencer. 1846. "4th July in Mountain Township." July 11.
Bauer, Karl Jack. 1992. *The Mexican War, 1856–1848.* Lincoln: University of Nebraska Press.
Daily Times News. 1965. "New Barbecue Establishment Opens." April 24.

Elie, Lolis Eric. 1996. *Smokestack Lightning: Adventures in the Heart of Barbecue Country*. Berkeley: Ten Speed Press.
Evans, Amy. 2005. "Interview with Pat Davis Sr." *The Mississippi Hot Tamale Trail*. www.tamaletrail.com (accessed May 28, 2007).
Ferris, Marcie Cohen. 2004. "We Didn't Know from Fatback." In *Cornbread Nation 2*, edited by Lolis Eric Elie, 97–103. Chapel Hill: University of North Carolina Press.
Fisher, Brian. 2002a. "Interview with James Willis." BBQ Oral History Project and the Southern Foodways Alliance website, www.southernfoodways.com (accessed September 27, 2009).
———. 2002b. "Interview with Nick Vergos." BBQ Oral History Project and the Southern Foodways Alliance website, www.southernfoodways.com (accessed March 22, 2009).
Herndon, Dallas T. 1922. *Centennial History of Arkansas*. Chicago: S. J. Clarke.
Higginson, Thomas Wentworth. 1861. "Nat Turner's Insurrection." *Atlantic Monthly*, August.
A History of Tennessee from the Earliest Times to the Present, Together with an Historical and a Biographical Sketch of Madison County. 1886. Nashville: Goodspeed. Transcription available at www.tngenweb.org/records/madison/history/goodspeed/.
Hughes, Louis. 1897. *Thirty Years a Slave: From Bondage to Freedom*. Milwaukee: South Side Printing.
Jackson Gazette. 1824. "Fourth of July." July 10.
Johnson, Greg, and Vince Staten. 1988. *Real Barbecue*. New York: Harper Collins.
Keogh, Pamela Clarke. 2004. *Elvis Presley*. New York: Simon and Schuster.
Kiple, Kenneth F., and Kriemhild Coneè Ornelas, eds. 2000. "Hogs." *Cambridge World History of Food*. New York: Cambridge University Press.
Memphis Commercial Appeal. 2005. "History of World Championship Barbecue Cooking Contest." Bar-B-Q Blog. blog.commercialappeal.com/bbq/archives/2005/05/history_of_worl.html (accessed January 4, 2009).
Memphis Daily Avalanche. 1868a. "Conservative Barbecue." July 27.
———. 1868b. "Mississippi: The Democratic Canvass." June 17.
———. 1868c. "Railroad Barbecue in Mississippi." November 26.
Morison, Samuel Eliot. 1965. *The Oxford History of the American People*. New York: Oxford University Press.
Raichlen, Steven. 2003. *BBQ USA: 425 Recipes from All across America*. New York: Workman.
Reed, John Shelton, and Dale Volberg Reed. 2008. *Holy Smoke: The Big Book of North Carolina Barbecue*. Chapel Hill: University of North Carolina Press.
Rose, Willie Lee Nichols. 1999. *A Documentary History of Slavery in North America*. Athens: University of Georgia Press.

Securities and Exchange Commission. 1966. *News Digest* 64–66 (April 4).
Shinn, Josiah H. 1908. *Pioneers and Makers of Arkansas*. Little Rock: Democrat Printing and Lithographing.
Time. 1963. "Profits for Mom and Pop." May 24.
"To the Editor." 1847. *Arkansas Intelligencer*, June 19.
Trillin, Calvin. 1985. "Thoughts of an Eater with Smoke in His Eyes." *New Yorker*, August 12.

3

Patronage and the Pits
A Portrait, in Black and White, of Jones Bar-B-Q Diner in Marianna, Arkansas

JOHN T. EDGE

A white man clutching a brown paper bag stands in the dirt-and-gravel lot that fronts Jones Bar-B-Q Diner in the Arkansas Delta town of Marianna. Grease splotches the bag, a stain that envelops the bottom and flares up the sides. The man appears to be sixty, maybe seventy. His face is wide and jowly. His hair is thin and comb-raked. He wears brown pants, a white shirt, and a baby blue windbreaker. He could have left a couple of minutes ago, could have jumped in his pickup and driven away, eating a barbecue sandwich from a foil wrapper, fighting the collapse of the two slices of white bread that contain, for the moment, a mound of hickoried and sauced ham and shoulder.

But the man lingers. The grease spreads.

He stares across the neighborhood. At rusted-out and busted-up trailer homes. At carbon-smudged chimneys that stand where clapboard bungalows once stood. At bottle-strewn ditches, flush with crabgrass and bull thistle.

The man is no barbecue pilgrim, questing for lost tribes and forgotten temples in this once-prosperous cotton kingdom. He's likely a native. The man appears at ease in this neighborhood, the one that some old and intransigent whites still call "Niggertown." Just as he appears at ease across the levee and down the blacktop in his neighborhood, where sentry pines and picket fences frame tidy farmhouses.

Integration came early to barbecue (and it remained, after the civil rights movement came and went, while schools and other public accommodations resegregated). That is the story we chowhounds tell, with a whiff of self-satisfaction. It's a narrative that lends a nobility to the restaurant trade. It reframes an industry built on a medieval hierarchy of labor, one that has, historically, tended to exploit the underclass. More important, it rationalizes that back-door white patronage of black barbecue restaurants foreshadowed an integrated present, when Jim Crow no longer lords over Southern tables. Such a story is built, in part, on the reductive belief that, as the late Lawrence Craig of Craig's Barbecue in nearby De Valls Bluff, Arkansas, once told me, "whites figured blacks were good at barbecue. Same as they figured we could sing and dance. They gave us the green light, like they did with heavy lifting, because they didn't want to do the work." (Craig said all of this without malice; he told me he was happy to have had the opportunity to cook.)

In *Southern Food: At Home, on the Road, in History*, John Egerton argues that "before schools, churches, sports teams, and even other restaurants in the South got around to lowering the barriers of racial segregation, many of the region's best barbecue pits maintained a thriving interracial trade." Egerton is right. A trip across the proverbial tracks to a barbecue shack offered whites early entrée to everyday black pleasures. At the back door, out of sight, racial barriers were relaxed, and white dollars were welcomed. The implication has always been that a shared appreciation for one of those pleasures, for smoked pig, was a catalyst that brought whites and blacks together. Yet I've begun wondering, in light of recent time spent in Marianna—seat of government for poverty-stricken Lee County—if that back-door patronage might be better understood as the culinary equivalent of a booty call. I've begun thinking of barbecue less as a cultural product and more as an ephemeral indulgence, entered into lightly, exited from easily.

Some incarnation of Jones Bar-B-Q Diner has been open, and relatively integrated, since the 1910s, maybe earlier. (If a firm opening date could be established, a task at which this writer has failed, Jones might prove to be the oldest black-owned restaurant in the South and, perhaps, one of the oldest family-owned black restaurants in the nation.) Walter Jones was the founder and first pitmaster. Along with a brother, Joe Jones, and a contemporary, Tobe Key, he is remembered, by both whites and blacks, as a sort of barbecue trickster, a master of the dark and fiery arts. "He was a drinker, always half in the bag," an octogenarian who grew up in Marianna tells me. "I can see him in a cloud of smoke with a bottle of sauce in his hand."

Others recall the dogtrot house in which Walter Jones lived, and from which he began peddling his barbecue on Fridays and Saturdays. "It was unpainted, just bare wood," says an older white patron. "There were barrels out back for burning down coals. They were set in the ground and cocked at an angle. And a pit, a block pit, in the ground. There was no real place to eat; everybody got their barbecue to take away." The original restaurant was nothing but "a screened-in back porch," recalls an older black patron. "If you wanted sauce, you brought your own pint bottle and he filled it for you. You could get skins for free; ears and tails, too."

Whole-hog was the standard in the early years. Hacked from the carcass and pulled into sandwich meat, Walter Jones sold it from a metal roasting pan, set on a kitchen table. Patrons could snag a free piece of smoke-blackened rind while waiting for him to weigh their purchase on a scale. In a book of Lee County history compiled in 1986 to commemorate Arkansas's sesquicentennial celebration, Hubert Jones—son of Walter Jones and father of present-day proprietor James Jones—recalled the family's initial barbecue setup, circa 1925, as "a hole in the ground, some iron pipes and a piece of fence wire and two pieces of tin."

"My brother and I would cook out at the farm, where we raised our pigs," recalls sixty-three-year-old James Jones, the gray-haired and gimlet-eyed grandson of the founder. "My father would sell the meat in town at this place they had. They called it the Hole in the Wall. That's what it was. Just a window in a wall where they sold meat from a washtub. That was it until he opened this place, in '64." Today, James Jones works the restaurant that his father, Hubert Jones, built. It's a white cinder-block shotgun on a corner lot. At the prow of the building, above a small dining room outfitted with a side-by-side refrigerator and two dinettes, is a second-story apartment, wrapped in asbestos siding. Lace drapes frame the downstairs windows. Wrought iron filigrees the storm door. Oversized oak and hickory trunks hunker by the side door. A thin feather of smoke trails, always, from a brown block chimney.

Between sandwiches, which he serves through a square service window—the tight confines of which call to mind both a ticket booth at a porn theater and a Catholic church confessional—you'll find Jones, propped on his elbows, tucked into the galley that runs the length of the rear counter. He keeps his back to the pit room where Theophilus Bannon, a twenty-five-year Jones veteran—known to friends as Spanky—works a long-handled shovel, ferrying coals to one of two block pits from a fireplace built so high and wide that you might expect to find

Sow with Babies by Luster Willis. Used with permission of the Willis estate.

it in a ski lodge. Above Bannon, oak and hickory burn-off lacquers the rafters and roof. In spots, stalactites of calcified tar have formed on the two-by-fours overhead. Viewed in the slanted afternoon light, they call to mind icicles of black licorice. The pits are swaybacked from the weight of time and the heft of tens of thousands of hogs. Rigged with a block-and-pulley system, they're topped with thin sheets of tin that, when lifted, loose a sweet pall of smoke (first you breathe deeply, then you hack and shudder).

Spanky Bannon and James Jones usually cook meat three days a week. Some of it is their own, destined for two-dollar-and-fifty-cent sandwiches on white Wonder Bread. (Jones recently suspended service of pan-fried bologna, sluiced with barbecue sauce. "It was too much trouble for a buck," he explains. "People wanted mustard. People wanted mayonnaise. To hell with it.") The rest of the meat belongs to others, hunters mostly, who bring in deer and coons and other creatures to be slow-smoked for thirty-five cents per pound. Open the back pit and

A Portrait of Jones Bar-B-Q Diner in Marianna, Arkansas

Hog Killin' by Luster Willis. Used with permission of the Willis estate.

you'll spy their consignments, wrapped in tinfoil, tagged with a name and a pickup date. (On a recent afternoon, a couple of Lee County School Board turkeys shared pit space with a brace of bacon-wrapped quail, property of a local auto-parts dealer.)

James Jones doesn't live upstairs like his parents did before him. But on the nights he cooks shoulders and hams, he sleeps in what was once their apartment. "I can't remember when I didn't smell like smoke," he tells me. "That's the price you pay. That, and a lack of sleep for going on twenty years." As he makes sandwiches, scooping chopped meat from an aluminum-foil-wrapped Crock-Pot, measuring each payload on one of his grandfather's old scales, drenching each in a paprika, cayenne, and red vinegar sauce, squirted from a repurposed Aunt Jemima bottle, James Jones drops his guard. "It's not so much about looking after the meat, keeping it from burning or something," he tells me, almost twisting his face into a scowl. "It's about keeping the meat from being stolen."

This is my fourth trip to Marianna in as many weeks. On past visits, Jones has declined, with both grace and finality, a discussion of his business history. He has deflected questions about his grandfather by dangling the prospect of a collection of family history, now in the possession of relatives in Chicago. "If we could get that book, you'd have your story," he has told me. "You'd be set. Without that, you've got all I got to give. There's not much to tell." But now, for reasons that are unclear, Jones is leveling with me. He's telling me about how his ancestors used to burn wood down into embers in old oil barrels. He's talking about the sense of accomplishment he derived from cooking his first pig. He's telling me that his son—who coaches at a nearby high school and moonlights at Wal-Mart—won't be following him into the business. And Jones is talking about how thieves have begun preying on his business, about how they've taken to stealing his meat, straight off the grill. "One night, this guy cut in here and tried to steal a whole hog I was cooking for someone," he says. "It was too big for him to lift, but he got away with three shoulders. Hauled them away in a meat box. Hell of a thing to happen, in your own neighborhood."

Early on, Lee County was a place of possibility for newly freed blacks, or at least it was purported to be. In the late 1800s, when Arkansas was heralded as the "great Negro state of the country" with "rich lands" and "meagre prejudice" and "opportunities to acquire wealth," the Arkansas Delta was pitched as a place where "sweet potatoes grew as large as watermelons" and "money could be plucked from the trees, like picking cotton off the stalk." It was also a place of political ferment. In 1891, when the Cotton Pickers' League called a general strike as a means of winning pay concessions from planters, only two places managed a work stoppage. One was Lee County. Nearly one hundred years later, in 1971, in the wake of the civil rights movement, black citizens of Marianna, trying to wrest economic control from the white oligarchy, staged a yearlong boycott of white-owned downtown businesses. (The flashpoint for the boycott was, appropriately enough, an argument over pizza service for a black patron at the local Mug and Cone drive-in.) Some believe that was the beginning of the end for Marianna's downtown vitality.

Today, on the town square, a third of the businesses are boarded. A funeral home, with two gold hearses standing at the curb, occupies the busiest corner. Inside the Lee County Courthouse, a janitor polishes the terrazzo floor, as if the sheen of the marble might somehow compensate for the dull pallor of the town. In a nearby office, at the close of a conversation about the economic climate, a local official observes, "Everybody on TV is talking about a recession. Maybe a depression. Where have they been? In Lee County, we've been in a recession for thirty years." It is true. Thirty percent of Lee County residents live in poverty. Other measures lag the state and the country similarly, including education and nutrition. The reasons for these statistics are clear to those with an understanding of the Mississippi River Delta region. Jobs associated with the manual harvest of cotton have vanished. So have middle-class whites and blacks. Neglect of public schools in favor of white-flight academies has fueled and sustained divides of class and race. For want of a well-educated and well-trained workforce, economic redevelopment has stalled.

The political ferment of decades past has subsided. And the local economy has ossified. New roads have bypassed Marianna. So have new immigrants. (While the Hispanic population has skyrocketed in other parts of Arkansas, it has flatlined in the Delta, where new job opportunities are few.) According to prevailing wisdom, economic and cultural stasis is good for barbecue, which is, after all, a vestige of the Bronze Age blowing smoke in the present. To eat in a proper barbecue joint is to engage in a time-travel exercise, wherein cookery is reduced to its most elemental, and the past—both good and ill—emerges from the smoky depths each day.

That, it seems, is what Jones Bar-B-Q Diner promises. And that is what Jones Bar-B-Q Diner delivers.

And that is why, not thirty minutes after an old white man stood in the parking lot, bag in hand, he was replaced by a younger white man, bearing his own burden, gripping his own bag, a similar stigmata of grease defining the barbecue within. That man, I might as well tell you, looked a lot like me.

Note: This chapter appeared in an earlier form under the title "In through the Back Door: The Nobility of the Restaurant Trade" in issue 64 of *Oxford American* magazine. It is reproduced here with the permission of the author.

4

Piney Woods Traditions at the Crossroads

Barbecue and Regional Identity in South Arkansas and North Louisiana

JUSTIN M. NOLAN

Just off lonely Highway 82 on the eastern outskirts of El Dorado, Arkansas, I park my pickup in the gravel lot in front of a nondescript roadside one-stop I remember well from my childhood. Karl Brummett, the store owner, greets me at the door with a ready smile and a sturdy apron.

"Down from the hills of the Ozarks comes the native son."

"Yessir! And thanks for taking time out for a local boy!"

"Now, I know very little about barbecue, but I'll tell you what I do know . . ."

In a sense, Brummett is right, of course: few people claim to know much of anything about barbecue down here in southern Arkansas, where I was born and raised. Partly this is because the region is known a bit more for its Louisiana-based flavors and soul food—neither of which, however, excludes barbecue, it might be noted. El Dorado, my hometown of twenty-two thousand, occupies the center point of Union County's broad, gently rolling pine forests. Driving south from Fayetteville, the swift blue-green streams of the upcountry had given way to the flooded forests and "gumbo backwaters" of the low country somewhere near Gurdon.

Anthropologists and folklorists have long realized the value of examining food traditions as systems capable of generating insights into the values, beliefs, and histories of human cultural and ethnic groups (Brown and Mussell 1984; Sutton 2001; Bower 2009). Because food sharing is an immensely social behavior, anthropologists might strive to understand how regional foods contribute to cultural memory and the subtleties of social identity. Here, at the edge of my hometown, at the door to the barbecue store before me, things felt familiar again. Evening shadows held long and lonesome in the twilight. Dense thickets behind the shop filtered the fading sunshine while crickets pulsed to a summer rhythm I knew well. An eighteen-wheeler roared by.

"Your grandmother was just in the other day! Now I trust you'll be talking to some of the folks in her generation, right?"

"Yessir, I plan to."

Certainly I wasn't the first anthropologist to work here. In fact, my career had long been inspired by the great cultural anthropologist Charles E. Thomas, who depicted the slow burn of cultural loss and modernization in *Jelly-Roll* (1986), his ethnographic account of an African American community in a rural mill town north of El Dorado. My father's parents and their relatives have deep roots here, and my mother became an acculturated insider after moving to El Dorado in 1957. My mission, as an anthropologist, was clear—I would revisit these Piney Woods with hopes of discovering something perhaps unseen in ordinary life, something meaningful about social relationships through a binding food tradition we celebrate, and fancy ourselves to have mastered. That tradition, of course, is barbecue.

Folks in North Louisiana, just fifteen miles south, share a cultural affinity with South Arkansas (Martel 1953; Good 1981). North Louisiana's parishes are mapped by highway signs as "Piney Hills Country" as travelers drive south over the state line at Lockhart, Louisiana. Here on the Arkansas side, the region is alternately referred to as "Piney Woods," "Timberlands," "Land of the Pines," "Tall Pine Country," or occasionally "Piney Hills." A cultural connectivity can be seen in the culinary traditions which erase the boundaries, momentarily, betwixt the cup and lip.

These Piney Woods are perhaps unique in terms of their enduring link to natural resources—namely, oil and timber, mainstays of the extractive economy—for which El Dorado was named the "city of pride and progress." El Dorado would eventually become a thriving crossroads of regional trade, industry, and development, particularly following the oil boom of the 1930s. Today, the cultural region of the Piney Woods encompasses roughly twelve thousand square miles of sandy, rolling coastal forests, spanning west to east from Lewisville to Crossett, and north to south from Fordyce to Ruston. The region's economic

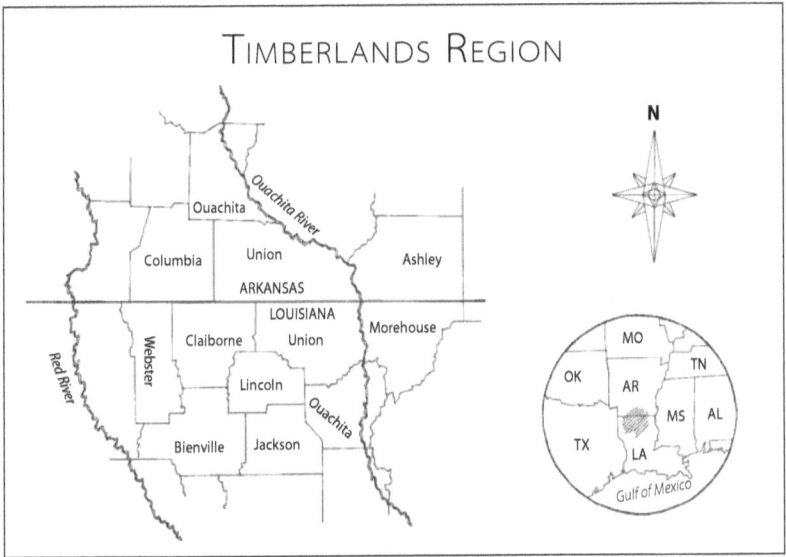

Map of the study area. Illustration by Katlin Jones.

prosperity has diminished substantially over the years, into hopes and promises that linger over yesteryear's dreams, and nostalgia for things forsaken but not forgotten—a mix of reticence, attachment, and longing among local sons and daughters. And still, there are those who never leave. The region's elder generations are venerable torchbearers of a distinctively proud Southern culture, steeped in antebellum patriarchy and posterity. This essay is one native son's attempt to provide an analysis of barbecue and its role in sustaining social history and group identity throughout South Arkansas and North Louisiana.

The Study Region and Scope of Work

The Piney Woods consist of roughly eight parishes in North-Central Louisiana, and four counties of South Arkansas. Though not particularly well known, the region is characterized by distinct cultural and ecological features, the latter of which include the broad, rolling coastal forests dissected by gentle "gumbo water"—dark, slow-moving streams laced like strands of molasses across the region. The culture of the region is a culmination of subsistence and survival. Defined by a shared sense of belonging, and grounded in Native American, French American, African American, Scots Irish, and other belief systems, folk life in the Piney Woods has been, and continues to be, sustained by a complex extractive economy entrenched in natural resources. The oil reserves of the region's geology, once ubiquitous but now elusive, combined with the sprawling stands of loblolly pine plantations, constitute the primary resources of the economy. For families native to the region, some fortunes have been made and some dreams have been lost, but mostly, lives have been sustained by connectedness to these Piney Woods.

Barbecue offerings are readily abundant here, and as such they vary by preparation and cooking styles and techniques, and by choices of wood for the right coals required for the indirect heat of a slow-burning fire and the ultimate smokehouse flavor. Barbecue traditions convey a portrait of cultural history perhaps not readily seen through other, more customary approaches to the anthropological study of American regions. Barbecue runs deep and wide here, and like a fair number of culinary mainstays originating in these rolling pinelands, it yields much more than a flavor; it brings forth stories of kinship, solidarity, and survival.

Mary Douglas, the late British anthropologist, envisioned foodways as critical to anthropological inquiry (see, e.g., Douglas 1997). Understandings of food are rooted in culturally constructed values and beliefs that guide which foods we readily consume and which we expressly avoid (e.g., Brown and Mussell 1984; Anderson 2005). Barbecue can be seen as one long-standing Southern cultural construction, laden with valuable messages about regional identity and belonging. Like other foods tied intimately to families and regions, barbecue (perhaps more than most others) is coded with insights about the nature of the relationships among all who participate in this immensely social, inclusive food event (Humphrey 1991). When shared socially, food items transform edible choices into events, transactions, memories, recipes, celebrations, and customs. Where barbecue is concerned, compelling understandings of social histories, subsistence strategies, group interactions, and patterns of adaptation are served up when the topic emerges in conversation about "what folks eat around here."

Like other forms of expressive culture in the region, barbecue transcends economic and ethnic boundaries, and therefore resides among the most dynamic artifacts within the constellation of culture—that is, everything involved in what we make, say, and do. Yet barbecue is also a time-tested mainstay sufficiently rooted in place, an American tradition

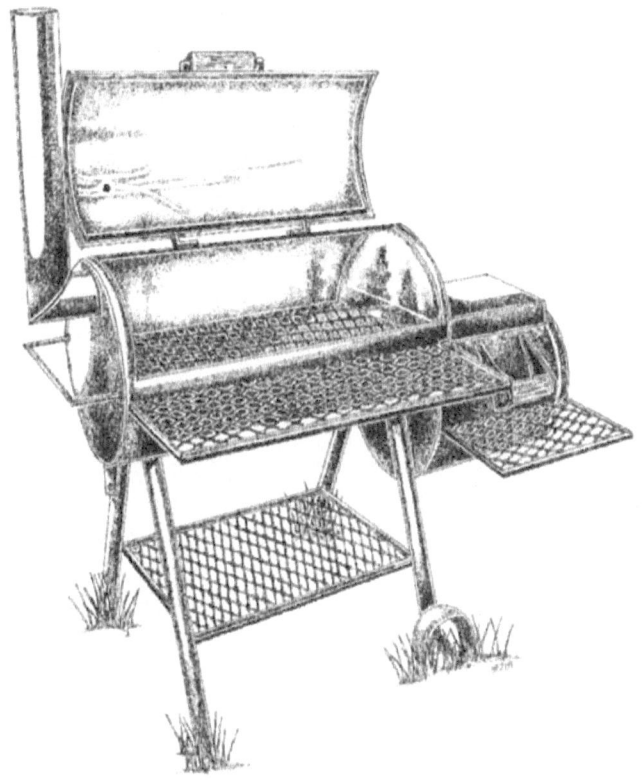

Smoker. Illustration by Katlin Jones.

rendered regional by specific combinations of flavors and techniques of preparation that remain moderately resistant to the forces of outside change. The Piney Woods represent a historic and geographic crossroads of sorts, a place in the world where black and white people have coexisted for many decades, where social boundaries exist mainly in the background of everyday life, where class lines are more evident in neighborhood architecture than social convention, and where Southeastern and Southwestern cultural traits interpenetrate to form a mosaic that's just subtle enough to overlook unless you're seeking to describe it.

My mission began with Karl Brummett, a third-generation sausage maker and barbecue master on the outskirts of El Dorado. The flash in his eye conveyed a hint of irony in his self-deprecating comment about his knowledge of barbecue, and I suspect he knew I'd sense it. Like his forefathers, who had honed their craft into an art appreciated by many, Brummett is known throughout South Arkansas and North Louisiana for his legendary barbecue brisket, pork ribs, and smoked sausages, and, of course, his savory family sauce. Unlike the thicker, rich brown chili-type sauces used by some of the Piney Woods pitmasters, Brummett uses a recipe more akin to the Delta's style—a light tomato-based concoction with vinegar, black pepper, and a vaguely smoky taste that's more tangy than sweet. We chatted about the virtues of ribbon cane and sorghum molasses syrup, two of many ingredients that bring indelible flavor to the sauces of the region's slow-cooked meats.

Ethnographic Methods

Fieldwork for this study was conducted from April to mid-September 2009 over six successive visits. Each visit consisted of about three days of travel in the region, and twelve pitmasters were consulted. Each of these experts were male, and all were selected according to reputation and chain-referral in the cities of El Dorado, Farmerville, Monroe, Ruston, Dubach, Homer, Springhill, Lewisville, Magnolia, and Camden. The pitmasters ranged from thirty-nine to seventy-seven years of age (mean = 55.2), and all had long-standing kinship ties to the area. Nine were of predominantly European American descent, and three were African American. All of them sell and or serve barbecue through their own businesses or otherwise, and they shared their personal narratives freely with me. Following the traditional mode of ethnographic inquiry, I opened each conversation casually, using loose, semistructured (and tape-recorded) interviews, with one recurring question integrated into all interviews: "What makes this region's barbecue distinctive, in your own words?"[1]

Results and Discussion

So what makes Piney Woods barbecue distinct? Table 4.1 lists the twenty-five most commonly mentioned characteristics of local barbecue in descending order, starting with those mentioned by eleven pitmasters ("beef brisket"), followed by those mentioned by ten ("pork ribs"), and so forth. Taken together, these components constitute a portrait of a culinary crossroads, where multiple area-specific barbecue features coalesce into a distinctive style. As one younger shop owner assured me,

Table 4.1. Barbecue characteristics mentioned, by order of frequency

Order	Item	Frequency	Percentage of respondents ($N = 12$)
1	Beef brisket	11	92
2	Pork ribs	10	83
3	Hickory smoked	8	67
4	Pulled pork	8	67
5	Tomato base	7	58
6	Mustard	6	50
7	Liquid smoke	6	50
8	Tamales	6	50
9	Oak smoked	6	50
10	Sorghum molasses	6	50
11	Pork tenderloin	5	42
12	Vinegar base	5	42
13	Vinegar slaw	4	33
14	Sweet beans	4	33
15	Flour	4	33
16	Pork and beans	4	33
17	Chili	4	33
18	Creamy slaw	4	33
19	Slaw on sandwich	4	33
20	Smoked chicken	3	25
21	Catfish	3	25
22	Mesquite smoked	3	25
23	Pork sausage	3	25
24	White beans	3	25
25	Pinto beans	3	25

"You can tell you're in Timber Country straightaway! All you gotta do is see what meats they serve! Mostly oak-smoked, hickory too, sweet sauce but not that sweet, I tell you, and don't let the slaw trip you up. Most folks aren't inclined to put slaw on the sandwich bread, and it's sometimes creamy—and then other times, it'll pucker you right up! Keeps you on your toes, I guess you'd say." Indeed, the barbecue of the region can be seen as a unique blend of "Texas" and "Eastern" styles, and as such it is decidedly different from neighboring regions. While I cannot claim the mandate to judge my home region's slow-smoked flavor, no self-respecting resident would deny that it's delicious.

Like other regions of the American South, a culinary pride of place is alive and well along the Arkansas-Louisiana border. Typical barbecue menus in the Piney Woods showcase beef brisket, sliced or chopped; smoked pork, sliced or chopped; sliced pork tenderloin; pulled pork shoulder; pork ribs (beef ribs are served at home mainly); pork sausage; and smoked chicken. Most meats run about ten to twelve dollars a pound. Combination dinners cost around eight dollars a plate. Choose two, sometimes three, sides: barbecue beans, brown beans, green beans, coleslaw, potato salad, tamales if you're lucky, peach pie, fruit cobbler. Most places have a story to tell; sometimes they print them on the menu for the curious customer or infrequent passerby to see. For instance, conversations revealed that chicken is a relative newcomer among the repertoire of smoked meats in the Piney Woods, perhaps not surprising given the significance of the poultry industry in the area's economy. An elderly barbecue master explained to me his situated vision of Piney Woods barbecue one sultry afternoon near Magnolia:

> Truth is, here's the truth—it's a melting pot here. Black, white, east, west: everything comes together in our barbecue. You got the Cajun spices and sweet ribbon cane from Louisiana, a hint of vinegar from the east, the sweet tomato sauce—that's ours! The beef brisket's so popular around here and chili notes that I suspect must come from Texas, along with their pinto beans. We're pretty tolerant around here. In fact, I think we've been adopting a bit of this and that from each other all along.

That all barbecue east of the Mississippi River is branded "Eastern" is itself an interesting point of contention. Clearly it conveys the Piney Woods' proximity to, and sociodemographic contrast with, the Delta and its perhaps better-known African American culinary staples. Mustard plays a curious role in the regional flavor of Piney Woods barbecue. It's prominent in Old Hickory Sauce—a thick, orange, almost astringently mustard-based concoction found on the shelves of supermarkets across Camden, Magnolia, and El Dorado. The sauce conjures images of its namesake, the Old Hickory restaurant, which has served as South

Arkansas's touchstone for the presentation, flavor, and experience of regional barbecue, right down to the sweet beans served in crocks.

While Old Hickory's mustard tones are well known by regional pitmasters, they choose to acknowledge its virtues rather than incorporate the spice into their own sauces. "It's too Eastern," said one pitmaster I interviewed, who practically denied its existence in any local recipes. Instead, regional choices highlight the revered tomato (generally in the form of ketchup), black pepper, vinegar on occasion, molasses in varying proportions, and the occasional chili seasonings, swirling into various rich brick-colored and orange-red sauces. Sauces seem to especially complement beef brisket, the meat that ultimately muscles out the pork shoulders and sausages, which are loved by many. After all, Southern barbecue is generally grounded in pork offerings, and even the Piney Woods experts recognize its symbolic value on the plate. The Piney Woods are a bona fide Southern region, I was repeatedly reminded—for instance, when the topic of liquid smoke occurred in conversations: "Shhhh . . . lots of us use it in our regional style, but we don't all like to admit that much, so tread lightly here. Liquid smoke, see it comes in several flavors. Me, I like the mesquite, and then again, my daddy might well shake his head in shame if he only knew."

The essence of the region's "staple flavor" is best understood as an aggregate of Southern barbecue: it's bluesy, soulful, spicy, smoky, and vaguely sweet and tangy. Respondents from Southwest Arkansas and Northwest Louisiana mentioned a number of features more commonly associated with Texas-style barbecue, such as brisket, chili, and mesquite smoked. Respondents from Southeast Arkansas and Northeast Louisiana discussed aspects more frequently connected to Eastern barbecue in the American South, such as vinegar and mustard. Those traits in the center of the study region, such as beef brisket, pork ribs, oak smoked, and hickory smoked, were mentioned most frequently by respondents who live there. Thus, the heart and soul of Piney Woods barbecue emerges spatially, geographically, in the stories told by the pitmasters about the smoked meats they serve, their patterns of preparation, and the dishes that traditionally accompany them.

Piney Woods barbecue is perhaps undiscovered by the outside world, but for these long-timers, that's just as well. While "Piney Woods barbecue" may not ring a bell in the mind of American food geographers, its hallmark feature is its inclusiveness, its shape-shifting habit of incorporating neighboring flavors from the Southeast, Louisiana, and

Texas. Unlike the great debate between Piedmont and Upcountry Carolina barbecue described in John Shelton Reed and Dale Volberg Reed's *Holy Smoke* (2008), the differences between Eastern and Western sauce flavorings do not constitute grounds for feuding in the Timberlands. To the contrary, most pitmasters who spoke to me were eager to acknowledge the virtues of "pulled pork," "dry rubs," and "Carolina sauces," even offering the occasional curious remark about "that white North Alabama sauce . . . that's supposed to be real, real good."

For this native anthropologist, the barbecue preparation patterns in the Piney Woods revealed a series of understandings about regional and cultural identity in this crossroads of the Mid-South. Interviews with the region's experts illuminated how "insiders" see themselves through an important, but understated, food tradition that is linked to the historic subsistence of the region. One elderly pitmaster near Ruston explained pork this way:

> We'd have pork all the *time*. And we'd cook it up every which way, you know. Raisin' hogs was a way to make a living, make ends meet, keep food on the table. Butcherin' hogs, smokin' hogs, now that's taking you back, way back. Guess it's no surprise we all got pork on the menu nowadays. Use to be, makin' sausage was an art, and the sausages, they'd be at "middle of the place" . . . ever heard that expression? And still, these folks, they love their beef around here. Don't make much sense to specialize in one or the other, gotta keep folks happy since everybody's got their taste, you know.

The Piney Woods, in some ways, constitute an ambivalent Southern culture. While clearly Southern, this country is neither upcountry nor coastal, neither Eastern nor Western. Aspects of many different ethnic and regional groups are visible among the colorful threads of its history and tapestry. Like the famous watery bayous of South-Central Louisiana's Cajun Country, the Piney Woods are a swirl of peoples whose memories make up an amalgam, stroked by Southern history, seasoned through hard times, change, chance, and choice. In Northeast Louisiana, one respondent recalled the days of twenty years ago, when one-man operations sold rib plates in a parking lot somewhere: "The trick was knowing where to look! They were mobile, you see, up this road one day and down that road the next. Just movin' with the flow, and you wanna talk about good barbecue. Those fellows, they might could've made a livin' that way, but in the long run, all they left behind was a memory of some first-rate cooking. I wonder what happened to their recipes, come to think of it."

The discourse surrounding barbecue reveals as much about regional culture as the varied slow-cooked morsels themselves (e.g., Humphrey 1991). Accordingly, a vast and colorful array of barbecue lore has emerged in the minds, lives, and stories of Piney Woods residents. I don't deny that my efforts to capture the essence of the region's barbecue are possibly constrained and confounded by my own sense of belonging as a native anthropologist. Expressive culture in the region, when viewed through barbecue, is revealed as both distinct from and similar to that of surrounding cultural areas. Contemporary residents of the Piney Woods describe themselves as "pioneer descendants" belonging to a place in the South that's entrenched in living history, brought sharply into focus through foodways. That history is conveyed via an indirect, circular pattern of storytelling, ribald jokes, and a healthy dose of Creole, Delta, Texas, and upcountry cooking tips and flavoring preferences. But nobody dared to share their recipes, and this much I know is true: it wouldn't be the right thing to do down here.

As the summer shadows lengthened, my culinary journey reached its conclusion. With the fall semester looming large on my horizon, I said goodbye once again to my beloved Piney Woods, but not before stopping off to visit Karl Brummett on my drive back to the University of Arkansas in Fayetteville. Brummett offered approbation for my work, much to my delight and relief, and he sent me on my way with three pounds of his smoked breakfast sausage. After walking to my truck and exchanging farewell pleasantries, our attention drifted back to his gravel parking lot off lonely Highway 82. Brummett could tell I was delighted by the diversity of his clientele that day, which as usual represented the demographic spectrum of Union County's residents here in the heart of the Timberlands. He shook his head and smiled, inspiring me to consider the sublime relevance of barbecue, how it beckons you home, how it binds people together. I got in my truck and rolled down the window with a thanks and a promise to return very soon. Half turning away, he shrugged and waved goodbye, calling out a final point of savory wisdom: "Folks seem to keep coming, and I mean all kinds of folks, every kind of folk you'd ever imagine! Keeps things interesting around here."

Barbecue bears resemblance to a number of illuminating folk cultural processes in the American South. Ritualized social events such as hunting and fishing traditions also illuminate social processes, call forth histories, and convey meaning to anthropologists working in this region of the American South (e.g., Robbins and Nolan 2007). Candid and meaningful interpretation of folk traditions is vital to cultural conservation as an ongoing process of invention and reinvention (Carney 1998). These processes are evident in the edible, material, and customary components of the Piney Woods and its largely understudied history and folk culture. Food-sharing events are central to kinship ties and social celebrations on several levels among regional and ethnic groups. The relevance of area-specific foodways (e.g., duck gumbo and mayhaw jelly in the Piney Woods) as usable and consumable traditions clearly warrants deeper discussion by food researchers and anthropologists in the years to come. Discourse might include the lesser-known food-sharing activities such as fish fries, chili cook-offs, shrimp boils, potlucks, and pie suppers. Accompanying drinking traditions should also be highlighted in the future, as several interviews led to lively exchanges about the virtues of regional potables such as muscadine wine and blackberry moonshine. There are many virtues of coming home for supper, and for the enthusiast of slow-cooked meats, they are by all means evident across the Piney Woods.

Notes

I would like to extend my sincerest thanks to Katlin Jones for providing the map and drawing for this chapter, and to Jim Veteto for his timely encouragement and constructive editorial guidance on several previous drafts of the chapter. My thanks to Karl Brummett, Worth Camp, Robert Nolan, Josie Marshall, Robin Carroll, Philip McDaniel, and the many talented pitmasters throughout South Arkansas and North Louisiana who shared their time with me. This chapter in spirit belongs to you.

1. Following a number of qualitative social studies of shared belief systems, text analysis was applied to the data (Bernard and Ryan 1998) in an effort to ascertain specific characteristics of Piney Woods barbecue shared among all of those who participated in the study. A list of fifteen frequently mentioned descriptive terms (e.g., beef brisket, hickory smoked) was generated and sorted into rows, and compared against the twelve respondents, sorted in columns, using the data analysis program ANTHROPAC 4.0. Each respondent was coded according to their respective regions of residence within the Piney Woods (e.g., Southwest Arkansas, Northeast Louisiana). To determine how specific regions of residence influence each pitmaster's rendition of "authentic" Piney Woods barbecue, correspondence analysis was applied to this "trait by respondent" matrix. The results of the corre-

spondence analysis were charted using multidimensional scaling to visually represent the patterns of barbecue trait distribution as mentioned by each respondent across the study region.

References

Anderson, Eugene N. 2005. *Everyone Eats: Understanding Food and Culture*. New York: New York University Press.

Bower, Anne L., ed. 2009. *African American Foodways: Explorations of History and Culture*. Urbana: University of Illinois Press.

Brown, Linda Keller, and Kay Mussell, eds. 1984. *Ethnic and Regional Foodways in the United States: The Performance of Group Identity*. Knoxville: University of Tennessee Press.

Carney, George O. 1998. "Introduction: A Geography of American Folklife." In *Baseball, Barns, and Bluegrass: A Geography of American Folklife*, edited by George O. Carney, 1–18. Lanham, MD: Rowman and Littlefield.

Douglas, Mary. 1997. "Deciphering a Meal." In *Food and Culture*, 2nd ed., edited by Carole Counihan and Penny Van Esterik, 44–53. New York: Routledge.

Good, James K. 1981. "The Vernacular Regions of Arkansas." *Journal of Geography* 80, no. 5: 1975–81.

Humphrey, Theodore C. 1991. "'It's a Community Deal Here, You Know': Festive Community Life in Rural Oklahoma." In *We Gather Together: Food and Festival in American Life*, edited by Theodore C. Humphrey and Lin T. Humphrey, 153–68. Logan: Utah State University Press.

Martel, Glenn. 1953. "Early Days in Northwest Louisiana." *Arkansas Historical Quarterly* 12, no. 2: 119–25.

Reed, John Shelton, and Dale Volberg Reed. 2008. *Holy Smoke: The Big Book of North Carolina Barbecue*. Chapel Hill: University of North Carolina Press.

Robbins, Michael M., and Justin M. Nolan. 2007. "What's Old Is New Again: Cultural Change in Hunting and Fishing in Missouri and Arkansas." In *Cultural Analysis and the Navigation of Complexity*, edited by Lisa Brandt, 85–102. Lanham, MD: University Press of America.

Sutton, David E. 2001. *Remembrance of Repasts: An Anthropology of Food and Memory*. New York: Berg.

Thomas, Charles E. 1986. *Jelly-Roll: A Black Neighborhood in a Southern Mill Town*. Little Rock, AR: Rose.

5

Priests, Pork Shoulders, and Chicken Halves

Barbecue for a Cause at St. Patrick's Irish Picnic

KRISTEN BRADLEY-SHURTZ

It is the end of July in small-town Tennessee. The midmorning sun rests high in the sky, and the sweltering humidity only rises with the sun's trajectory. On days like today, the locals say, it's a hundred degrees in the shade, and you're beginning to think this is not an exaggeration. You park your car in a large grass field with what must be hundreds, maybe thousands, of other cars. Reluctantly, you leave that cool, air-conditioned vehicle and walk toward the festival grounds. The smell hits you immediately: burning wood, smoke, barbecue. That same smoke floats above you in the air, beckoning you to partake in the feast. As you draw closer, you see the crowds gathered, the lines forming, and the men—all those men—shoveling red-hot coals, building fire, preparing meat, working so hard on this hot, humid day.

This is St. Patrick's Irish Picnic in McEwen, Tennessee. Every year, on the last Friday and Saturday of July, the tiny St. Patrick's Church and School puts on this festival of epic proportions—nay, *Guinness Book of World Records* proportions.[1] Every year, as they will surely tell you, this small Catholic church and school causes the town's dwindling population to grow more than ten times in size, if only for one weekend. Estimated visitors have totaled more than twenty-five thousand people over the course of the weekend (Trolinger 1988), though recent estimates reflect an average of fifteen to eighteen thousand visitors per year over the two days of the event. People come from all over the country. Remarkably, one couple travels from Canada every year to attend. The couple happened upon the picnic one year during their tour of the Southern United States; now they volunteer to help cook the pork shoulders and serve dinners. When the picnic is over, the many visitors return to their homes, only to return again year after year. It has been this way, though admittedly on a smaller scale, since 1854.

McEwen, Tennessee: A Brief History

McEwen, Tennessee, lies approximately twenty-three miles east of the Tennessee River and fifty-eight miles west of Nashville in Humphreys County. In 1842, two Catholic men from New Orleans settled in the area to raise sheep, bringing with them several Irish Catholic families to help with the herd. In 1845, a traveling missionary, Father Aloysius Orengo, found this small Irish community and settled in the town. Father Orengo built St. Patrick's Church in 1849, and St. Patrick's School was built in 1855 ("A Community Study," n.d.; Lehman 1949). In 1861, with the onset of the Civil War and the near completion of the railroad between Nashville and Memphis, many of the mostly Catholic railroad workers settled in the area (Telli 2004). St. Patrick's School was the only school in the area until 1882, when the local public school was founded (Lehman 1949). McEwen was first incorporated as a town in 1907, and the first full nine-month public school was founded in 1917. In 1932, the State of Tennessee built State Highway 1 (now U.S. Highway 70) through the town. The town continued to grow in the decades after the building of the highway, but the population has been declining in recent years. According to a 2007 census, the town of McEwen has a population of 1,683 (Sperling's Best Places, n.d.). Despite the town's small Catholic population, St. Patrick's Church and School are both still thriving.

St. Patrick's School is operated through the Catholic Diocese of Nashville. It is the only Catholic school in Humphreys County and receives students from the surrounding three counties. It teaches grades prekindergarten through eighth, and currently has an enrollment of approximately seventy-five students. The school has a low student-to-teacher ratio and focuses on religious as well as academic studies. While the school does employ lay teachers, in 1937 administration was assumed by the Dominican Sisters of St. Cecilia in Nashville, and the school is continuously staffed by three Sisters from this convent. In

1949, a four-room building was built to house the school, and it remained there until 2004, when a progressive capital campaign raised the money to open a new school building. Today, the school features one of the lowest tuition rates of all the schools operated within the Nashville Diocese. School parents are offered further tuition incentives if they pledge to help with the Irish Picnic. This generous break in tuition and fees is made possible by the funds raised by the picnic each year.

St. Patrick's Irish Picnic and Homecoming, as it is known today, first began in 1854 (*News Democrat* 1993a). In that year, the people of the parish held a chicken supper as a fund-raiser for the church (to purchase a new bell, according to local folklore). The event was originally known as the St. Patrick's Chicken Supper, but in 1878 it became St. Patrick's Irish Barbecue Dinner. The change reflected a need to differentiate the St. Patrick's event from those of other local groups, who often held chicken suppers and were not known for their barbecue. The change may also have reflected growing attendance at the event, as more individuals could be fed from a single pig or goat than from a chicken. The new meat choice was also reflective of the socioeconomic environment of the town. Many McEwen families and St. Patrick's parishioners were farmers who raised their own pigs and goats. While the meat is purchased today, in the early years each family donated animals from their farms to be barbecued (though goats likely went out of fashion in the area by the 1960s). The barbecue and free square dancing were the main attractions of the picnic for many years (*News Democrat* 1993a). In 1948, WSM, a radio station in Nashville, provided music entertainment for the picnic, and Grand Ole Opry stars Minnie Pearl and Uncle Dave Macon were among the performers (*Tennessee Register* 1948).

In 1988, the Irish Picnic was listed as a Tennessee attraction at Disney World's Epcot Center in Orlando, Florida—the first such listing for the state (Trolinger 1988). That same year, the Irish Picnic was honored by the *Guinness Book of World Records* as being the World's Largest Outdoor Barbecue. Father Charles Ney, known to the parish as Father Charlie, was the priest at St. Patrick's Church that year. Father Charlie stated, "We don't hold the barbecue to set records, but to raise money to operate our school . . . but the Guinness recognition does give us grounds for bragging" (Oldham 1988). That year's picnic saw an influx of at least twenty-five thousand visitors and featured the cooking of sixteen thousand pounds of pork and 1,500 chickens (Trolinger 1988).

McEwen, Tennessee, has hosted St. Patrick's Irish Picnic and Homecoming since 1854. Photo by Kristen Bradley-Shurtz.

All of this meat was cooked on the picnic's 237 feet of barbecue pits (*News Democrat* 1993a).

In 1993, a grease fire destroyed the picnic's permanent barbecue pits, and an estimated 16,700 pounds of meat were lost. According to a local newspaper, the picnic that year was expected to use three and a half truckloads of hickory slabs, eighteen thousand pounds of pork, and four thousand chicken halves (News Democrat 1993b, 1993a). Despite the nearly complete destruction of the picnic's meat supply, the picnic was still a success, thanks to cooperation and support from community members and local businesses. Volunteers at the picnic worked "extra hard" to salvage what meat was left unscorched. Local residents and businesses donated barbecue for the picnic to sell. Many patrons returned pork shoulders they had already purchased, while others went to local barbecue restaurants and bought additional meat to help replace the picnic's diminished stock. Mike Bradley was in charge of the dinner stand that year and said, "When you look at the number of shoulders the dinner stand had to sell and how many they actually sold, it was like the fishes and the loaves." Bradley's example effectively demonstrates the community's support of the Irish Picnic.[2]

The Catholic Community

Local support and volunteers from the residents of McEwen, from Humphreys County, and from other Catholic parishes in middle Tennessee are still essential to the Irish Picnic's success. In 2005, it was estimated that more than three hundred volunteers worked to make the 151st Irish Picnic a success. The former pastor of St. Patrick's Church, Father John Sims Baker, said, "There wouldn't be an Irish Picnic without the people who contribute so much of their time and energy to this event" (qtd. in Grimes 2005). Because all the money from the Irish Picnic goes to support St. Patrick's School, parishioners and school parents, friends and family join together to form the picnic's all-volunteer workforce (Trolinger 1988). The event has become so large that the parish and school simply cannot furnish enough workers to operate the entire event. The Association of Religious Data Archives estimated in 2000 that St. Patrick's Church, the only Catholic church in Humphreys County, had approximately 310 members. Using their numbers, only approximately 3 percent of Humphreys County is Catholic. The church's 2009 report to the Nashville Diocese, however, estimates a congregation of approximately 420 members. Both numbers match data compiled by Glenmary Catholic Missions (n.d.), which estimated the area to be 1–5 percent Catholic in 2000.

Though the picnic is a Catholic event, it is obvious from the numbers that the event is attended and worked by people outside of the Catholic community. It is estimated that approximately 50 percent of the picnic's workers are either non-Catholic community members (including friends and family of St. Patrick's parishioners) or Catholics from other parishes. For many years, St. Patrick's Church was the only Catholic church between Memphis and Nashville. Now, however, there are neighboring parishes in Dickson, Tennessee, approximately fifteen miles east of McEwen, and in Tennessee Ridge, approximately twenty miles to the northwest. Both of these parishes started as missions of St. Patrick's Church. Members from these parishes, along with others in Nashville and Ashland City, Tennessee, volunteer at the picnic every year. Each of these volunteers has his or her own reason for participating: some are former parishioners, some are school alumni, many are relatives, and some simply wish to help with this amazing event.

The event is open to the community and is attended by people from across the entire country. There is no estimate as to what percentage of visitors is Catholic; however, as the numbers above indicate, the majority of the surrounding community is Protestant. This Protestant community anxiously anticipates the picnic each year. Like the numerous Catholic churches of Owensboro, Kentucky, St. Patrick's Church is known for its barbecue. Despite concerns about the chaos that can emerge from such large crowds, for many the picnic is a yearly highlight. This is hardly surprising as the slow-cooking process fills the air with a delightful smell that lingers throughout the town. When the smell of wood smoke and cooking meat hits, the community knows that the Catholics at St. Patrick's are barbecuing.

The Secret Recipe

Volunteers and community support are not the only factors responsible for the success of the Irish Picnic. One key component of the Irish Picnic that continues to draw crowds every year is its barbecue sauce. Frank Walsh, former chairman and head barbecue pitmaster, called "Mr. Frank" by those who knew him, "concoct[ed] a tangy, unforgettable barbecue sauce" (Trolinger 1988). All of the meat served at the picnic is prepared using this sauce or some variation of the sauce. Over the past few years, Mike Walsh, Mr. Frank's son, has overseen the preparation of thousands of gallons of this barbecue sauce.

Making nearly seven hundred gallons of the sauce each year, Walsh has quickly become an expert. He reserves two or three Saturdays during the summer before the picnic strictly for making barbecue sauce. On these days, the sauce is cooked in two large aluminum pots stationed in a permanent construction on the picnic grounds. These two pots hold 200 and 250 gallons each, and they are heated over a wood fire. Walsh works from the early morning hours into midafternoon preparing, mixing, and keeping heated this amazing concoction. Around 6:00 a.m., Walsh and typically six volunteers work to start the cooking. The pots are tended by members of the Walsh family throughout the day. Allowing for cooling time, the sauce is cooked for approximately seven hours. Around 3:00 p.m., other workers arrive to help with the bottling. A table and a valve-operated PVC-pipe construction are used in this process. The pipe construction pulls the sauce from the pot through its tubes, and the valve allows the flow of sauce to be shut off and on as bottles are filled. Approximately six people work around the table in assembly-line fashion, with two people operating valves and filling bottles, two people wiping off any spillage and attaching lids, and two people securing labels and placing the bottles into boxes. Others work loading and unloading bottles.

The sauce is divided among 250 gallon-size containers and 2,500 to 2,800 pint-size bottles, which are sold during the picnic. Mike Bradley said, "In a good year, we sell out of all of the sauce before Saturday evening." Another thirty gallons are used with plate dinners and barbecue sandwiches. The remainder is reserved for basting the meat. The barbecue pork requires approximately sixty-five gallons, while twenty gallons are set aside to serve as a base for a separate sauce for the chicken. The last two to three gallons from each pot are always in high demand as the "bottom of the barrel," or the hottest of each batch of sauce. These last bottles are not sold but are usually given to volunteers or key donors.

The sauce is based on ketchup, vinegar, and red and black pepper. Its consistency and taste fall somewhere between that of sweet ketchup-based sauces and thinner vinegar-based sauces. While the sauce is reflective of its geographic location, its exact ingredients remain secret. According to Irish Picnic legend, the Walsh family brought the recipe with them from Ireland in the 1850s (*News Democrat* 1993a). This family was one of the first to settle in the area, and Mr. Frank's father served in the Confederate Army. Today, this family serves as keeper of the secret recipe. As reported in the Nashville *Tennessean* in 1988, "The recipe is almost as closely kept as the Coca-Cola recipe. Mr. Frank keeps the recipe in a bank vault. Only he and his sons have access to it" (Oldham 1988).

Legends regarding secret sauces are common in the world of barbecue; Jack Hitt writes, "Chefs guard their secret recipes (which tend to involve strangely commonplace ingredients like A-1 Steak Sauce or red wine vinegar or margarine) with paranoia worthy of Coca-Cola or KFC" (2001). Despite the frequency and fervor of master chefs guarding their secret sauce recipes, the legends surrounding St. Patrick's Irish Picnic barbecue sauce are likely untrue. Pete Tarpy, longtime parishioner and alumnus of St. Patrick's School, recalls that Mr. Frank and Cleve Bradley, an African American man and former pitmaster, concocted this distinctive sauce in the 1920s. This is interesting to note because the picnic, in recent years, has stemmed from a community with a very small African American population. The 2000 census reveals that only 0.49 percent of the population of McEwen is African American, and this presence is completely absent from St. Patrick's Church.

While stories purport the picnic's secret recipe to be the product of white Irish Catholics, it was likely the virtually unnoticed influence of African Americans that helped developed its flavor. Others recall that Mr. Frank created the sauce around 1925, lending credence to the tale of Cleve Bradley's influence, as he served as pitmaster at this time (Oldham 1988). Further debunking barbecue lore, Tarpy asserts the sauce recipe is not housed in a bank vault. Rather, according to Tarpy, the recipe has been "stored in the hearts and minds of Mr. Frank, his son Mike Walsh, and Tommy Hooper." Hooper is the current barbecue-pork pitmaster at the picnic. Whatever the details of its history, the sauce recipe is still veiled in layers of barbecue secrecy.

The Meat

Every year, the Irish Picnic "boasts mammoth amounts of food consumed by hungry visitors" (Trolinger 1988). In 2004, the year of the 150th Irish Picnic, they cooked twenty-one thousand pounds of pork shoulder and 4,200 chicken halves (Telli 2004). Likewise in 2009, they cooked approximately twenty thousand pounds of pork and more than four thousand chicken halves. The pork is cooked in one session on two large, stationary barbecue pits; one pit measures 138 feet long and five feet wide, and the second measures 134 feet long and five feet wide. Early on the Friday morning of the picnic, volunteers assemble to net the pork shoulders, salt them, and place them on the enormous pits. The task requires a tremendous number of workers.

When I arrived at the grounds for the 2009 Irish Picnic, it was just before 7:00 a.m. A handful of men were gathered around a table positioned at the head of the barbecue pits and next to a refrigerated truck. The truck contained the approximately 1,200 pork shoulders which would be cooked that day. Numerous other volunteers, including women and children, formed a line that wound between the two pits. At 7:00 a.m., the priest from St. Patrick's Church, Father Michael Baltrice, came to the grounds. The priest, assisted by an altar server, led a prayer for a successful picnic. Using the traditional aspergillum and aspersorium, the priest blessed both the meat and the workers with holy water. This is a yearly tradition which marks the beginning of the picnic's unique process of meat preparation. Following the blessing, three or four men worked to unload the shoulders from the truck, handing them down to the next person in line. They then cut the shoulders from their wrappers and passed them on to one of two men holding cotton elastic nets. These nets are slightly smaller than the shoulders and work to hold the meat together as it cooks to tenderness. Once the shoulder was encased in a net, it was passed to the next pair of men, who rolled the netted shoulder in salt. The shoulders were then passed, one person at a time, down the entire length of the barbecue pit and placed to cook. Within the hour, all 1,200 shoulders had been placed, and the pits were ready to be fired.

Chicken halves are prepared in a similar fashion, but on a much smaller scale. The chicken halves are cooked in three separate batches on a smaller set of barbecue pits to the left of the pork pits. These pits measure fifty feet long by six feet wide. The cooking of the chicken starts on the Thursday before the picnic. Arriving just after 10:00 p.m., I found a group of men, women, and children gathered around the smaller, but still impressively sized, chicken pits. They were preparing to begin the first round of cooking, two of which would be complete before the picnic grounds officially opened the next morning. Working in pairs of younger, less experienced people matched with older, more experienced people, they quickly unboxed and unwrapped the chicken halves and placed them bone-side down on the pits. They must start cooking long before the picnic begins as the chicken is sold on Friday, while barbecue pork is sold on Saturday. Both the barbecue pork and the barbecue chicken are cooked using the secret-recipe sauce, but for the chicken, the secret-recipe sauce is mixed into yet another secret recipe before being slathered onto the meat.

While the sauce is certainly one secret to making good barbecue, the real trick lies in the method of preparation and manner of cooking. First, both meats are cooked over beds of burning hot coals. The barbecue pits are lined with larger fire pits on either side. These pits burn hardwood taken from local sawmills. When the hardwood burns down to coals, the workers shovel the coals out of the fire with long-handled shovels and place them under the meat through openings in the barbecue pits. The cooking of the barbecue pork takes approximately twenty to twenty-six hours to complete. The meat cooks slowly because it is cooked over coals and not over open flame (Oldham 1988). Each batch of barbecue chicken takes approximately five hours to cook. Because of the length of cooking, workers cook in shifts, but there is one expert on the grounds at all times. This expert pitmaster is Tommy Hooper for the barbecue pork, and his cousin Wayne Hooper for the chick-

Tommy Hooper, pork pitmaster at St. Patrick's Irish Picnic, stokes the fire. Photo by Kristen Bradley-Shurtz.

ens. Tommy's crew consists of approximately thirty people. Wayne's crew consists of approximately nine people and is followed by another chicken-cooking crew on the Friday afternoon of the picnic.

All the Fixin's

Beginning Saturday morning, barbecue pork can be bought by the pound, in sandwiches, or as part of a plate dinner at the dinner stand. In the plate dinner, the barbecue pork is served along with fried chicken, green beans, coleslaw, potato salad, and dessert. Most of the food served at the dinner stand is donated by school families and parishioners. Each of these people is asked to bring one fried chicken, one gallon of green beans, one gallon of vinegar slaw, one gallon of potato salad, one gallon of ice tea, three cakes, and a twenty-five-dollar donation to help offset the cost of the meat. Previously, this donation was enough to offset the costs, but no longer. Additionally, several families donate produce from their gardens, especially tomatoes and cucumbers for use at the dinner stand. A refrigerated truck is brought on-site for food storage. Two out of every three cakes are reserved by the cake booth, a carnival-style game which gives out cakes as prizes. The remainder of the donated food is used exclusively in the dinner stand.

Like the rest of the picnic, the dinner stand is operated entirely by volunteers, and there are usually around twenty volunteers working in the dinner stand at all times. These include four people pulling and chopping barbecue shoulders, two people on ice and drinks, six people on the serving line, four or five in the kitchen, one taking money, and another on tables and general help. The volunteers in the kitchen cook the many gallons of green beans, mix enormous vats of coleslaw and potato salad, and work to keep the serving line supplied with food. There is no good estimate as to the amount of food the dinner stand uses, but they typically serve 2,400 to 2,600 plate dinners and pull and chop approximately seventy-five shoulders to serve with the dinners. They serve plate dinners from 10:00 a.m. until they run out of food or customers, whichever comes first. Typically, they close between 8:00 and 9:00 p.m. Any leftover prepared food is donated to local groups that house special-needs adults and children and to other local churches. Leftover canned food is kept to be served in the school cafeteria.

Other food stands at the picnic include the hamburger booth, the barbecue sandwich stand, the ice cream booth, and the St. Christopher's Knights of Columbus booth. Like the dinner stand, the barbecue sandwich stand serves barbecue pork. In this case, however, the barbecue is served on buns, with dill pickle slices, and the stand also sells potato chips. Based on the number of buns ordered each year, it is estimated that the sandwich stand makes and sells about 3,500 sandwiches. For this, the workers chop and pull approximately 175 pork shoulders. Additionally, they use approximately five gallons of dill pickle slices and seven cases of chips. The sandwich stand is staffed by six people who pull and chop barbecue, four or five selling and taking orders, and another six to eight making sandwiches. The barbecue is, of course, the main draw for the Irish Picnic, but other food stands provide alternatives.

Gender Roles and Masculinity

It is important to note that the cooking crews are not entirely men, though they are certainly male dominated. Tommy Hooper says there have been a few women in the past who have taken part in the meat cooking and some who participate year after year. He says St. Patrick's certainly does not discriminate: their crews consist of male and female, young and old alike. Typical foodways studies, however, often place significant emphasis on the division of gender roles in food preparation. This is particularly true in barbecue scholarship. Jonathan Deutsch notes that women have been the primary cooks and nurturers in most cultures, but that barbecue is an exception. Deutsch writes, "On the other side of the continuum, we have also accepted and embraced the idea of men cooking recreationally. Backyard barbecues, complete with 'kiss the cook' aprons, are as masculine a phenomenon as mowing the lawn or scowling under the hood of a car in suburban Middle America" (2005, 92). Tony Whitehead has written that "women are seen as the ideal preparers of food, except in the case of barbecues" (1984, 123). This could be explained in part by the festival-type setting of many barbecues. Deutsch cites Kathy Neustadt as finding that in festival settings, "women tend the food while men tend the fire" (2005, 110).

While gender divisions of sorts may exist in the majority, they are hardly ubiquitous. Tommy and Wayne Hooper's barbecue crews consist mostly of men, but women do participate in the meat cooking. Perhaps even more telling, men increasingly participate in other food preparation activities at the Irish Picnic. More men work on the serving line and in the kitchen at the dinner stand than have in years past, and much of the food donated to the dinner stand is brought in by men in the parish or fathers of schoolchildren. The sandwich stand also has men and women working alongside each other to make sandwiches, despite this task being stereotypically seen as a woman's job. Dinner stand chairman Mike Bradley asserts that this is because food preparation roles, and all roles, at the Irish Picnic are divided by family rather than by gender. Further showing the reliance on division by family, Wayne explains that he learned the skills needed to take over the cooking of the chicken from both his aunt and his uncle. Pete Tarpy has observed the change throughout the years of his participation in the Irish Picnic. He notes that in the early days, the gender roles were exclusive: men tended to the fire, and women tended to the kitchen. The times, of course, are changing.

When Wayne and Tommy Hooper set foot on the picnic grounds, they face the daunting task of cooking thousands of pounds of meat, supervising crews of workers, and, above all, making sure they get it right. Sure, the men revel in it, and they both enjoy what they do, but they do it because they care about St. Patrick's Church and School. Perhaps the seriousness of the work and the danger of it all—literally—going up in smoke serve as some latent cultural expression of masculinity, but this cannot be the only purpose or meaning of the barbecue. The men in charge of the pits certainly do not see it as such. In fact, they do not believe that an individual must be masculine, or even male, to participate. According to Tommy, anyone can learn, but it takes both knowledge and skill to get it right. In explaining this knowledge and skill, both men called what they do an art.

Tradition and Skill

The workers at the Irish Picnic have developed over time the skills required to create their barbecue masterpieces, and these unique methods of meat preparation are what make St. Patrick's barbecue memorable. Time, practice, and repetition have allowed Wayne Hooper and his family to develop the sweet barbecue sauce which gives the picnic's barbecue chicken its unique taste. Because the regular picnic sauce is usually too hot to be used on barbecue chickens, the chicken sauce is made by combining the original secret-recipe barbecue sauce with undisclosed ingredients. The result is a thick, rich, sweet, tangy sauce, which is prepared by the Hooper family in the same pots as the regular Irish Picnic barbecue sauce. Wayne says this double-secret recipe is "what makes the chicken so good." Wayne and his crew cook the halves completely prior to basting them, which keeps the sauce from burning. They do, however, heat the halves slightly after putting on the sauce. This allows the sauce to stick to the chickens and gives the meat the good sweet taste that people enjoy. Wayne and his crew also have ways of cooking that give the chicken the tender, juicy qualities barbecue is expected to have. They first slow cook the chickens for three hours with the bone-side down. They then flip the halves and cook them for the next two hours with the meat-side down. This "holds the juices in better," creating the tender, juicy meat people want.

Both the pork and chicken preparations require significant skill to accomplish. The cooking crews work constantly to regulate the temperature each hour and to make sure the meat is always cooking. Tommy Hooper explains, "If you heat meat and allow it to cool down in the process before it reaches its doneness temperature, it will spoil. That's why we always have a steady firing of the meat." To accomplish this, the workers must shovel the embers and coals from the hardwood fire pits and spread them out under the meat. Tommy describes this process as "another art" that people have to learn. As the workers shovel coals, another individual walks behind with a rake stick to keep the embers from

Wayne Hooper, practicing the art of barbecuing chicken. Photo by Kristen Bradley-Shurtz.

piling up under the meat. If the embers are allowed to pile up, the meat will char. According to Tommy, "Handling the meat, firing the meat, and regulating the temperatures is the hardest thing we do with the picnic. That's what fascinates a lot of visitors that come to our picnic.... They watch us with our ten- and twelve-foot shovel handles, how we manage the embers and the firing of the pits, and they're amazed at how we can regulate the temperature the way we do."

All of this work is done by volunteers from the parish and school, who Tommy calls "really talented helpers"; however, each shift of workers is always supervised by a "knowledgeable person." For the barbecue pork, these knowledgeable people include Tommy, who is there at all times during the cooking of the pork; Mike Walsh; Wayne Wells; and Tommy's two sons, Scott and Paul. Tommy says, "One or two of us are there at all times to oversee." The same approach is used for the cooking of the barbecue chickens—either Wayne Hooper or Phil Ross is present at all times. All of these individuals have been working at the picnic and learning these skills for many years. In Wayne Hooper's and

Tommy Hooper's cases, their experience exceeds thirty years. Tommy says, "How you keep the meat cooking and keep the temperature rising on the meat is something that is learned over time and studying and helping at the picnic grounds." Here we witness Gerald Pocius's idea that skill is tied to group, emotion, and tradition (1995). These skills are developed as mechanisms for producing a product that is aesthetically pleasing according to the group's needs and ideals. This product then evokes an emotionally positive response in the people of the group, in this case keeping the people coming back year after year for more barbecue. The skills needed to produce the barbecue year after year are the same skills that have been needed to do so for many generations.

Traditionally, the cooking of the meat and the managing of the fires at the picnic "is an art that the people of St. Patrick's [have] sustained since it started as a Church Picnic and Homecoming," according to Tommy Hooper. He has been cooking it that way since the 1970s, and it was done that way before he came to St. Patrick's. This statement is reflective of the idea that the meat is cooked in a particular way at St. Patrick's simply because it has always been cooked that way. The tradition is seen, as Michael Owen Jones (1989) would say, as continuity in human thought and behavior across time. Jones's ideas are reflected also in the manner in which the workers at the picnic have learned the skills that the cooking of the meat requires. Tommy explains, "It is an art that myself and Mike Walsh learned from Mr. Cleve Bradley, who was over here when I first came over and who was cooking the meat with Mike's daddy, Mr. Frank Walsh. And we learned from two of the master chefs of barbecue." Wayne Hooper also describes having learned his "art" from his Aunt Judy and Uncle Jerry Smith, who "were over the cooking at that time." Both men describe learning through interaction with their teachers. Wayne recalls his aunt and uncle letting him "get in there and help" and essentially learn through working alongside his elders. Tommy now does the same thing with his sons and grandsons. They participate and learn from him, and it is hoped that they will one day take over the cooking so he can concentrate on being exclusively an overseer.

Tradition plays an important role in the Irish Picnic. Of course, variations on traditional themes have arisen as the times have changed. Most notably, the chicken sauce is made from a variation on the original secret recipe. Other variations on tradition have occurred throughout the years of the Irish Picnic as well. Originally, hardwood slabs were placed in the pits by hand. Now, a front-end loader has become a new tradition—and the operation of it a new skill—used in the preparation of the Irish Picnic barbecue. Tommy Hooper's grandson Blain has been learning to use the front-end loader through interaction with his grandfather for years. Additionally, the barbecue formerly took on its distinctive flavor as it was cooked by being buried in the ground. The building of permanent above-ground pits altered that tradition. Further, after the devastating fire in 1993, the wood building sheltering the above-ground pits was replaced with a metal construction.

Finally, the cooking of barbecue at St. Patrick's relies on skill and tradition rather than on exact measurements. Speaking of this, Wayne Hooper says, "We don't do it by thermometer. We do it by sight. It's almost an art." Hooper estimates they keep the pits for the chickens around three hundred degrees, but he has never used a thermometer to check. He says you can tell how the chickens are cooking by watching the color of the smoke. He says, "If it's a light blue smoke, we're doing well. If it starts getting darker, then we have it too hot." Tommy Hooper makes the same assessment when describing the cooking of the barbecue pork. He estimates they keep the pits somewhere between 225 and 275 degrees. He says he could use a thermometer, but "no one does." Rather than cooking by exact temperature, Tommy cooks "by knowledge of cooking from the past forty years." He watches how the meat drips and how the meat smokes. Tommy says,

> We cook the meat until the process of the dripping stops. When that stops . . . the meat starts to absorb, suck in the smoked flavor from the embers, and that's the process that will start pulling in the barbecue sauce. So after about eighteen to nineteen hours of cooking would be the first time we would start basting the meat with our barbecue sauce, and that is so it will absorb the sauce as it finishes cooking until we start to sell it that morning.

If the sauce is applied too early, the ketchup in the sauce will blacken and make the shoulders look burnt. Applying the sauce at an exact point during cooking keeps the shoulders moist and adds flavor to the pork.

Tommy and his crew are also innovative in the method with which they baste the meat with sauce. The sauce is applied to the shoulders using a custom sprayer with two spray wands. This sprayer holds the barbecue sauce in a central vat, which rests on top of a cart with wheels. The sprayer is pulled down the center of the two barbecue pits, and workers use the wands to spray sauce on the shoulders on both pits. The knowledge of when to apply the barbecue sauce and the development of this unique method of application was, of course, learned through time and practice.

Conclusion

All of this work—not to mention wood, coals, smoke, embers, sauce, and, of course, meat—serves to create a unique barbecue event. The dominant characteristics of St. Patrick's barbecue certainly distinguish it from other barbecues. Most important, however, the picnic raises money to support St. Patrick's Church and School. While the wonderful barbecue keeps people coming back year after year, it is almost certainly its worthy cause that has perpetuated its success. Every year, thousands of people flock to this otherwise small town to enjoy thousands of pounds of barbecue pork and chicken, purchase gallons of secret-recipe barbecue sauce, and spend a day reveling in the rustic nostalgia that has been a part of the church since 1854. They come to support St. Patrick's Church and School, and they come to have fun.

Now, the sun has set on the last Saturday in July, the heat and energy finally dissipating from the recently hectic picnic grounds. With the picnic drawing to an end, visitors begin to trickle home, and the workers begin to wrap up their responsibilities. Another twenty-thousand-plus pounds of barbecue have been painstakingly crafted by the picnic's expert pitmasters and happily consumed by all who attended. The trash is swept away, leftover food is packed into refrigerated trucks, and numbers are tallied: more than $90,000 has been raised for the tiny Catholic school. And now, with the sun gone and the artificial lights being sporadically extinguished, the picnic is over. Until next year, of course.

Notes

This article is dedicated to my uncle Pete Tarpy, who sparked my interest in the Irish Picnic as a research topic and taught me, above all else, the importance of humor.

1. The Irish Picnic was featured in the 1988 *Guinness Book of World Records* as the largest barbecue (p. 405).
2. In this project, I have interviewed countless people to whom I am greatly indebted. The ones cited here include former picnic chairman Mike Bradley

and his daughter, Mary Bradley; Pete Tarpy (Mike Bradley's uncle); and the two pitmasters, Tommy Hooper (Pete Tarpy's son-in-law) and Wayne Hooper (Tommy Hooper's cousin).

References

"A Community Study." n.d. Photocopy, Humphreys County Archives, Waverly, TN.

Deutsch, Jonathan. 2005. "'Please Pass the Chicken Tits': Rethinking Men and Cooking at an Urban Firehouse." *Food and Foodways* 13:91–114.

Glenmary Catholic Missions. n.d. "Catholic Church: Adherents as Percentage of the Population." *www.glenmary.org/grc/RCMS_2000/maps/Catholics.jpg* (accessed February 15, 2010).

Grimes, Alexia. 2005. "Volunteers Key Success of St. Patrick's Irish Picnic." Diocese of Nashville. July 15. *www.dioceseofnashville.com/article-stpatrick_picnic.htm* (accessed November 15, 2008).

Hitt, Jack. 2001. "A Confederacy of Sauces." *New York Times Magazine*, August 21.

Jones, Michael Owen. 1989. *Craftsman of the Cumberlands: Tradition and Creativity*. Lexington: University Press of Kentucky.

Lehman, John. 1949. "McEwen Parish to Commemorate Centenary on May 29." *Tennessee Register*, May 15.

News Democrat. 1993a. "139th Irish Picnic July 30–31." July 16.

———. 1993b. "Thousands of Pounds." August 6.

Oldham, Paul. 1988. "'World's Largest' Barbecue to Boost Parochial School." *Tennessean*, July 27.

Pocius, Gerald L. 1995. "Art." *Journal of American Folklore* 108, no. 43: 413–31.

Sperling's Best Places. n.d. "McEwen, Tennessee." *www.bestplaces.net/McEwen-Tennessee.aspx* (accessed November 24, 2008).

Telli, Andy. 2004. "Family Tradition: St. Patrick Irish Picnic Celebrates 150 Years." *Tennessee Register*, July 16.

Tennessee Register. 1948. "Irish Picnic Set in McEwen Parish." July 25.

Trolinger, Shannon. 1988. "Picnic Plans Underway." *News Democrat*, July 22.

Whitehead, Tony Larry. 1984. "Sociocultural Dynamics and Food Habits in a Southern Community." In *Food in the Social Order: Studies of Food and Festivities in Three American Communities*, edited by Mary Douglas, 97–142. New York: Russell Sage Foundation.

6

Identity, Authenticity, Persistence, and Loss in the West Tennessee Whole-Hog Barbecue Tradition

RIEN T. FERTEL

Although the Southern iconoclast W. J. Cash seemingly could not appreciate barbecue, he did honestly understand its foundational importance to the region. He blamed pork consumption for the degeneration of the South. "Increasingly," the amateur, but well-admired, sociologist wrote of the Southern frontiersman, "his diet became a monotonous and revolting affair, of cornpone and the flesh of razorback hogs" (1941, 25). For better or worse, hog flesh defines, today as for centuries past, the Southern palate. The present and historical lives of Southerners and swine are intertwined; the people identify with and have been identified with the pigs. The tradition of smoking meat, mainly hog, and eating barbecue has been accepted as the most authentic of Southern customs. Barbecue culture is Southern culture. Or as John Egerton writes, "Barbecue in these parts is ever so much more than just the meat; it's also the preparation, the ritual, the social occasion, the fellowship, the anticipation, the realization, [and] the memory . . . of Southern history" (1990, 68).

Whole-hog barbecue is exasperating and dangerous to prepare, and thus increasingly rare. Barbecue guru Lolis Eric Elie, following a cross-regional smoked-meat trek, declared whole-hog to be "perhaps the most difficult technique for the barbecue cooks to master" (2005, 136). Smoking a pig that can weigh up to two to three hundred pounds requires extra time, space, observation, and muscle. The process demands complete attention and control of the fire, which must be distributed so that the heat properly smokes both the thicker hams and shoulders of the hog and the thinner sections evenly. Blazing hardwood coals are shoveled continuously under the pig, while plumes of lung-searing smoke choke the pitmaster. Whole-hog barbecue necessitates patience and endurance, as the size of the carcass and slow-smoked technique entail an eighteen- to twenty-four-hour cooking cycle. Beginning skin-side up, the massive, sizzling hogs are finished with a fantastic denouement, a careful flipping that rotates them muscle-and-fat-side up for the final hour or two of smoking. Preparing whole-hog barbecue is much like lifting weights in a sauna for nearly an entire day.

Traditionally a fixture of large-scale family and communal gatherings, though it appears less often now, and the competition circuit, where it continues to thrive, whole-hog barbecue is also professionally prepared in restaurants scattered throughout the South, especially the Carolinas, Arkansas, and West Tennessee. In the western Volunteer State counties of Chester and Henderson, West Tennessee whole-hog barbecue achieves a nearly mythic status. Barbecue is whole-hog. Whole-hog barbecue defines West Tennesseans, pitmasters, and consumers alike. It forms a vital contribution to individual and community identities. Here whole-hog is history, society, and custom. It's featured at family reunions and Fourth of July celebrations. It's eaten for breakfast, lunch, and dinner. Whole hogs plague the nightmares of one Lexington pitmaster, and have sent a Henderson pitmaster to the hospital. To partake in West Tennessee whole-hog barbecue is to observe the rituals, symbols, and pageantry of tradition; participate in a community; and devour the most authentic culture in the area.

In the summer of 2008, as part of a larger project including Memphis and its environs, I conducted twenty-five oral history interviews with individuals—pitmasters, restaurant and slaughterhouse owners, and one legendary waiter—involved in the professional West Tennessee barbecue trade. The project was undertaken in support of the Southern Foodways Alliance's Oral History Initiative for inclusion in the archives at the University of Mississippi. The oral history interviewees were chosen not for the taste of their barbecue but for their historical and regional importance. For this chapter, ten members of the West Tennessee whole-hog barbecue culture, from eight establishments, will be featured. They include Liz and Ike Kinchen, owners and pitmaster (Ike) of the whole-hog joint Liz's Bar-B-Q; whole-hog barbecuer Chris Siler of Siler's Old Time BBQ; Billy Frank Latham of Bill's Bar-B-Q; Joe Joyner, former owner but still the pitmaster at Jacks Creek Bar-

B-Que; Richard Hodge of Richard's Bar-B-Que, who does not smoke whole hogs but fondly remembers doing so as a young man; Crystal and Derek Norwood, young co-owners of Hays Meat Company; Curt Blankenship of Curt's Smoke House; and Ricky Parker, the legendary pitmaster of Scott's-Parker's Barbecue.[1]

This chapter will deconstruct oral history transcripts in order to put the whole-hog players in dialogue with each other, imaginarily seated at the same table, resulting in an interdiscursive history of the region's barbeculture. In West Tennessee barbecuedom, the past is always linked to the present, in real and imagined ways; myth and memory are wrapped in whole-hog barbecue's regional origins. The identity of pitmasters and customers must also be considered: place and function—that is, rural farm communities and consumption of barbecue—create unique personal and communal identities that are entirely based on region. Cooks and consumers treat the hog in diverse ways. I will investigate both the literal and symbolic role of the pig in West Tennessee barbecue culture. The action of barbecuing is more than a process of cooking; pitmasters create or brand a distinct identity through the keeping of secret recipes and the intense labor and danger associated with this special species of barbecue. In conclusion, I will focus on the recent changes to local whole-hog culture that threaten to end the practice. Pitmasters Billy Frank Latham and Joe Joyner have recently ceased to smoke entire hogs. In the face of a disappearing barbeculture, several other pitmasters—old and new—have resisted change by strengthening their own ties to the hog and insisting on the authenticity of whole-hog barbecue. Despite a multitude of economic, technological, and societal transformations, West Tennessee whole-hog barbecue persists.

Origins, Myths, and Memory

As historians and anthropologists continue to speculate on the origins and etymology of barbecue, West Tennessee pitmasters create and circulate their own stories, their own regional myths (see, e.g., Warnes 2008). Richard Hodge of Richard's Bar-B-Que in Bolivar explains the origin story he learned. When asked whether Tennessee barbecue was a rural invention, he answers, "I understood the way that barbecue was established was people used to let their hogs run loose out in the yard sometimes. And a house fire trapped some hogs underneath it, and when the fire was out, somehow they decided to sample the meat and that's where I heard the origin of barbecue came from. And it was in the

South." According to Hodge's genesis tale, which he can only remember as once hearing "a long time ago," a completely passive act generated not just whole-hog barbecue but also the act of eating smoked pigs. Though Hodge gives no indication that he believes the story, he determinedly emphasizes that the event occurred in the South. Thus, whole-hog barbecue is a wholly Southern miracle.

Origin stories are also used to justify the location of a whole-hog restaurant. Chris Siler's Old Time BBQ takes up a mythic acreage in local barbecue lore. Siler's inhabits a spot halfway between Memphis and Nashville, conveniently located just south of Henderson in a scenic bend in Highway 100 East, the old main route that connected western and central Tennessee. But more important, local patrons claim that the location's barbecue history goes back more than 150 years. Siler's customers maintain that his recently purchased restaurant occupies the site of the very first barbecue. "It's been here forever," says Siler.

> Local people, they hold that this is the first barbecue pit ever made, which I don't know about that totally. I think it maybe just started out some good old boys just started cooking, and they really didn't pay attention if it was barbecue or not. . . . They used to just cook outside, under holes in the ground, and under the trees out here. This was, at one point in time, it was kind of an oak grove, so everybody would cook out here and they'd just dig a hole in the ground and start cooking the hog. And they've been doing that for years.

The relationship of memory to eating is important. Siler, despite being in his early thirties, designates his restaurant as "Old Time BBQ"—he, with the aid of his customers, draws a connection between a porcine past and present.

Unsurprisingly, the owners of barbecue establishments often claim a lineage to a previous pitmaster, business, or recipe. Barbecue businesses are rarely ever new, and very few entrepreneurs or cooks just up and establish a whole-hog barbecue restaurant. Ricky Parker of the formerly named B. E. Scott's Barbecue in Lexington started working at a young age for Early Scott and finally acquired the restaurant in 1989. A pair of barbecue enthusiasts once proclaimed, "Of all the pitmasters we met . . . none was more serious about his barbecue than Early Scott" (Staten and Johnson 2007, 81–82). According to Parker, his revered mentor Scott—a former Lexington school bus driver—acquired the smoke

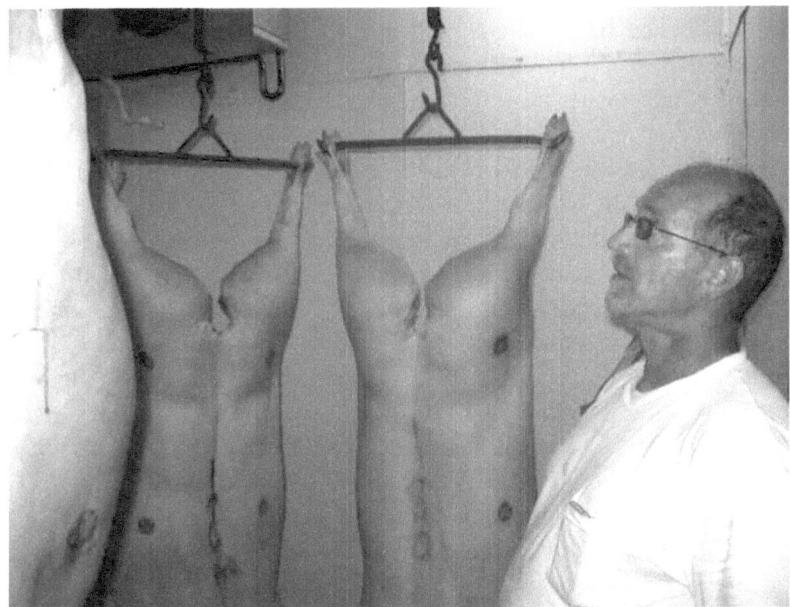

Ricky Parker inspects the pigs to be put on that morning.
Photo by Rien Fertel.

shack on Lexington's Highway 412 West in the early 1970s, trading two school buses for it. As with many other pits, no one remembers the name of the previous incarnation.

Like Scott, other whole-hog pitmasters have also set up shop in previous barbecue houses. In 1997, Joe Joyner bought a restaurant nestled in the crossroads of Tennessee Highways 22A and 100 East. Customers knew to buy their whole-hog from this new pitmaster because it had always been sold at this intersection. "There's been barbecue sold here for many, many years . . . ," Joyner recounts. "There's probably been barbecue—I'm not for sure the number of years—but we're at least looking at sixty years plus. . . . But [the pits have] always been known as Jacks Creek Barbecue." Billy Frank Latham, Joyner's father-in-law, remembers dining at the site: "Been a barbecue place before I ever remember." In 2000, Latham left his five-plus decades as a farmer to buy the recently shuttered Thomas and Webb pit house (which he renamed Bill's Bar-B-Q) and continue that venue's whole-hog tradition. The location's history appealed to him: "I've eat at it a whole lot."

Whole-hog barbecuers also form linkages to the past by training under established pitmasters. Chris Siler learned from and worked for pitmaster and owner Chad Sellers, who in turn gained tutelage under previous proprietor Bobby Sells. After five years, Siler purchased Bobby's Bar-B-Q—Sellers had kept the name—and renamed it for himself. Additionally, Siler kept on Ronnie Hampton, Sellers's renowned pitmaster. With the purchase Siler gained not only a piece of mythical barbecue property and its equally lauded pitmaster, but also the all-important sauce recipes once brewed by Sells. Like the name of the business, Siler also altered the sauce: "Everybody has different tastes so they alter the recipe just a little bit to suit themselves, and I've done the same thing. You know it's like my hot is a little . . . bit hotter than Chad's hot was, and my mild is a little sweeter. . . . Everybody who does it, does it to their own taste." By keeping the methods and recipes relatively unchanged but claiming the business name and sauce spice levels as his own, Siler has joined a long-standing community of whole-hog pit cooks and owners.

The transmission of techniques and recipes may be seen with other whole-hog establishments. Ricky Parker's education under Early Scott is an often-told story. The mentor discovered his future successor, a precocious fourteen-year-old from Memphis, working the local pump at Morgan's Service Station. Parker helped Scott at the pits late nights and early mornings, before and after school; he would also leave school to work the busy lunch shift. Scott and his wife adopted teenage Ricky following a violent incident at the Parker home between father and son. Barbecue soon became Parker's mission, and he transformed into a true barbecue saucerer's apprentice: "At the age of seventeen and a half, I was three months [from] graduating from high school, and Mr. Scott told me, 'Why don't you just quit school and you come to work?' He said, 'You done learned all you going to learn in school . . . now let me learn you about life.'" Along with some minor tweaks that Parker made to the smoking process, the sauce remains nearly the same. Parker is presently grooming his son Zach for the trade.[2]

Rather than a chain of linkages, the whole-hog barbecue community in rural West Tennessee may be seen as a web of interconnections.[3] At the center of this interconnectivity is the mini whole-hog empire established by Dennis Hays. Until just recently, Hays operated his own abattoir, which supplied whole hogs to the Lexington-Henderson barbecue corridor, and up the road he smoked his own hogs at Hays Smoke House. Hays had retired from both businesses by 2007. Curt Blanken-

Chris Siler prepares a whole hog for the pit. Photo by Rien Fertel.

ship purchased the smokehouse, having previously worked at Scott's under Ricky Parker. At Curt's Smoke House, he carries on the smoking process and sauce recipes learned from Hays. Derek and Crystal Norwood, a young married couple from Florida, have since purchased the slaughterhouse, Hays Meat Company, and continue to supply Scott's-Parker's, Siler's, and others with butchered whole hogs. Whether through timeworn myths or more recent memories, pitmasters locate their own origins and find their place within the West Tennessee barbecue order of things.

The Pitmaster and His People

Both historically and at present, the barbecue ritual provides extensive social synergy within a localized sphere. As several classic studies of Southern eating show, barbecue has historically been smoked and served at family gatherings, church picnics, and political rallies (Bass 2008; Egerton 1987; Reed 2004; Taylor 1982). Most of the participants in this study remember whole-hog communal assemblies as part of West Tennessee's traditional social and cultural structure. Whole-hog cooking typically takes the effort of several men (the whole-hog event is usually gender specific) to prepare the hog, flip the carcass, and watch for periodic heat-on-fat combustions during the long smoking process. Nearly all of the interviewees grew up on farms, many of which raised hogs, and in such settings holiday and Sunday family gatherings were commonplace. This spirit of community translates into the restaurant business in the Tennessee whole-hog triangle. Everybody eats whole-hog in Chester County and Henderson County, Tennessee. Those that cook and serve the hog become locally prominent. The relationship between a pitmaster and his people is a connection that defines community in whole-hog Tennessee.

One Tennessean, writing about his state's barbecue, sacralized it as "that element which binds us into a community. Barbecue is a social cause, something which gives meaning to our existence" (Egerton 1987, 164). For citizens of the western third of the state, whole-hog barbecue is a home-cooked, special-event meal. Curt Blankenship recalls killing hogs with his family during the fall harvest season and notable holidays: "I can remember back from when I was a little boy, you know when it's cold out . . . you had to go kill hogs and stuff. . . . Plus my family, we have a big family, and we always do a Fourth of July thing of where we barbecue." Richard Hodge, as a boy in Hornsby, Tennessee, took an interest in whole-hog cooking during the town's yearly celebrations: "They had an annual Fourth of July picnic for the community, and the entire West Tennessee would show up at it. It would literally be hundreds of people, and the elders would get under a barn in case it rained, and dig a hole in the ground, and put their pigs on, and stay with them all night. I'd go up there when I was very young and kind of enthused

Ike Kinchen examines a hog halfway through the smoking process.
Photo by Rien Fertel.

about what they were doing, and watched to see how the process was done, and it kind of went from there." Likewise, Ike Kinchen, growing up in the delectably named Sweet Lips—a tiny farm community east of Henderson—reminisces about these special-occasion cookouts: "From the time I was real little, I followed behind them [the pitmasters] and started, learnt what I know now about cooking hogs."

These whole-hog barbecues transcend mere gathering and feasting. They symbolically serve as a ritualistic event—the hog becomes the host for the community's communion. Richard Hodge describes the whole-hog gathering as "just a community effort. There's no competition, no nothing." Ike Kinchen labels it "a big outfit . . . a family get-together." Curt Blankenship partakes in "grill[ed] hamburgers and hotdogs" at his family's barbecues—that is, they eat while waiting to eat. The most ethereal description of a communal hog smoking goes to Joe Joyner: "We would cook three to four hogs a summer, and it was just a community-type thing. . . . It was just fellowship for the community. A lot of family basically is what it was; it was fellowship for the community." This fellowship of the porcine united the community and transformed it into a family.

Most of the Henderson-Lexington community comes from the multitude of farms that dot the area. The region is well suited to hog farming, which helps explain why rural Tennesseans eat so much of the animal. As geographer Sam Hilliard explained, swine has been the majority of Southerners' "first choice" for food since the early nineteenth century (1972, 92). He calculated that most white Southerners ate pork almost every day during the antebellum era. In West Tennessee this statistic carries over to the present; pork still predominates today. The public's consumption of swine continues to astound Chris Siler, despite his being a native of the region: "The only thing I can say is this has got to be the most barbecue-crazy bunch of people in the world I've ever seen in my life. I have never seen people who love barbecue so much as in this area." Billy Frank Latham remembers when small-scale commercial whole-hog barbecue first started thriving in his area: "You didn't have to do it at home anymore." The new restaurant culture meant that hog-mad Chester County citizens could get it whenever they wanted; Latham fondly recalls, "You'd eat barbecue all day."

Consider this story told by Liz Kinchen. Her husband Ike's illness forced the couple to close their previous establishment, the Friendship Barbecue, in early 2003. The following year, in her words, "was miserable." Former customers begged them to reopen; they were ravenous, stopping the couple at every outing. "We couldn't go shopping, and we couldn't go to the funeral homes. . . . You couldn't go nowhere. . . . They wanted whole-hog cooked right, barbecue to eat." Fed up, the Kinchens finally relented, reopening a whole-hog house down the street, purely, in Liz's perspective, "to satisfy the people." Her husband agrees: "Yeah, for the people. They want it."

Sociologist John Shelton Reed suggests that Southerners will frequently reinforce their community by emphasizing the differences from outsiders (2004). In whole-hog country, locals habitually "otherize" the nearby metropolitan mecca of Mid-South barbecue: Memphis. West Tennesseans disdain Memphis for three culinary reasons. First, the city does not produce whole-hog, at least not commercially. Second, the city is littered with franchise barbecue chains that cook a supposedly inauthentic and inferior product. And worst of all, these faux barbecues have attempted to locate, always unsuccessfully, in whole-hog territories. In addition, the interviewees consistently responded that the people of West Tennessee all eat barbecue, and that those who do not should be regarded with suspicion. Locals do not just consume barbecue; it also consumes them. As Billy Frank Latham communicates, "Anyone that lives in a place as small as Henderson in Chester County now is going to know about barbecue."

Though whole-hog barbecue defines the identity of West Tennesseans, outsiders also come to taste the authenticity and the tradition of their old-style barbecue. The interviewees frequently related how well their barbecue travels, how often outsiders enjoy taking whole-hog to other places, or even having it mailed. The Kinchens' customers "carry it, ship it, freeze . . . barbecue from here to about near every state in the Union." Chris Siler estimates that 25 percent of his business comes from out-of-towners. Though he believes in the quality of his barbecue, it still "amazes [him] sometimes how far some people have come to get barbecue." Ricky Parker is not surprised by the success of his product outside of its local context: "The first of June, I shipped out a half a hog to Illinois, and then I shipped some to New Jersey. . . . The furthest I've ever shipped any was Japan. And I've shipped some to Switzerland. Ain't sent none to Hawaii yet." Parker's barbecue transcends geographic and cultural boundaries. He understands that a food that is deemed authentic (and tasty) is universal. By the time it reaches Hawaii, Parker's barbecue will have nearly conquered the whole world.

The Ubiquitous Pig

Life in West Tennessee weaves the existence of hogs and humans together. All of the people interviewed for this project were either farmers or the children of farmers. The pitmasters were all white males. According to 2000 U.S. Census data, whites outnumbered African Americans nearly nine to one in both Chester and Henderson counties. In and around Memphis, however, African American pitmasters and barbecue restaurant owners are much more prevalent than in the West Tennessee countryside. Today, just as at the end of the nineteenth century, limited social and economic mobility keeps African Americans confined to the twin metropolises of Memphis and Nashville and largely absent from the state's agrarian midsection.

Billy Frank Latham farmed before becoming a pitmaster. Ike Kinchen came from a long line of farmers: "That's the only way they [his family] had of making a living." Joe Joyner, Chris Siler, and Richard Hodge grew up on farms. The Norwoods fell in love on neighboring family farms in Florida. Ricky Parker, though born in Memphis, was the son of sharecroppers. Like all the other interviewees, Curt Blankenship has "pretty much been around a farm all my life."

Many of the interviewees' families farmed hogs, typically not to sell but to eat. Joyner remarks that on his family farm, "it was fairly common to have a few hogs running around." An abundance of pigs naturally defined what Siler's family ate: "It's just been an old family tradition out here to cook barbecue just 'cause . . . this area is surrounded by farms, and it used to be if the farmer wanted to go eat that's what they did." Pigs still mean sustenance and survival in rural Tennessee. But for the whole-hog pitmasters, pigs also signify economic sustainability—in Henderson and Lexington hogs mean business.

Like any good capitalist, whole-hog business owners see their product in terms of numbers and statistics. Though an important cultural commodity, West Tennessee commercial barbecue is also ultimately about how many sandwiches are sold. One result of smoking hundreds of specimens a year is that pitmasters see pigs almost solely as carcasses ready for the fire. Unlike on a family farm, commercial pitmasters may rarely see their pigs alive and often describe them in terms of weight. Billy Frank Latham illustrates a pig in the following terms: "Anywhere from about 180 up to about 250, it's a whole hog." Breeding does not define a whole hog like poundage does. Others define a hog by how much meat it produces following cooking. Chris Siler says, "You can figure a hog that's about 190, you're going to get just a little bit less than half of that weight in barbecue. You wouldn't quite get ninety-five pounds out of it, but you know it will be less than that. It will be closer to eighty; it just fluctuates." Ricky Parker, among other pitmasters, tells time by how many whole hogs he sells. Like a professional athlete or big-shot restaurateur, Parker can tick off his records. Fourth of July weekend, 2008 (the national holiday is the busiest time of year for all barbecuers): forty-four whole hogs smoked. All-time Fourth of July record: sixty-seven whole hogs. He and his son Zach hoped to beat that record in 2010, when the long holiday weekend ends on a Sunday, a day when he is normally closed. For whole-hog pitmasters, swine becomes a figure in the ledgers of enterprise; the pig is ubiquitous (Nissenson and Jonas 1992).

Whereas the pitmasters, at most times, treat the pig with notions of entrepreneurial concern, their customers view it as something altogether remarkable. Whole-hog barbecue is prized by eaters over other smoking techniques that focus on specific cuts of meat, normally shoulders, hams, and ribs. "Everybody loves [whole-hog] because it's moister" than ordinary barbecue pork cuts, according to Liz Kinchen. "They don't like just shoulders and hams." On the full pig, in the words of her husband, Ike, "you can find meat that you like the best. . . . You can get any part of the meat you want." For consumers the possibilities associated with the whole hog are of utmost importance—the opportunity to devour every part of the pig allows customers to participate in a ritual going back to the earliest farm smoke-outs. Ricky Parker runs down the cuts: "You get your whole hog, you got dark meat, white meat, you know, outside brown meat. You got just a little bit of everything."

It may seem obvious, but it is this "everything" that gives whole-hog its name—except the head and feet, the whole pig is smoked and eaten. The phrase "whole-hog" seems to have first appeared in William Cowper's 1779 poem "The Love of the World Reprov'd; or, Hypocrisy Detected." In it, Mohammad (here, "Mahomet") declares a prohibition on eating a particular part of the hog, but tests his worshipers by refusing to name the cut:

> But for one piece they thought it hard
> From the whole hog to be debarr'd,
> And set their wit at work to find
> What joint the prophet had in mind.

As the Muslims debate over the forbidden piece, some "choose the back" and others eat the belly. Some postulate that "He meant not to forbid the head," while a few "piously prefer the tail." Interpreting the hog differently, the followers promptly "eat up the hog" (Cowper 1836, 323–24).

Customers likewise "eat up the hog" and codify their passions by labeling the barbecued pig's anatomy with a whole multitude of nicknames and preferring one part over another. One cut of meat can carry many different and "unusual" monikers, according to Chris Siler. "Middlin" is one of the more common designations for what laypeople call bacon, the fatty underside of the hog, which gets its nickname for its location midway between the shoulders and hams. Perhaps because of its popularity—it is among the most requested parts of the barbecued hog—middlin, or belly meat, carries several semantic designations: "I've heard it [called] belly lean; let's see, stringy . . . I hear them call it rib meat, side meat, just different things like that."

Patrons fight over more limited cuts of flesh. According to Ricky Parker, the "catfish," a piece of meat found under the tenderloin, is "the most tenderest part of the hog" and the most in demand at Scott's-Parker's Barbecue. The amount of catfish in a pig can fill only two sandwiches worth. Customers who do not arrive soon enough to reserve their catfish and other favorite cuts often choose to leave hungry. Eaters dedicate their appetites to certain portions of the whole hog. Curt Blankenship sees his share of picky customers who insist on certain cuts: "If you don't have it, they're not going to eat it." If Liz's has run out of middlin meat, patrons choose to leave with empty stomachs and return even earlier the following day. Ike Kinchen says, "They come in here, and I can be out of it, and they say, 'Well, if you'll have some tomorrow or the next day . . . I'll just wait on it.'" Chris Siler experiences the same type of anatomy-specific customers at his barbecue. He considers it his duty to correctly identify the cuts of meat to his patrons and not to sell them another cut under pretense: "I tell them, 'I'm not going to lie to you; I'm just going to be honest with you and tell you what I got.' They're not real mad about it, but that's all they'll eat is their particular cuts. And they'll usually leave. And most of the time they tell me before they leave, 'Well, hold me a pound of it tomorrow.'" Though he smokes hundreds of hogs a year, Siler's customers, like Cowper's eaters, continue to search for that one special cut.

Barbecue in Action

Whole-hog, like all traditional barbecue, demands four universals: meat, wood smoke, a steady fire, and plenty of time. All West Tennessee whole-hog pit businesses use pig, hickory, slow fires, and sixteen to twenty-four hours of smoking. The final products are decidedly different in taste, each manifestation being unarguably unique. In the face of homogeneity, whole-hog pitmasters express their individuality. Through eponymous naming practices, secret recipes and techniques, and communicating the distinctiveness and arduousness of their labor, these barbecuers create a unique identity—while at the same time participating in those uniform practices that make whole-hog an authentic, regionally based cuisine.

The names of whole-hog pits evince an individualistic identity. At Richard's, Bill's, and Curt's, establishment and entrepreneur are synonymous. Although Ike Kinchen oversees the pit at Liz's, his wife prepares the plates, sandwiches, and sides, and gets her name on the signage. Joe Joyner ran Joyner's Jacks Creek until selling the business in May 2008; its new owner, Jo Hilton, reverted to the old name, Jacks Creek Bar-B-

Que, thus referencing the location's historical roots. Similarly, at Siler's Old Time BBQ, Chris Siler named his recently purchased restaurant after himself while drawing attention to the historical, old-timey cooking style. Both Ricky Parker and Crystal and Derek Norwood kept their establishments' existing names to honor former owners. Early Scott and Dennis Hays had trained them and were long-standing Lexington-area barbecue icons themselves. Shortly before being interviewed, however, Parker decisively changed the name of the restaurant he has owned and operated for nearly two decades since taking over from Scott. Claiming distinctiveness while still venerating his former boss, Parker compounded past and present to form Scott's-Parker's Barbecue.

Throughout Southern barbeculture, secrets, like names, allow pitmasters to stand out as individuals and hitch their recipes to history. Every pitmaster acknowledges that he or she possesses classified recipes, thus making every pitmaster the sole keeper of a piece of arcane information. Sauce recipes are some of the most closely guarded barbecue secrets. Curt Blankenship remembers eating Priest Ellis's barbecue as a Lexington teenager. Ellis's sauce made him renowned in the area: "He has a sauce that nobody knows how he made. I guess his wife says that she knows how to make it, but she won't give anybody the recipe. So everybody says that Priest carried it to his grave with him." Pitmasters frequently describe their sauce as sweet, vinegary, or spicy but add few other explicit details (e.g., see Veteto, Chapter 10, this volume). In his hunting-trophy-filled office behind the pits, Richard Hodge tells of acquiring his sauce recipe: "Well, that deer up there on that wall, I killed, and a friend of mine wanted a hind quarter of deer, and he duck hunted, so he traded me three ducks and a gallon of barbecue sauce for the hind quarter of that deer. And the next time I saw him I wanted to know how to make that sauce. And he said, 'I'll tell you what I put in it, but I'm not going to tell you how to make it.' . . . I started gathering up all the stuff I remembered that he made and started experimenting with it, and about five hundred gallons later I finally come up with a pretty good sauce."

Secrets extend beyond sauce concoctions to all aspects of West Tennessee barbecue. Speaking on the hazards of a pit fire, Ike Kinchen says, "Three things that will put it out, and I ain't going to say what they are but they'll put it out, if you catch it in time. And you can beat yourself to death and still not get it out." He will not identify any of the three methods, confirming that they are his secrets. Ricky Parker coyly reveals that a farmer who breeds hogs specially for Scott's-Parker's Barbecue feeds the animals a "special diet" of the pitmaster's choosing. When quizzed as to what the diet contained, Parker, laughing, states, "Well, that I can't say. Yeah, it's just a different supplement. It's 'bout more than just corn-fed." Parker and others assert their identity by controlling the distribution of information and protecting and confirming barbecue prescriptions as their own.

By articulating the labor intensiveness of commercial barbecue, West Tennessee pitmasters express the importance of their work and the fraternal aspects of their trade. Parker might just be the hardest working man in the business. In fact, he claims as much: "There is nobody else that works harder than I do." He works sixteen to twenty hours a day, six days a week, rushing back and forth between his barbecue pits. He survives on little rest: "I've been doing this so long that if I sleep more than three hours a night I feel bad. I absolutely feel bad." In interviews he repeatedly states, "I'm married to this place more than I am my wife." Parker suspects that his customers cannot appreciate the toil and stress of professional barbecuing: "I think they take it for granted a lot of the times, and they don't actually see the work that's involved in it. . . . This is not no easy job for nobody. It really ain't." These sentiments are echoed by Parker's former assistant Curt Blankenship: "Some people don't realize how much work actually goes into barbecue. They think it's like a hamburger or something; you just put it on and [in] a few hours it's done." The physicality of whole-hog barbecuing allows the pitmaster to establish his identity, while also separating himself from the masses.

Perhaps no other aspect unites pitmasters more than fire. As Chris Siler remarks, "There's a long joke that you're not really a barbecuer till you've burnt your pit down once." He has witnessed two pit fires: "If it ever does light, it's gone in five minutes; it'll burn the entire building down . . . and you lose all your hogs in less than five minutes. . . . It's amazing to see how fast that will burn." Ike Kinchen likens the explosive combination of hog fat dripping on burning coals to "setting kerosene or gas on fire." Richard Hodge responds that fire can change a pitmaster's life: "You pay attention after you burn the place down." The terror of conflagration is most evident in the dreams of Ricky Parker. In those few hours of sleep he enjoys each night at home, Parker frequently has nightmares of "the pit catching on fire and the hogs catching on fire." A fire can end a pitmaster's career: "The way that we cook you can't get insurance on the building, and I try my best when I do leave to know that there ain't nothing going to catch fire." No insurance company will indemnify a structure in which hogs are being smoked as the risk is too great. Faced with exploding buildings, two-hundred-pound pigs, and a fickle economy, whole-hog barbecue is far too much excitement for all but the hardiest of pitmasters.

Persistence and Loss

Whole-hog barbecue is disappearing in West Tennessee. Fewer independent farmers are raising whole-hog swine, which are markedly different from those modern breeds specifically grown for anatomization. Some whole-hog barbecuers have recently made the switch to smoking modern cuts of pig. Shiny metal appliances—less wood fuel needed, less smoke produced, less labor required—have mechanized barbecue, moving its production from the sooty smokehouse to the sterile kitchen. A new generation of eaters order their smoked pig not by the cut of meat—middlin or shoulder, brown or white—but as at a fast-food chain: "One barbecue sandwich with medium sauce." Despite rising prices and technological advances, several pitmasters, old and new, remain dedicated to the whole hog. These whole-hog pitmasters resist change by striving for authenticity and tradition.

Since the 1980s, the rise and spread of agribusinesses—massive corporations that control all facets of the farming industry from land to seeds to machines—has eliminated most of the small family farms in West Tennessee. Before opening Bill's Bar-B-Q, Billy Frank Latham became the last in his long lineage of family farmers. He discloses, "Your small-time farmer has had to get out of business, for he can't compete with the larger ones that can grow so much more stuff than he could. And in fact, I was one of them; I had to get out of farming." Many of these small-scale farmers provided hogs for the local barbecue industry, as Chris Siler points out: "Local farmers, there's fewer and fewer every year . . . who do whole hogs, or who raise hogs." According to Joe Joyner, local whole-hog culture competed with large-scale capital and lost: "Six to eight years ago, there was a period when the price of pork just got so dirt cheap that it run so many of the little people out . . . and it's all big corporations now, and some of these big-time hog farmers. That's the only ones you see that have them now." Eventually, pitmasters like Latham "couldn't find a good whole hog to cook." It became "harder to find hogs" and "easier to find shoulders and hams," says Siler. Industrial processors now focus on butchering the more universally popular cuts of meat rather than the regional, very esoteric whole hogs demanded in West Tennessee. Ike Kinchen remembers a time when "everybody had a hog, you might say." Today, however, "you might go one hundred miles and not even find one. It's that way nowadays." The corporatization of the Southern heartland, symptomatic of America's farm crisis, has created a whole-hog swine crisis.

The mechanization of the farm and restaurant industries has altered the West Tennessee cultural landscape, calling into question the ideal of authentic whole-hog barbecue. Joe Joyner and Billy Frank Latham have equipped their restaurants using the very latest in smoking technology. Latham says, "They're called Hickory Creek Bar-B-Q Cookers, and they have four smokers on them, and you got your timers and all that you set up. And once you build the temperature up, it holds it there for any amount of time you want to cook it." The Hickory Creek Bar-B-Q Cooker is a rectangular steel box with a hinged door that opens up like a car hood; its dimensions are large enough to fit an entire hog. The cooker uses just "two pieces of wood, about one inch square and about ten to twelve inches long, to cook a whole cooker full of hog." Joyner adds to the illustration: "The heat is generated through electricity, but it does have smoking capabilities where you put your wood in smoke tubes and it'll just smoke overnight." Joyner swears by the economic savings the electric pit provides and the added benefit of decreasing the risk of fire: "It's a lot cleaner, safer, and more efficient; the temperature is always steady. It doesn't fluctuate like you get from the fire and with coals." These two barbecuers defend their modern smokers from detractors; they believe that the cooker provides a similar taste to open-pit barbecue and does not remove the pitmaster from the process. At one point, Latham opened his pit's hood, pulled out a glistening chunk of pork, and handed it over: "See how tender that is? Even though I cook on a cooker, you still got to know what you're doing, or you won't come out with very good meat."

Because of their reliance on modern smoking technology, Joyner and Latham abandoned whole-hog barbecue for prepared hams and shoulders. At the time of interview, Joyner had not cooked whole-hog for two and a half years. He blames the disappearance of local whole-hog production and also cites the cost-effectiveness of dealing with smaller portions: "Where the expense comes is, you know, labor costs, waste associated with a whole hog comparing it with shoulders and hams, you really cut your throwaway stuff out a lot. . . . The whole hog has a lot of excess material that you cannot put in your barbecue . . . the bones, the skin, the fat." Latham agrees; portioned barbecue is "easier and simple[r]" than whole-hog. Large meat-supply corporations have helped change his mind: "There's no end to the supply of [hams and shoulders] as long as you've got your Swift and Excel and all those big companies you see putting them out." Both Joyner and Latham also blame the immensity of whole hogs. Joyner says, "I was getting older and it was sort of harder for me to handle them by myself." Latham's body is actually a casualty of whole-hog; the day-to-day strenuous lifting of hundreds of pounds of pork took a toll on his health. He suffered a hernia and was forced to take medical leave for several weeks: "See, you strain bad on whole-hog, and I just had a rupture come in my side, and I had to quit handling that whole hog." These two pitmasters, now content to work with their electric smokers, used to labor alone with the masses of whole-hog meat, whereas Ricky Parker, Ike Kinchen, Chris Siler, and Curt Blankenship all use assistants when lifting, flipping, and altogether struggling with their whole hogs. Perhaps whole-hog barbecue should never be a solitary exercise.

For every West Tennessee pitmaster that quits whole-hog, others remain. Long-standing pitmasters (such as Ike Kinchen and Ricky Parker) continue the tradition, while members of a younger generation (such as Curt Blankenship and Chris Siler) are just beginning to wrestle with the barbecued hog. These resilient pitmasters believe that the local community will always demand whole-hog; as Blankenship states, "There ain't no other way to do it around here." For Siler, the whole-hog ritual trumps questions of economics and ease: "Everybody has always done [whole-hog] here, and sticking with the old way, people like that. It's definitely a more expensive process, but it pays off in the end. . . . You have a better reputation with it; you have something that's a little bit unique, because fewer and fewer places are doing whole-hog anymore, and that gives us like our little niche in the market." Even though whole-hog barbecue is most likely the original form of Southern smoked swine, Siler and others see it as "unique." Parker, like Siler, realizes that uniqueness sells and that he himself has become an icon of authenticity: "I'm the oldest. I'm the oldest at this kind of business in West Tennessee if you count years to years."

Parker and his peers resist change and become both more real and more mythical in the process. "We do it the old-fashioned way," says Parker. "We don't use ovens and stuff to cook our barbecue in. . . . This place ain't never changed." He considers himself "the real deal" and "a dying breed," a cook who survives on instinct and "know-how" instead of "gauges . . . [and] thermometers." He curses the need for "that damn cooker." Other pitmasters openly express contempt for those pitmasters who cannot resist change. "There are people that got lazy," rebukes Ike Kinchen. "It's work to cooking the whole hog, and the other you can just put it in the electric cooker and cook it overnight, and don't have to smell all the smoke or breathe it and everything else." To a man who smokes three hogs daily in a barely ventilated, low-ceilinged, converted two-car garage, anything less might certainly be considered "lazy." In Parker's view, an authentic pitmaster not only controls the smoking process with fire but also smells, looks, and talks the part, exuding what can only be called barbecuity. His customers "like the whole idea of the type of person I am," though he believes many consider him "a damn nut" for putting his "life on hold to do something like this." Parker's description of how others perceive him seems incorrect, however: barbecue has not interrupted the life of this pitmaster extraordinaire, barbecue *is* his life.

According to swine enthusiast William Hedgepeth's treatise, "Throughout history and down the throat of time, the hog has been one of the most persistently transcendent symbols in human culture" (1978, 183). It remains so in Henderson and Lexington, Tennessee, despite the pessimistic prognosis of several pitmasters. Billy Frank Latham thinks whole-hog barbecue will revert to its earlier form of rare backyard smoking: "I think in the next few years you'll only have just special occasions where you'll have whole-hog done on an open pit." He advises newcomers to not "even try it, on count of the extra hard work. Plus, you got to keep you a supply of good hogs." Joe Joyner agrees that a good swine is hard to find: "Now there's just not a lot of hog raisers around here." Even whole-hogger Liz Kinchen concedes that she and husband Ike are the last of a generation: "There's not anybody going to get out and hunt it up and cook it." Relatively new arrivals to the area, Crystal and Derek Norwood insist that whole-hog is "just good food, and as long as they keep cooking it like they do, people are going to want to eat it." To raise the issue of disappearance with Ricky Parker is to be showered with friendly derision; as long as he smokes pigs, the tradition lives on. Undoubtedly, the future of whole-hog barbecue lies with the youngest generation of pitmasters and consumers who believe in it. Take eighteen-year-old Zach Parker, for example, who, when school is out, assists his father from the first flip of the hog—at around seven in the morning—to the final spreading of the coals, way past midnight. He insists that he is ready and willing to open an authentic whole-hog pit just like the one he grew up in.

Notes

The author thanks the Southern Foodways Alliance, and especially John T. Edge and Amy Evans, for allowing a green oral historian to carry their exemplary banner into the field; the Coleman family for providing shelter, sustenance, and all kinds of support in Memphis; proofreaders Shome Dasgupta, Jay Coleman, Jonathan Large, and Dr. Randy Fertel; the editors of this volume; and most of all, each of the Tennessee barbecue practitioners who sacrificed their time to speak to me in the summer of 2008.

1. Full transcripts of the oral histories and locations may be found at www.southernbbqtrail.com, part of the Southern Foodways Alliance's website, www.southernfoodways.com.
2. In his interview with the author, Ricky Parker says he left home to work for Early Scott at the age of thirteen; however, several other interviews with Parker refute this timeline (Edge 2000, 209–10; Gelin 2008, 132–33; Leith 2008, 252–55).
3. John Shelton Reed and Dale Volberg Reed call North Carolina's similar, but decidedly more complex, interrelatedness of pitmasters and barbecue restaurants the "Briarpatch" (2008, 68–69).

References

Bass, S. Jonathan. 2008. "'How 'bout a Hand for the Hog': The Enduring Nature of the Swine as a Cultural Symbol in the South." In *Southern Cultures: The Fifteenth Anniversary Reader*, edited by Harry L. Watson and Larry J. Griffin, 371–88. Chapel Hill: University of North Carolina Press.

Cash, W. J. 1941. *The Mind of the South*. Repr., New York: Vintage Books, 1991.

Cowper, William. 1836. *The Works of William Cowper, Esq.: Comprising His Poems, Correspondence, and Translations*, vol. 13, edited by Robert Southey. London: Baldwin and Cradock.

Elie, Lolis Eric. 1996. *Smokestack Lightning: Adventures in the Heart of Barbecue Country*. Repr., Berkeley: Ten Speed Press, 2005.

Egerton, John. 1987. *Southern Food: At Home, on the Road, in History*. Repr., Chapel Hill: University of North Carolina Press, 1993.

———. 1990. *Side Orders: Small Helpings of Southern Cookery and Culture*. Atlanta: Peachtree.

Hedgepeth, William. 1978. *The Hog Book*. Garden City, NY: Doubleday.

Hilliard, Sam Bowers. 1972. *Hog Meat and Hoe Cake: Food Supply in the Old South, 1840–1860*. Carbondale: Southern Illinois University Press.

Nissenson, Marilyn, and Susan Jonas. 1992. *The Ubiquitous Pig*. New York: Harry N. Abrams.
Reed, John Shelton. 2004. "Barbecue Sociology: The Meat of the Matter." In *Cornbread Nation 2: The United States of Barbecue*, edited by Lolis Eric Elie, 78–87. Chapel Hill: University of North Carolina Press.
Staten, Vince, and Greg Johnson. 2007. *Real Barbecue: The Classic Barbecue Guide to the Best Joints across the USA—with Recipes, Porklore, and More!* Guilford, CT: Globe Pequot Press.
Taylor, Joe Gray. 1982. *Eating, Drinking, and Visiting in the South: An Informal History*. Baton Rouge: Louisiana State University Press.
Warnes, Andrew. 2008. *Savage Barbecue: Race, Culture, and the Invention of America's First Food*. Athens: University of Georgia Press.

PART II

Old/New Barbecue Moving Forward

7

The Changing Landscape of Mid-South Barbecue

Edward M. Maclin

On a Friday in June near my parents' home in West Tennessee, my brother lit the grill to prepare for his wedding rehearsal dinner. He had borrowed the grill from a friend, and it was spectacular: a trailer-mounted behemoth with multiple hanging racks, all attached to an electric motor drive designed to move the barbecue slowly and continually through a cloud of hot smoke. Family members walked past with beers in their hands admiring the machinery. The ribs were seasoned with "number five rub" from the small West Side Grocery in Covington, Tennessee. The beer-can chicken was falling-off-the-bone tender, and the barbecued bologna was succulent and thoroughly smoked. This was not just barbecue in the pulled-pork sense—it was *a barbecue*, and as at most such events there was plenty of food to go around. When planning the wedding rehearsal dinner, the couple had been clear: they didn't want to go to a restaurant, and they didn't want to limit the guest list to immediate family—they wanted something that all the family members and friends involved with the wedding could attend, and my brother wanted to be in charge of the food.

Cut to Georgia, several weeks earlier. The annual Old Timey Seed Swap at Agrarian Connections Farm in Crawford, Georgia, includes seed exchanges among small farmers in Georgia, Tennessee, Alabama, and the Carolinas. It also includes music, storytelling, and a large barbecue event. That year's barbecue included West Tennessee–style pulled pork, because I was recruited to do the smoking, and this is what I know. The pork was raised locally by Tad Brown and Susannah Chapman—who also happened to be anthropology graduate students at the University of Georgia. In previous years my coeditor, Jim Veteto, and

I had shared barbecue duties, but this year Jim was in the field investigating heirloom vegetable varieties, so another anthropologist, David Himmelfarb, took his place. With over two hundred attendees, copious amounts of pork were required, along with a quart of homemade sauce—made from a recipe that was still being field-tested, since Jim's family recipe was unavailable (see Veteto, Chapter 10, this volume). The experience of West Tennessee barbecue doesn't begin with the first bite: smoke poured from our dual fires starting just after sunrise. In the afternoon when people began to arrive, they circled the smokers periodically, already beginning to taste the pork through the smoke. Despite our discouragement, dogs found the pork fat dripping from the bottom of the smokers into delicious puddles on the ground. When the smokers were opened, the lines of people formed before the meat was even pulled. Though the event was hosted and sponsored by faculty at the University of Georgia through the Southern Seed Legacy Project, the skill of the pitmasters was equally important in drawing large crowds.

Smoking meat is not just a restaurant activity; West Tennessee has a long and proud tradition of homestead barbecuing. Smokers may be simple constructions for whole hogs, converted barrels, commercial side-box smokers, or grand trailers with lights. Smoking meat is a daylong affair: a full day or more for a whole hog, less for smaller cuts. Hickory, oak, and wine- or whiskey-barrel staves, often soaked in water, are the raw materials that lead to a pinkish "smoke ring" just beneath the surface of the meat. Chemical process aside, smoking has a certain Zen quality: minimalist, with an abiding awareness of temperature, smoke concentration, and the particulars of the meat. It is a meditation on time, smoke, and flesh that requires nonaction as much as decisiveness. Producing good barbecue—meat that is tender, moist, and smoky—is a skill that can earn local (or familial) fame, even when the results are never entered into a contest (Veteto and Maclin 2009).

All that said, the barbecue culture of West Tennessee (and the Mid-South in general) is changing. James L. Watson and Melissa L. Caldwell, in *The Cultural Politics of Food and Eating*, write that "food is not just a topic worthy of inquiry in its own right; food is a universal medium that illuminates a wide range of other cultural practices" (2005, 1). As such, barbecue can serve as a lens to illuminate other cultural practices, such as those surrounding marriage and gender. Barbecue is also instrumental in numerous political projects and as such can illustrate shifts in the distribution of power. Here I will discuss barbecue in terms of a shifting "barbecue landscape"—a potentially useful description, since the idea of landscape brings with it the concepts of perspective, scale, and position.

The Politics of Barbecue

Following the Civil War, the U.S. government began a journey that led from land giveaways to near protectionism. The beneficiaries were, to a large extent, corporate entities—particularly banks and railroads. Vernon Parrington has compared this national shift to a "Great Barbecue": "A huge barbecue was spread to which all presumably were invited. Not quite all, to be sure; inconspicuous persons, those who were at home on the farm or at work in the mills and offices, were overlooked; a good many indeed out of the total number of the American people. But all the important persons, leading bankers and promoters and business men, received invitations" (1927, 7). More recently, the idea of an "invisible barbecue" has been used to describe deregulation and government subsidies for telecommunications industries and the Internet since the 1980s (Moglen 1997). As in the 1800s, such an event promises widespread feasting, while the largest actual benefits accrue to a small corporate elite.

These barbecue metaphors are easy to make partially because of the history of barbecue within politics.[1] Here I use politics in its common sense—relating to politicians and elections. In the South before the Civil War, barbecues were commonly used as gathering events for meeting political candidates (Dupre 1994; Moss, Chapter 2, this volume). In antebellum Madison County, Alabama, in 1827, contention arose regarding political barbecues, which some believed to be places "where sobriety is exchanged for intemperance . . . and liberty chastened to licentiousness" (Dupre 1994, 479). To barbecue detractors, these events were illustrative of a new disorder arising from the collapse of older institutions and connected to new forms of social mobility and industry (Dupre 1994). Political barbecues continue in the South; in West Tennessee, a recent *Fayette Insider* article (2008) described controversy following a Democratic Party rally at Bozo's Bar-B-Q in Mason, Tennessee. An opponent of candidate Bob Doll was circulating a photograph of Doll taken at the event; Doll, a Republican, had run as a Democrat in the 2006 election. Electioneering may have been the subject of the photograph, but the fact that its context was a barbecue restaurant shows again that, come election time, barbecue goes hand in hand with making speeches, kissing babies, and "gripping and grinning."[2]

During the twentieth century, barbecue in the South was affected by shifts in hog production and distribution. These changes resulted in fewer small and local farms raising hogs. In the early part of the 1900s nearly every farm raised some hogs, but from 1940 until 1992 the number of farms raising hogs decreased from 3,768,000 to 188,000. The largest hog producers were now large firms running operations at multiple sites and using contract growers to produce in excess of fifty thousand hogs annually (Rhodes 1995). Changes in hog production and distribution meant that meat available for local restaurants increasingly came from farther distances. In the famous case of Ollie's Barbecue in Alabama, the U.S. Supreme Court decided that federal desegregation regulations applied to this small, family-owned establishment, partially because their meat came across state lines (Weiner 2003). As large-scale hog producers expanded, the government introduced tax credits for the construction of new facilities (Rhodes 1995). The Great Barbecue continued.

Pork and Power

During the 1960s, consumers purchased two-thirds of their food in grocery stores and one-third from food-service operations; by the 1990s, more than half of consumer food was purchased at food-service operations (Thu and Durrenberger 1998). In terms of barbecue, some of these restaurants are small, family-owned operations. Increasingly across the South, though, the top-ranked barbecue restaurants in urban areas are franchises or chain restaurants, according to local newspapers: in Knoxville, Calhoun's was voted number one, with Buddy's Barbecue as a runner-up; in Memphis, the number two spot went to Corky's Barbecue; and in Little Rock, Chili's and Corky's were both runners-up for best ribs.[3] All of these restaurants offer efficiency, predictability, and control—in short, they have been McDonaldized (Ritzer 2008). Here there are no handwritten signs advertising "pie today," no uncertainty about store hours.

While McDonaldization allows for expansion and regularity, it does so at a steep price: increased constraint on creativity and diversity. I recently visited Bozo's Bar-B-Q in Mason, Tennessee, on a rainy afternoon for lunch. The wind was blowing, the rain was coming down in a steady downpour, and I was craving a barbecue plate for inspiration. Walking in the door, I was greeted with "sit wherever you want" from one of the waitresses. I took a cursory look at the menu to see whether anything had changed. Then I noticed one of the chairs had a large bucket in the seat—positioned to collect rainwater dripping from a leak in the roof. There were no "Danger!/¡Pelligro!" signs, no "please pardon our puddle." The food was delicious, particularly on such a rainy day. My server was pleasant, but obviously not reading from a script. Contrast this experience with one at large restaurant chains, where employee training videos, management guidelines, and corporate branding attempt to deliver not just food, but a complete prepackaged experience of safety, fun, and efficiency.

As restaurants change, so do their menus (and the food itself). Looking at restaurant menus provides insight into social class stratification (Wright and Ransom 2005). At Corky's, for example, the glossy menu is decorated with images of succulent food and advertises a pulled-pork sandwich with regular or sweet potato fries for ten dollars, a barbecue plate for sixteen dollars, or ribs and pork for twenty-two dollars. Any vegetarians can order the pasta primavera, sautéed in a light cream sauce. Compare this to Craig's Barbecue in De Valls Bluff, Arkansas, where the menu above the register spells out choices with adjustable plastic letters:

SANDWICHES	DINNERS
PORK: $3.28	PORK: $6.83
BEEF: $3.40	BEEF: $7.29
HB: $2.70	RIB: $7.44
HB DELUXE: $2.83	POLISH: $6.85

These restaurants cater to different publics, and although the quality of the barbecue might possibly be similar (a matter of taste that I will not address here), the rise in prevalence of chain restaurants has social and economic effects. The shift toward large-budget barbecue firms also results in the commodification of Southern culture (Girardelli 2004). In this version, Southern culture is both homogenized and cleaned—freed from its dynamic tensions and complicated history. At the same time, the prices—both in dollars and in required cultural capital—at many chain restaurants serve to re-establish and strengthen historic economic and ethnic divisions within communities by welcoming some customers and excluding others. Historic barbecue restaurants may present the same exclusiveness in terms of cultural capital; I have been warned away from several Memphis restaurants by friends and family because they are in a "bad" part of town. In addition to structural inequalities, restaurants may also perpetuate racial and regional tensions through the discourse of restaurant staff as they interact with diverse customers (Mallinson and Brewster 2005). Economically, these shifts toward chain restaurants have increased efficiency—which also means a decrease in the number of people employed and a widening gap between the wealthy owners of firms and the lowest-paid employees.

Shifts away from homemade products and toward chain restaurants also have potential health effects. Home-cooked barbecue, particularly whole-hog barbecue, is a time-consuming endeavor requiring stamina and strength. The time commitment and opportunity cost (in giving up meat that could otherwise be preserved or sold) for a rural farmer to kill and cook a whole pig makes it an infrequent occurrence. This is probably good because, as delicious as it may be, barbecue is healthy only when consumed in small and infrequent doses. Recent research, most notably that of Eric Schlosser (2005), has pointed to the negative health effects of the modern American restaurant industry. Eating in a Memphis-area barbecue restaurant recently, one person commented, "I'm watching what I eat—but not today!" The spread of chain restaurants makes the consumption of the barbecue feast possible on a weekly, or even daily, basis. Barbecue, particularly when coupled with fried side items, may be appealing specifically because it makes no pretensions toward health-food status, "green" production, or sustainability.

For example, Watson and Caldwell (2005) present organic food as an important area for future food research, and organic food is marketed as sustainable and healthy. Yet organic barbecue is virtually nonexistent. A Google search for "organic pulled pork + Memphis" yielded only six results, including three duplicates, and none of those links were actually for products located in Memphis. While chain barbecue restaurants in particular tend to have "light" or "healthy" alternatives, they have not yet made the leap to organics. Organic pork is more expensive than conventional pork to produce (Larson, Kliebenstein, and Honeyman 2001). Pork has—for the most part—so far escaped the new hegemony of organic "yuppie chow" seen in other markets (Guthman 2003) as well as the new industrialization of the organic movement.

In the context of restaurant barbecue, power is distributed in complicated ways. Steven Lukes (1974, 2007) describes three facets of power: the power to make decisions directly, the power to set agendas, and the power to shape beliefs and attitudes. The rise of chain barbecue restaurants in the heart of barbecue country points toward the first and second modes of power. Large restaurants carry economic weight that enables their owners to make direct decisions about location, advertising, and even who their customers will be. At the same time, those restaurants must conform to the sense of tradition and authenticity developed by small-scale local enterprises. Some measure of beliefs and attitudes continues to be shaped by older landmark barbecue institutions—though increasingly, attitudes about pork in general and barbecue in particular are influenced by dedicated advertising campaigns.

Meat, Gender, and Food Pornography

Like the landscape along an interstate highway, the barbecue landscape increasingly includes numerous advertisements. Food pornography is the idealized representation of food. Along with the expansion of foodservice companies has come a flood of barbecue-related products and advertising. An increasing number of publications and television programs dedicated to barbecue are festooned with images of meat, shimmering with oils and sitting suggestively among green leaves and colorful vegetables or atop chrome cooking implements. Unlike tofu and other light fare, barbecue is dangerous—a leather-clad mistress waiting to be devoured.

More than that, in a time when politicians stress the virtues of family values, barbecue is the new commodification of desire—a desire that is attainable only through immersion in the market. The idealized image of pork, like other pornography, attaches monetary value to a natural good in a way that also sends normative messages: about what we should value, what is considered as standard, and what our aspirations should be. The shift in marketing of pork—the *other* white meat—focuses on leanness, made achievable through industrialization and selective breeding (Rhodes 1995). Just as other forms of pornography focus on body parts to the exclusion of the whole (Adams 2004), food marketing disassembles the hog into clean, healthy bits. You don't want to know where the other parts go. The result is presented in glossy full color as an ideal that masks the messy nature of barbecue. More than just a marketing twist, the system of marketing pork, restaurants, and processed meat serves as a form of bio-power (Foucault 1990), in which large-scale hog operations can claim public demand as a justification for physically restraining and reshaping the bodies of their herds (Thu and Durrenberger 1998). The resulting ultralean pork bears little resemblance to its slop-fed precursor.

The production and consumption of pork also highlights the dynamics of gender relationships. The cooking of meat in general has been described as a largely male activity, linked in multiple cultures to patriarchy and domination (Adams 1999). Television programs and magazines dedicated to grilling and barbecue are often studded with advertisements for do-it-yourself car repair and beer, while magazines dedicated to a wider range of cooking carry less stereotypically masculine advertisements. Within vernacular American English, we hear of women feeling like "a piece of meat," the euphemistic use of the term "pork" (which also appears in the title of a series of sexually charged films, *Porky's*), and the use of the term "pigs" to describe both chauvinistic men and the police. The use of sexual language by men when assuming the traditionally female role of cooking has been documented in other settings (Deutsch 2005), and barbecue in particular serves as a lens for viewing gender relations (see Deutsch, Chapter 8, this volume). If barbecue is a gendered food, then it is gendered in its consumption as well as its production; whereas men have some license to disregard health when consuming ribs, pulled pork, and the like, women have much less. This is curious, especially considering that women at times have a biological need for iron and other components of a meat diet (Adams 1999). Gendered representations of barbecue serve to both recreate and reflect perceptions of gender within Southern culture, an area that is deserving of additional study.

Pork Futures

The Mid-South barbecue landscape continues to shift in ways that are driven by local tastes, individual initiative, and large-scale changes in technology (Maclin and Veteto, Chapter 11, this volume), economy, and governance. As the current volume illustrates, pockets of resistance remain. The resurgence of heritage breeds, the Slow Food Movement (Knipple and Knipple, Chapter 9, this volume), and the development of virtual food communities (Maclin and Veteto, Chapter 11, this volume) provide a small but growing counterbalance to the economic engine of the hog industry. While chain restaurants spread through Southern cities, many small barbecue restaurants continue to thrive. And, in backyards, at church picnics, and at family reunions, small-scale barbecue continues to be made. At the same time, the relationships between food, culture, and industry continue to change in a multitude of various ways that merit future study.

As my wife and I returned from our honeymoon along the Blue Ridge Parkway a few years ago, we noticed a small box sitting on the porch of our house. Another wedding present, no doubt. Tired and hungry from the last leg of our trip, we walked to the door and saw the package in more detail—an overnight mail-delivery box, from Corky's in Memphis. Inside was pulled pork, slaw, baked beans, and sauce. There was enough for dinner that night, and the next. The rich flavor of the sauce and the smokiness of the pork were undulled by their flight, untainted by their cardboard packaging. Several weeks later, we had a party for friends who had been unable to attend the wedding. On the menu: Memphis-style pulled-pork barbecue. The shoulders bought were from a chain store near the house. The hickory was purchased in a plastic bag, already cut in chunks and supplemented with charcoal briquettes. Music played and friends ate way too much barbecue while sharing stories of fieldwork, other meals, shared experiences past, and hopes for the future. Authenticity, it seems, is in lived experience—even when that experience is built on shifting ground.

Notes

1. Although the events are metaphorical barbecues, they are not barbecues in the Mid-South tradition; Parrington discusses the wealth of the metaphorical barbecue in terms of beef: "To a frontier people what was more democratic than a barbecue, and to a paternalistic age what was more fitting than that the state should provide the beeves for roasting" (Parrington 1927, 23).
2. Ties of politicians to barbecue also call to mind excess government spending on local projects—typically called pork—although there seems to be no etymological connection to barbecue itself.
3. *Metro Pulse*, "Best of Knoxville 2009," *www.metropulse.com*; *Memphis Flyer*, "Best of Memphis 2008," *www.memphisflyer.com*; *Arkansas Times*, "Best of Arkansas 2008," *www.arktimes.com*.

References

Adams, Carol J. 1999. *Sexual Politics of Meat*. New York: Continuum International.
———. 2004. *The Pornography of Meat*. New York: Continuum International.
Deutsch, Jonathan. 2005. "'Please Pass the Chicken Tits': Rethinking Men and Cooking at an Urban Firehouse." *Food and Foodways* 13:91–114.
Dupre, Daniel. 1994. "Barbecues and Pledges: Electioneering and the Rise of Democratic Politics in Antebellum Alabama." *Journal of Southern History* 60, no. 3 (August): 479–512.

Fayette Insider. 2008. "Bob Doll Addresses Running as a Democrat." August 5. *fayetteinsider.com*.
Foucault, Michel. 1990. *The History of Sexuality*. Vol. 1, *An Introduction*. Victoria: Penguin Books.
Girardelli, Davide. 2004. "Commodified Identities: The Myth of Italian Food in the United States." *Journal of Communication Inquiry* 28, no. 4 (October 1): 307–24.
Guthman, Julie. 2003. "Fast Food/Organic Food: Reflexive Tastes and the Making of 'Yuppie Chow.'" *Social and Cultural Geography* 4, no. 1: 45–58.
Larson, Ben, James Kliebenstein, and Mark Honeyman. 2001. "Cost of Organic Pork Production." Iowa State University Extension, Ag Decision Maker, File B1-80, January 2003.
Lukes, Steven. 1974. *Power: A Radical View*. London: Macmillan Press.
———. 2007. "Power." *Contexts* 6, no. 3: 59–61.
Mallinson, Christine, and Zachary W. Brewster. 2005. "'Blacks and Bubbas': Stereotypes, Ideology, and Categorization Processes in Restaurant Servers' Discourse." *Discourse and Society* 16, no. 6 (November 1): 787–807.
Moglen, Eben. 1997. "The Invisible Barbecue." *Columbia Law Review* 97:945.
Parrington, Vernon Louis. 1927. *The Beginnings of Critical Realism in America, 1860–1920*. Vol. 3, *Main Currents in American Thought*. Online at xroads.virginia.edu/~HYPER/parrington/vol3/toc.html (accessed October 1, 2009).
Rhodes, V. James. 1995. "The Industrialization of Hog Production." *Review of Agricultural Economics* 17, no. 2: 107–18.
Ritzer, George. 2008. "The McDonaldization of Society." In *An Investigation into the Changing Character of Contemporary Social Life*. Thousand Oaks, CA: Pine Forge Press.
Schlosser, Eric. 2005. *Fast Food Nation*. New York: Harper Perennial.
Thu, Kendall M., and E. Paul Durrenberger. 1998. *Pigs, Profits, and Rural Communities*. Albany: State University of New York Press.
Veteto, James R., and Edward M. Maclin. 2009. "Introduction to Tennessee Barbecue." Southern Barbecue Trail, Southern Foodways Alliance. *www.southernbbqtrail.com/* (accessed February 9, 2010).
Watson, James L., and Melissa L. Caldwell, eds. 2005. *The Cultural Politics of Food and Eating*. Malden, MA: Blackwell.
Weiner, Mark S. 2003. "The Semiotics of Civil Rights in Consumer Society: Race, Law, and Food." *International Journal for the Semiotics of Law* 16, no. 4: 395–405.
Wright, Wynne, and Elizabeth Ransom. 2005. "Stratification on the Menu: Using Restaurant Menus to Examine Social Class." *Teaching Sociology* 33, no. 3 (July): 310–16.

8

Swine by Design
Inside a Competition Barbecue Team

Jonathan Deutsch

For most, exposure to barbecue is limited to ordering a plate from the customer side of the counter or barbecuing some ribs on a few sweltering summer Saturdays per year. Most leave the rubbing, sweating, smoking, fire tending, and mopping to the pros. After all, we can appreciate a symphony without spending countless hours practicing until we can perform a passable Mahler tuba solo.

But for some—usually men—appreciation is not enough. They see barbecue as something to be mastered. They strive not merely to make *good* barbecue, but to make the best. They want to do it not in a flimsy egg-shaped smoker from the hardware store but in an elaborate contraption with valves, gauges, and vents—a culinary performance not for a family's accolades but for a shot at trophies and prize money. These are barbecue competitors, and they are in it to win it.

As part of a larger project on cooking and masculinity, I spent a season with a competition barbecue team (nice work if you can get it)—as well as conducting some fieldwork in seasons preceding and following the complete season—in an attempt to understand the culture, the motivations, and the processes of competition barbecue. Underlying this research was a central question, a reductio ad absurdum often voiced at the competitions: "Why not just buy some good barbecue and call it a day?" Indeed, the enthusiasts on the team I followed, all amateur cooks, spend hundreds of hours and dollars each season to pursue a hobby that their wives complain about, and that involves late nights, lost weekends, sweating, stinking, and losing more often than winning.

It produces an oversmoked barbecue that may fare well in competition by distinguishing itself from the other entries on the judges' fatigued palates, but which the competitors acknowledge they "wouldn't want to eat a whole plate of."

The methodology used in the study consists of ethnographic methods for subcultural groups, largely outlined by Margot Ely and colleagues (1991), who in turn draw heavily from the work of John Lofland and Lyn H. Lofland (1995) and Robert Bogdan and Sari Knopp Biklen (1998). Interviews, by contrast, use an adaptation of the *charlas culinarias* technique promulgated by Meredith Abarca (2007), in which food becomes the springboard for more complex discussions. The presentation and analysis of data in this chapter also draw heavily from Ely and colleagues (1997), in that (1) edited field notes are presented, (2) creative representations of data are used to show the texture of a field site, and (3) analysis is recursive and tied to data presentation; that is, there are not broad discussion and theoretical sections following the presentation of data, but rather themes drawn from the data themselves are presented in sections along with the supporting data.

This chapter explores the *what* and *why* of competition barbecue by sharing excerpts of field notes from a competition weekend with Swine by Design, the pseudonymous barbecue team that I followed. Interspersed with the descriptive details of the *what* of barbecue is some discussion of themes that emerged from the fieldwork under the broader topics of gender and performance. The chapter is not an attempt to fully answer the (ultimately unanswerable) *why* question, but rather an opportunity for readers unfamiliar with competition barbecue to have a peek inside.

A Weekend in the Life: First Competition, DC Barbecue Battle

Shortly after seven in the morning on Saturday I arrived at the Barbecue Battle in Washington, DC. Most team sites had been set up already, though some people were still arriving, trying to squeeze their trucks and trailers in between others. No one was at the Swine by Design rig. But at the neighboring site, Zeke, whom I had met the previous night on a stroll to sketch the layout of the competition site, was there with a woman, arranging his site. I asked him if he knew where Andrew, from Swine by Design, was. He said that Andrew should arrive soon. I explained through the chain-link fence surrounding the site that Andrew had asked me to meet him but that I wasn't allowed into the site without an armband. The woman gave me her armband to use to get in. I showed it to the guard, who this time graciously let me in. I returned it to the woman, thanking her. Zeke began to joke about where Andrew was, saying, "Where's that lazy piece of shit? . . . I'm gonna call and get that fucker out of bed." He took out his cell phone. I said, "You don't need to call him. Thanks, but I'm happy to wait." He smiled and said, "I insist," dialing his cell. Obviously, these competing teams are relatively close, I thought. "Hey sleeping beauty, you've got a visitor. What'd you say your name was?"

"Jon."

"Jon. Hold on, talk to him."

"Good morning, Andrew," I said. "I told Zeke not to bother you but he insisted. So I'm here, Brian should be meeting me shortly, and I look forward to meeting you."

I hoped that waking him up, however unintentionally, would not put him in a bad mood. I took a walk, looking at some of the other team sites and taking pictures. I was fascinated by the team names, like "Close Encounters of the Third Swine," and "Fuhgeddaboutit, the NYC Barbecue Team." I was also taken with the backyard-like decorations—pig lights, picnic tables, checked tablecloths, pig candy dishes, road signs, lawn chairs, and inflatable recliners filled the teams' areas, which measured about twenty feet by twenty or thirty feet. I also noted the corporate presence, ranging from a sausage company's "world's largest grill" and a giant peanut sponsored by the peanut board to ice cream, pizza, tires, detergent, and pens. The list of sponsors and scope of this competition seemed much larger than others I had read about.

When I returned to the Swine by Design site, Brian, another team member, was there with the back of his minivan open, along with a woman named Deirdre. Shortly after, Andrew walked up and introduced himself and his wife, Eileen. Eileen smiled, got into a yellow pickup truck that was parked next to the rig, and drove off. Meanwhile, Andrew went up on the rig and started sorting through supplies, and Brian and Deirdre began to unload the minivan. I observed for a bit, then helped unload the van—hoses, boxes of supplies, cutting boards, shoes, hats, juice, empty coolers, and other odds and ends. I told Andrew that although I was here as a researcher, I didn't need to stand at attention the entire time. He thanked me. "Actually," he said, "see that hydrant over there with the spigots sticking out? You can hook this hose up." I did, and we filled the rig's water tank. When the van was unloaded, Brian asked Deirdre where she parked, and drove off to find a parking place.

I walked back from the hydrant with Brian, who was returning from parking his car. I was carrying one of his hoses that I ended up not needing, which I had coiled haphazardly. I said to Brian, nodding at the hose, which looked nothing like his own neat coils, "You can tell who the architect is." Brian said, "Yeah, that's the compulsive engineer in me." I asked him to show me how he coiled them so neatly, and he did, laying the hose on the ground instead of holding it on his arm as I had done. He talked to Deirdre as I recoiled the hose, and I listened in. I gathered that this was Deirdre's first competition, and that she wasn't really connected with anyone on the team. She had been to the Barbecue Battle before and had spent some time with Swine by Design through contacts on a barbecue online discussion board. She was an avid backyard barbecue cook and had decided this year to join the team. Brian congratulated me on a good job of coiling the hose, and I said, "See, I have a lot to learn this weekend."

At this time, I think I should describe the cast thus far. Andrew is the founder and leader of Swine by Design. He is about six feet tall, blond, and in his late thirties. He isn't obese but has a heavy chest and stomach. He is an architect and came up with the concept of Swine by Design about seven years before. His wife, Eileen, is petite and quiet. I later learned from Andrew that she is a web designer and that she "begrudgingly designed and maintains the Swine by Design website." They have no children.

Brian is an engineer by training who works for the state as an administrator. He is about five foot six, stout, bald, and in his mid-fifties, with a gray beard. He wore sandals and a hat throughout the weekend, along with a tank top and a foam neck cooler that he chilled in the drink cooler with the ice. Brian told me that he is married to a lawyer, who doesn't much approve of his barbecue activities but does not actively oppose his participation. They have no children.

Deirdre is a fifty-something slim woman who is new to competitive barbecue and seems eager to learn. She was familiar with the team, chatting with them online previously and stopping by their site at two previous competitions. She is recently separated, has no children, travels often, and has recently stopped working.

Also present was Frank, another architect who works with Andrew and is a founding member of the team. He is in his late forties, single, and of average height and build.

All of the Swine by Design team members are Caucasian. I will continue to describe the members as they come up.

Next to arrive was Ed, another architect and founding Swine by Design member. He is in his forties and of average build. He was accompanied by his wife and twin boys. He brought chicken thighs with him and a small black kettle smoker, separate from the large one affixed to the rig. He too went off to park his car, asking Brian for advice on where to park, and told him to ice the chicken down in preparation for meat inspection. Brian said that he would do so as soon as the ice truck came.

Andrew insisted on giving me a tour of the rig to help me observe safely during the weekend. The rig was bought from a professional caterer, who had a problem using it commercially. It did not meet health department regulations, because it is not screened-in and has Formica rather than stainless steel cabinets. The caterer, in turn, bought it from a championship barbecue team, who did well with it in competition. I was fascinated by this provenance of competitive cookers. Looking at the classified ads in the barbecue newsletters emphasizes this heritage as well—who owned which cooker that is for sale and what awards they won with it.

Andrew first showed me the water tank, which I had previously filled that morning. He explained that it provides its own pressure, though the water is not potable. The cold water goes directly to the sink, bypassing a now defunct filter. The water for the hot water tap is routed around the back of the rig, through the cooker itself, which heats the water, and back to the sink, providing hot water while the cooker is being used. On the side of the rig, between the sink and the cooker, is a long black counter with cabinets and drawers beneath it. The drawers are filled with supplies such as utensils, plasticware, paper plates, and a stereo that plays music through speakers that Andrew attached to the rig. The cooker itself is opposite the sink and works on a three-chamber system. At the bottom is the firebox, where the team burns maple, cherry, and hickory, with no particular system other than using mainly maple—the most neutral of the three—to get the fire going. Use of gas or electric heat is not allowed in competition, though propane ignition sometimes is. Above the firebox is a trough of about ten gallons of water, which boils and steams the meat once the fire gets sufficiently hot. The water also tempers the heat to keep it even. Above the water, the meat sits on racks. The smoke comes up the left side of the cooker and goes across the water and meat and out a smokestack on the right. The Swine by Design team made one modification to the original cooker by adding an additional smokestack on the left, which allows them to release some excess smoke and heat before it goes across to the meat. The desired cooking temperature is between 200 and 250 degrees, and there are thermometers on each side of the cooker indicating the temperature. Andrew said that by opening the left-hand stack, the cook can lower the temperature by ten or twenty degrees very quickly.

Soon after, Andrew left to go get the meat from the meat truck, run by a local vendor who sells regulation competition meat from a freezer truck. Teams may purchase their own meat elsewhere, though getting it at the competition from the official vendor is often seen as insurance that the meat will pass the judges' inspection. Judges look to ensure that the meat is safe and kept iced or refrigerated; that the teams have not yet begun to marinate, rub, trim, or otherwise prepare the meat; and that the particular cuts of meat are approved by the sanctioning body for that particular competition.

Andrew returned, visibly upset, and said, "These guys are such a rip-off. We complained last year and they asked them back again."

"Frozen?" Brian asked. I guessed he was referring to the meat.

"Worse. Freezer burnt with shiners [exposed bits of bones on the ribs] all over. And they want $4.59 a pound for 'em."

"How are the shoulders?"

"OK, I guess," Andrew said dejectedly. "They only want $1.49 for them so I think I'll go ahead and get them and we'll go to the warehouse store or something for the ribs. . . . Also they want cash or check only. Anyone have a check?"

Brian said, "I knew I got cash out for a reason. How much do you need?"

"They said we could refuse the ribs. The shoulders come to $147.81."

Brian counted out exact change and gave it to Andrew.

"Why don't you guys come with me and take a look," Andrew said, "to see if you agree."

So Andrew, Brian, Deirdre, Frank, and I walked over to the meat truck, which is a refrigerated truck parked about two blocks from the site and staffed by a man with a son on a child leash. Sure enough, the ribs looked terrible to my eye. They looked like they had been defrosted and refrozen, which causes moisture release. And as Andrew had said, they were not very meaty, with "shiners," and had freezer burn. Though I know that as a researcher I should not have cared, I was relieved when the group decided to refuse them. The shoulders, however, looked good to me—pink and long cut, with good fat marbling. Andrew paid for the shoulders. He and Frank loaded them on a dolly that Swine by Design was sharing with Zeke's team and headed back to the site.

Back at the site, there was some discussion of who would go to the store for the ribs, and where would be the best place to get them. The viable options narrowed quickly to various supermarket clubs, and the deciding factor was who had memberships at which stores. Andrew decided he would go to get the ribs and asked who wanted to go with him. Deirdre volunteered. While they were discussing the meat, Zeke came over to Swine by Design's site and Andrew told him his problem. Zeke said, "Yep, that's why I always bring my own meat to these things. Not getting screwed again."

Meanwhile, Grant arrived. He is tall and lanky and does not say much. He told me later that he and his wife are both architects and that his wife used to work with Andrew, which is how he came to the team. He also told me that his wife was eight months pregnant with their second child.

I soon noticed Zeke bringing over bags of ice on his trolley. Brian noticed as well from atop the rig, where he was still setting up, and said, "Ice is here. You wanna go, Frank?" Brian pointed out a luggage cart and some wooden boards he had, and Frank got ready to get the ice. I offered to come along, so that I could see the ice setup. We got the ice, 160 pounds of it, and took turns hauling it back on Brian's luggage cart. When we returned the meat inspector was there. Brian explained the problem with the ribs, and the inspector said to come find him when Andrew and Deirdre returned.

Brian and Deirdre returned without incident, with ribs that Brian described as "beautiful," and Brian flagged down the meat inspector as he passed by in a golf cart. The meat inspection took less than a minute and seemed fairly cursory. "OK, good luck," the inspector said, checking boxes on his clipboard, and left. With the setup in place, the cooking began around ten o'clock in the morning. Brian took the shoulders out of the cooler and with a large knife began to trim them. He had previously strained a half-gallon jug of marinade into an aluminum pan and as each of the total of six shoulders was skinned, Frank injected it with the strained marinade using a brine pump—a large syringe that shoots brine from many angles and depths—inserting the pump every two inches or so to allow the marinade to penetrate the meat. Once the shoulders were brined, they were placed in a black plastic garbage bag inside a cooler and allowed to sit for six hours or so. They were to be cooked around five o'clock in the evening.

Once finished with the pork shoulders, Brian asked Deirdre if she would like to skin the ribs. She agreed enthusiastically and he showed her what to do. On the underside of each rack of ribs is a membrane that peels off easily when one end is gripped firmly. Deirdre used a paper towel to hold one end and peel off the membrane. Brian explained that removing this "skin" allows the smoke to better penetrate the meat and creates a tenderer product. Just as he did for the shoulders, Frank—along with help from Brian—injected marinade into the ribs, this time using strained bottled Italian dressing rather than a homemade marinade and using a smaller syringe to inject the marinade between each rib rather than the larger brine pump. Once marinated the ribs too were stored in a cooler until it was time to cook them, around five o'clock the next morning. Meanwhile Ed prepared a small home-style smoker for the chicken.

Swine by Design competes in competitions sanctioned by two different bodies, the Kansas City Barbecue Society (KCBS) and Memphis in May (MIM). Both have a series of regional competitions with winners advancing to a national championship. The competition I attended is actually a set of two subcompetitions—an MIM-sanctioned competition and a local competition without a sanctioning body. At the local competition, foods that are not sanctioned by MIM are prepared. These foods are chicken, beef, lamb, and sauce. Teams can compete in any or all of these divisions, but Swine by Design elected to compete only in the chicken category, which had been their most successful item in the past, as well as the sauce category, which was a new division at this contest and involved pouring eight ounces of their barbecue sauce into a water bottle and submitting it for judging. Because chicken was not part of the sanctioned competition and the first contest was on Saturday, items for it could be premarinated.

There was some downtime around noon, once the pork ribs and shoulders were marinating. The small smoker for the chicken was set up alongside the big rig—the fire in the big cooker was not yet started—and all of the other business attended to. During this time the team members continued setting up the site, wiping down the counter, unpacking boxes, and icing cases of sports drink, bottled water, and beer.

Brian produced some chips and salsa and sat down to snack and chat with the other team members.

A bit later in the afternoon, Ed began working on the chicken, which was to be judged that evening. He burned some charcoal in a pail alongside the small smoker and, when it was no longer flaming, added some of it to the smoker. Ed brought forth chicken thighs marinating in zippered plastic bags. He took the thighs from the marinade, trimmed the excess fat, and applied a dry rub—a mix of spices. When the small smoker was up to the proper temperature, he put the chicken on the smoker, dropping a digital temperature probe into the smoker from a hole in the top. The chicken cooked for about two hours at 225 degrees.

Hugh joined the group in the afternoon with cases of beer. He is also an architect, has a "beach bum" look, wearing shorts and large colorful shirts, and is rarely seen without a cigar. He is married, with three children, and has an average build.

When the chicken was cooked the thighs were removed from the smoker and carefully placed on an aluminum tray. Ed carefully painted barbecue sauce on each thigh and then returned them to the smoker to brown, cooking them for another thirty minutes or so. When they were finished the six best-looking thighs—evenly browned, trimmed of fat, and plump—out of the twenty cooked were submitted for blind judging in a Styrofoam clamshell. This strictly blind style of judging was different from the combination blind and on-site judging that was to take place the next day.

Around the same time the chicken thighs were finished cooking, the fire in the big cooker was started. The shoulders were dry rubbed and went on the fire around five o'clock in the evening; they were to finish cooking around midmorning the next day. Otherwise, the evening was a fairly slow time. Each team member ate one remaining chicken thigh, and Brian put the rest on a paper plate to share with competing teams. Zeke stopped by with his chicken for Swine by Design to taste. The team wouldn't know the results of the day's competition until the next day, so the members seemed to have little to do. The shoulders were basted and rotated every hour or so and as long as the fire was at the right temperature, things were under control. Between six o'clock and nine o'clock most of the day crew started to leave. Some went home if they lived within driving distance, while others slept in the team's hotel room nearby.

Around seven o'clock in the evening, Andrew took out some ingredients from a cooler including pork chops, bananas, macadamia nuts, lime, and sugar. I hadn't eaten much but was reluctant to leave the site to eat, so I hoped he was cooking dinner. I remember being repeatedly surprised that the team didn't really eat while they cooked or at other times at the site. Andrew explained to Brian that their winning "Anything But" (a category for non-sanctioned items such as vegetables, fish, or steak, sometimes spelled "Anything Butt," as a pun on pork butt) recipe for barbecue Thai bananas would not be allowed into the national competition because it was a dessert, which the contest organizers had disallowed. He said, "So I'm gonna try a macadamia-crusted barbecue pork chop with Thai banana sauce for 'Anything But.' You think that will work?" Brian was encouraging, and Andrew started preparing the pork. He lit the small smoker that they used for the chicken, told Hugh to make the sauce, and asked Frank to make candied macadamia nuts and toasted coconut for garnish. Andrew grilled the pork and put the components together. He then made two servings of the pork and the team cut it up and tasted it. They all commented that they thought the recipe was "a winner," but voiced their frustration that their banana dessert, which had won the regional competition and been published by the sponsoring company in their marketing materials, would not be approved for the upcoming national competition.

Around nine o'clock in the evening, Cam and James arrived to run the overnight shift. Cam is a tall man around forty years old. He works for a university as an administrator. His wife, a food professional, is not involved at all in the barbecue world. He has two teenage daughters. James is a young man, in his midtwenties, with a small build. He is also an architect and is single. He often volunteers for the night shift. The night shift's main job is to monitor the cooking temperatures of the meat, keep the fire going, and get the site ready for inspection. Cam immediately went to a cabinet on the rig and set up a small coffee maker.

The two different sanctioning bodies—KCBS and MIM—have a number of differences with regard to competition rules and procedures, the most obvious of which is on-site judging. At KCBS competitions, judging is done strictly by "blind box." The meat is placed in a numbered Styrofoam clamshell container, and a team member brings it to a judging tent, where its identifying number is changed and the meat is tasted by a table of six judges—usually a combination of nationally certified judges and local food professionals. At MIM-sanctioned competitions there is blind judging as well—by three judges—but an additional three judges taste the food on site, inspect the rig, listen to a presentation by the team members about their process, and are served by the team. Because this Barbecue Battle was an MIM competition, much of the night crew's energy was devoted to cleaning the rig and site to get it ready for the on-site judging. Just before dawn the ribs went on the grill and the shoulders were wrapped in foil and basted with apple juice so they could continue cooking while staying moist until judging in the early afternoon. (Andrew tells me that most barbecue teams deny foiling the meat but most do it.)

The rest of the crew arrived early on the morning of the second day. The second day is the serious judging day, and the tone was decidedly more serious as well. Some of the team members arrived in their official red Swine by Design polo shirts, while others brought them on hangers to change into later. Cam debriefed Andrew and Brian regarding the shoulders that had been cooking all night: "The spreadsheet says they should cook till six but they looked done so we foiled them early." Andrew seemed tense to me. "You foiled them early. Are you sure they were done?" Brian and Andrew checked the ribs, while Ed and Deirdre continued straightening up. Cam and James announced that they were going home to sleep, but James said that he would return in the afternoon for the award presentations.

Meanwhile, Hugh rehearsed his presentation for the on-site judging. He paced back and forth in the middle of the fairway, cigar in hand, rehearsing his talk. Later in the morning, the team converted the site into a "set" for the judging and did a full dress rehearsal. They folded the numerous chairs and hid the coolers, boxes, cooking equipment, and personal items behind a tarp. They put up red tarpaulin walls, which Andrew said would enhance the appearance of the meat, and set a table in the center of the site. They set the table with a table cloth, a vase of flowers, and silverware for two settings—the judge's and Hugh's. Opposite the judge were two easels with posters of the Swine by Design principles, which guided Hugh later when he gave his presentation. Behind the judge's place was a wall of about twenty-five trophies from past competitions. There was an effort to make everything clean and polished, despite the fact that the team was competing on a city street and there was smoke everywhere. Deirdre polished the trophies. Brian swept the pavement frequently throughout the morning. Andrew even swept the dust off the wood samples that they would show to the judge when explaining the Swine by Design barbecue process. Shortly before each judge came, Ed placed leaves of kale and whole bell peppers on the grill to garnish it as well.

The team asked me to step away and observe the actual judging from afar, so I was unable to listen in. In the past, Hugh explained, they had the entire team lined up inside the rig watching the judge's tasting. Now, however, the team shakes hands with the judge and steps back because of Andrew's suggestion that too many people watching the judge might make her or him feel uncomfortable. Since I was not allowed to closely observe the judging, I asked to observe and tape the rehearsal, in which Hugh ran through the process with Deirdre playing the role of the judge:

> *Hugh:* I'll ask the judges to step over here. I'll briefly mention a couple of the trophies, and I'm gonna put the judge over here in this position.
> *Andrew:* I don't even know if I'd mention the trophies if I were you.
> *Hugh:* Well, I refer to 'em as the wall of trophies. And that's about all I say about it. Nothing else.
> *Andrew:* OK.
> *Hugh:* And then I'll bring the judge over here and I'll put the judge there. Here. *[to Deirdre]* Wanna stand up for a second? The chairs'll be pushed in. I'll bring the judge in and next I'll go through the design goals. And then I'll take him over to the rig. And then after we do the whole smoker routine we'll bring him back out here. And then the meat'll come out from you. I guess then I'll sort of recap our goals. The plate of meat will be right here. And I'll have my rubber gloves on. I'll show the meat, give it to you [Deirdre, as judge]. I'll play with the meat. Talk about it. And then while talking about it I'm gonna recap these [principles]. I'm just reminding you, we talked about this nice red smoke-ring appearance. And I'm gonna be showing you the meat, I'm gonna be showing you the smoke ring. I'll be showing you the moistness. 'Cause really, I'm telling him what our goals are, I'm telling him how we're gonna do it. I'm gonna show them how we do it. And then I'll bring 'em back and, you know, show them that it was done. So I'm just gonna kind of hit everything very quickly. Probably about three minutes down here. Probably about four minutes up there. And then probably have about seven, eight minutes to sit and taste the food. And then they're out. So it goes really quick. And that's what's nice about this *[points to posters of design goals that form the backdrop for the presentation]*. It's an outline for me to follow.

After the blocking with Deirdre, Hugh asks for a more formal rehearsal with the other members of the group:

Hugh: Brian, you're going to introduce everybody.
Brian: Ladies and Germs, welcome to the Swine by Design. We're glad to have you with us today. This is the Swine by Design competition barbecue team.

Sunday after the rehearsal was a frenzy of activity. Blind judging came first, and each category was separated by thirty minutes. The teams had a five-minute window on either side of the official time in which to submit their blind boxes. Whole-hog, a category in which Swine by Design did not compete, was first, and followed by shoulder and ribs. The presentation of the food in boxes was strictly defined. Acceptable garnishes were lettuce, parsley, and cilantro only. Sauce could not be pooled, which was defined as sitting with an area larger than a fifty-cent piece, or drizzled—especially in a pattern, which could be used to communicate with the judges, as if Swine by Design wrote "SD" in sauce, for example. Sauces could be "striped" in a straight line across the meat. Meat from the shoulder could be pulled, shredded, chopped, or minced, provided there was enough of each style for the judges to taste.

After the blind boxes were submitted, the team quickly straightened up to get ready for the on-site judging. The team members who had been wearing other shirts changed into their team polo, and all members congregated in front of the site. The judges arrived one at a time in fifteen-minute intervals. Contestants are downgraded for delaying a judge, so the team was very conscious of having their routine move smoothly. As each judge arrived, Brian introduced himself and welcomed him or her to the team site. He then announced that the remaining Swine by Design members would introduce themselves. The team stood in a semicircle, and each member beginning with Deirdre and ending with Hugh introducing themselves. Hugh ended his introduction by indicating that he would be leading the tour of the site. He walked the judge under the tarpaulin roof of the rig, where Deirdre offered a drink of iced tea or water, and the extensive spiel rehearsed earlier began.

About an hour after the on-site judging for each category ended, there was a gathering outside the judge's tent. It was there that a staff member wrote down the three teams that were finalists in each category. These teams had a second on-site judging in the finals round, and the winning teams in each category received prize money as well as eligibility to compete at the national MIM competition. Andrew waited outside the judge's tent but came away looking dejected both times. Swine by Design did not make the finals in shoulder or ribs. Out of thirty teams, Swine by Design placed fourth in shoulder and sixth in ribs, missing the prize money and finals in both categories—but still making the top seven, the magic number for being announced at the awards ceremony and winning a trophy. They did not place in the top seven for chicken, which surprised the team, as they seemed to feel that this was traditionally their strongest category. Overall the team seemed neither overly happy nor overly disappointed with their placement, but acknowledged it was a tough competition and good time.

Men, Women, Masculinities, and Femininities

When I began interviewing the Swine by Design team members late in my fieldwork with them, I often began my interviews with a seemingly simple question, the answer to which served to provide some insight into the team members, their personalities, backgrounds, and stories, as well as the origins and history of the team, and their perspectives on barbecue culture in general. Though I had a short list of possible interview questions prepared, the first, "How did you come to join Swine by Design?" was typically the only scripted question that I needed.

Hugh and I were sitting drinking beer one evening at a competition later in the season. Andrew and Frank were up on the rig working again on their "Anything But" submission. Not happy with the pork, Zeke suggested rare tuna steaks with the same sauce. Andrew and Frank were practicing with swordfish steaks—thinking that rare fish could alienate some of the judges, who may be hesitant to eat rare fish cooked outdoors in the summer heat or have questions about the quality of the fish. Andrew, Frank, and Hugh are the founding members of Swine by Design, and the men collaborated to share the history of the team with me:

> *Jon:* How'd you get involved in this?
> *Hugh:* Andrew and I used to work together at the firm. And Frank.
>   A few of us used to work together. Ike. A couple other people.
>   And Andrew's brother, who I think Andrew may have lived with

in Memphis for a little while. Andrew's brother lived down there for a while and used to cook at the Memphis in May contest every year. And he had helped out his brother's team. And he had gotten Andrew interested in it. So I think Andrew had heard about this contest. I think the team formed in '93. He heard about it, and I guess he called just to see what it was about. What do you need to do to have a barbecue contest? Or a barbecue team? So they sent out some information, and they said, "Oh, by the way, we have one spot left if you want it." And uh, they didn't actually. Hey Andrew, when you first talked to the competition guys did they tell you it was closed out? Or did they tell you there was still spots left?

Andrew: When I first talked to the guys? Somebody died on another team or something. Had a heart attack. That was it *[laughing]*. And so they had an opening.

Hugh: And so Andrew calls me and says, "Hey, are you interested in doing a barbecue contest, and I had just bought a New Braunfels Offset Smoker for my dad for Father's Day. This was like two or three weeks before the contest. And I said, "Sure." So we ended up borrowing my dad's New Braunfels smoker and brought it out here. And cooked. We got a ribbon in chicken or something. Fifth place chicken.

Jon: Had you been barbecuing yourself for a while?

Hugh: He [Andrew] had. I hadn't really cooked a whole lot, no. A little bit. Backyard stuff. Like any other American. But nothing serious. But that was the whole beginning of it. We just had this little New Braunfels smoker and just filled it with charcoal every thirty minutes. We had to rent a tent. You know, you need some type of canopy here. And we ended up spending like five hundred bucks just on the tent rental. So we did it that way for like three or four years. We just got another New Braunfels smoker. And we cooked one full-size shoulder and tried to serve it to all the judges. And the judges would come up to us and say, "You know, it's really nice to pull the bone out of the shoulder for each and every judge." Well there's only a couple bones in a shoulder so you basically just need a whole shoulder for every judge. It just wasn't possible for us to cook that much meat. So we slowly built this here with a few hundred dollars. And the last year that we used it [the old setup] was the year that we were grand champions. And so we decided we needed something bigger. And we found this [rig]. A local caterer had it. So we figured, god, you know, it'll pay for itself in a couple years by not having to rent the tent and chairs and everything else.

Though each team member obviously has their own story regarding how they joined the team, the interview excerpt above is representative of the underlying reason that many Swine by Design members say they connect with the team. Most had no initial intentions of competing in barbecue, but rather were seeking guidance in a hobby where it seemed challenging to acquire mentorship. Barbecue, when done at home, is largely an individual act. Though it is often used in entertaining, true barbecue—meat slowly smoke roasted over indirect heat—takes hours or even days to prepare, and the actual cooking is often done individually. Furthermore, unlike many hobbies that are more easily learned from books, barbecue is probably best learned through a multisensory, hands-on experience. Even the best food writing cannot teach someone how something should taste. These qualities manifest themselves in team members joining Swine by Design not to compete per se, but rather to learn. This distinction is further belied by the fact that Swine by Design's members—largely white, suburban, middle-class or upper-middle-class professionals, many transplanted from other parts of the United States—are fairly unlikely to come from a barbecue tradition, where techniques are typically passed down from father to son as is done in African American and other Southern foodways traditions, as discussed in this volume and elsewhere (e.g., Elie 1996).

Indeed, it is this mentoring, learning environment that James finds so valuable in Swine by Design's receptivity to new members. Both Hugh and Brian speak of joining the team with regard to the distinction between grilling—quick, direct-heat cooking as for hamburgers, chicken breasts, or vegetables, done "like any other American" (Hugh) or "like most people" (Brian)—and barbecue, a skill not as easily learned. Deirdre, the newest member of Swine by Design—and the only woman member—also joined not to compete but to learn more about barbecue, meeting Brian and Andrew via an online barbecue discussion board.

Swine by Design is, for several reasons, not the obvious choice of a team to join in order to learn more about cooking traditional or competition barbecue. First, all of the members are amateur cooks. Some members of competing teams are food-service professionals, and some teams even boast barbecue cookbook authors, restaurateurs, and hosts of television cooking shows. Swine by Design is composed of design and other office professionals. Second, none of the Swine by Design members identify themselves as a barbecue expert or offer formal instruction in the form of barbecue classes, a side occupation of some successful teams. Third, Swine by Design, while good, is not generally considered to be an upper-echelon barbecue team, nor do they claim to be one. Swine by Design members seem to self-select on the basis of education level, occupation, class, and an educational rather than a purely competitive interest in barbecue. Members' interest in learning barbecue seems to be prominent within Swine by Design not because the team members *know* more than other teams, but because they engage in active online and face-to-face discussions about barbecue nuance and are willing to share what they have learned. There is very little information that the team holds proprietary, and Andrew's off-season experimentation makes him a popular coworker at his office, often carrying in racks of ribs and pulled pork to share at the office on Monday morning. These are educated people who like to cook, talk, and think barbecue.

I asked Grant to elaborate on how he joined the team:

> *Jon:* So your wife works with Andrew, that's how you got into this?
> *Grant:* Yeah, it kinda came about that way.
> *Jon:* Is she into barbecue?
> *Grant:* Yeah. Well, she used to help out. We had our daughter about four years ago. In fact her last contest would have been '97, I guess. The last time she helped out she was pregnant and didn't know about it and was sick the whole weekend. Plus it was about ninety-nine degrees. So it just took a toll on her system. And that was it for her.

Women

Grant's discussion of his wife's previous involvement with competitive barbecue, as well as the group's makeup of mainly male participants, raised many questions for me regarding the role of women in Swine by Design. There is no question that despite the recent addition of Deirdre to the team, Swine by Design is—however unofficially—very much a men's organization. Most of the team members come alone to competitions—"getting away" from their families, as Hugh put it—and women, while frequently discussed, are much less frequently seen at the Swine by Design site. Almost as evocative as the question of how each member joined the team is the question of women's roles in competition barbecue. I asked Hugh for his take on the issue:

> *Hugh:* You don't see too many barbecue wives, do you? My wife doesn't like it.
> *Jon:* Why do you think she doesn't like it?
> *Hugh:* My wife doesn't like it because I'm away overnight. Or an entire day really. So I only do a couple contests a year now. Because if I'm not around she's alone with the kids so it's a little tough. I think most of the wives love it when you *cook*. They like the food. But they just don't like the time it takes. It's a very time-consuming thing. If the other guys' wives feel the same way I don't know. It's a lot of money. Last year we brought in over five grand in prizes.

Significant in Hugh's comments is the distinction between the wives loving it "when you cook" and their feelings about the men being absent for part or all of the weekend to cook competitively—often, in the case of Swine by Design, sandwiched between two full weeks of work away from home. On the surface, the distinction seems less about the activity itself than the time commitment involved. Would Hugh's spouse have the same concerns if he hunted, fished, or mountain climbed with friends rather than being with his family on weekends? Or is there added tension because Hugh is doing something—cooking—that can be done at home or nearly anywhere?

I asked Deirdre—a woman in competition barbecue—about the issue. The collaborative nature of the on-site interviewing allowed the discussion to spread out from there:

> *Jon:* So how is it being a woman in this man's world of barbecue?
> *Deirdre:* Excellent *[laughing]*.
> *Jon:* Do you have any difficulties?
> *Deirdre:* Well, you know, this is my first season really. People are really friendly.
> *Brian:* Well, we'll change that *[laughing]*.
> *Deirdre:* I know.
> *Jon:* Why do you think there aren't more women at the competition or on the team?
> *Deirdre:* Because it's so time consuming. They really don't have time.

Because they're busy taking care of children. And a house. And everything else. And cooking because they have to and not because they want to.

Jon: Are you single, Deirdre?

Deirdre: I'm separated from my husband. So I'm *not* single. And I'm not married either.

Jon: Did your barbecue interest start after your separation?

Deirdre: No, no, my barbecue interest started about four years ago.

Jon: And you're married, right, Brian?

Brian: Yes.

Jon: Did your wife come to this?

Brian: No. Won't have anything to do with this.

Jon: Nothing at all?

Brian: Nothing.

Jon: She's obviously supportive by letting you go.

Brian: She tolerates it.

Jon: Why is she not into it?

Brian: It's just not her thing. She don't see the sense in it. She has a stereotyped view of barbecuers. And it's not particularly favorable. Our team is a bunch of professionals. White-collar people. The stereotype barbecuer is almost 180 degrees out from that. And it's not her thing.

Jon: Even in competitions?

Brian: [emphatically] The stereotype of that is one-eighty opposite of that. It's just like every stereotype. There's a grain of truth. And a whole lot of not necessarily true.

Jon: It just seems like a pretty expensive sport for a blue collar, um—

Brian: You'd be amazed. I don't know what some of these folks do but it's not a white-shirt-and-tie event. It's a good ol' boy event. Whether you are one or not. She works for one of the big law firms in town. And lives in a very white-shirt-and-tie environment. All day long. And this just isn't her thing.

While I had anticipated discussions about the usual issues that arise in any type of qualitative field research—gender, race, and class—I had not expected such strong feelings expressed within the team itself. Again with Brian, his spouse's feelings concern not the cooking itself, but the "good ol' boy" aspect of the competitions—which, while admittedly expensive, consist mainly of participants that Brian's wife identifies as rural working class. I asked to speak with Brian's wife to learn more about these powerful feelings, but Brian anticipated that she would decline and she did. I wondered, then, whether any of these men's wives or girlfriends encouraged their partner's role in Swine by Design. Even Deirdre, after all, joined the team once she was separated. Cam mentioned that his wife is a food-service manager, so I wondered whether she had more positive feelings about his participation than the other wives did:

> *Jon:* So what does your wife think about all this?
> *Cam:* Actually, she's pretty supportive. It's only about five weekends a year that we do it so, you know, she's pretty supportive of it.
> *Jon:* Does she come to these competitions?
> *Cam:* Actually I have yet to get her to come to one. I took the judging class this summer, and I actually tried to get her to take it earlier in the spring. I tried to get her to take the judging class so that then when my daughter is in college we could. Yeah, there's a lot of contests down in the mountains of North Carolina and stuff, we could go down, get a B&B. Make a weekend of it. I might still get her to take the class. We'll see. She's done some other food judging, so I think she'd enjoy it, so we'll see. Judging really only takes a couple hours so yeah, we'll see. But nah, she's pretty supportive of it.

I was struck by the fact that even though Cam identifies his wife as supportive, her support is somewhat tacit. She, like Brian's wife, does not object to his participation but chooses not to participate, despite Cam's encouragement. At the competition following this interview, Cam told the group he was berated for coming home so tired last time after doing an overnight shift, then having to drive three hours to pick up his daughter from summer camp.

I also asked Ed's wife, Glenda, how she feels about Ed's involvement with Swine by Design. She responded, "I mean, it's fine. Men need a hobby, you know. And this one at least is one we can visit with the boys. And it's good for them to see their father doing this. Relaxed. With the guys. On a team. You know, it's a lot of money. And time in the summer. But he likes it. We've always done stuff. Like fraternities, groups of friends, activities. So this is kind of the same." Glenda seemed more positive in her support of Swine by Design. For example, she was interested in my project and happy to talk with me. Part of her support seemed to come from the fact that she has always had the role of supporting her husband's endeavors. In a later informal interview she told me that she and Ed met in college, and that she and her girlfriends were the boosters for Ed and his fraternity brothers. Of the spouses with whom I spoke, Glenda is unique in discussing the positive aspects of the boys seeing their father as a Swine by Design team member, rather than seeing his involvement as time spent *away* from the family. At a later competition Swine by Design hosted a party for their sponsors on site, and the majority of the crowd consisted of Ed and Glenda's college friends, reinforcing what she had said about their relationship.

Finally, Andrew's wife, Ann, plays a highly involved role with Swine by Design—as their webmaster—as well as being the spouse of the leader, who the team acknowledges invests the highest amount of emotional and physical energy into the team. I asked Andrew what Ann's involvement in the team is. He answered, "She came down last night. She's kind of like Brian's wife. She's just tired of the whole barbecue thing. It's one of those things she just doesn't see the point. Oh, my wife is just sick of the, oh, you know, the *heat*, and just *why* would you wanna *do* that."

Why?

The question of "And just *why* would you wanna *do* that?" resonates. These men and one woman each spend hundreds of dollars in a weekend on gas, meat, lodging, dues, and supplies. They drive hours to competitions; spend weekends in the summer heat next to a fire; complain about heat, bugs, logistics, and competitors; lose sleep to tend a fire; and share hotel rooms with four or more of their sweaty and smoky companions. Though most of the team members may join to learn about barbecue, they do not pick up what they need to know and then move on. Rather, they pay dues, wear the uniform, travel to competitions, and compete. The ultimate question to me, then, is "Why?"

In one instance Andrew mentioned that the local fire department was charging a twenty-five-dollar permit fee to ignite competition cookers with propane. Hugh commented that for twenty-five dollars the team could buy a case of beer instead. "Good beer." Andrew ended the discussion by saying, "For twenty-five dollars we can buy barbecue from a restaurant and just go ahead and submit it." This sentiment underlies much of what I learned in my fieldwork. These amateur cooks invest huge amounts of time, money, energy, and emotion into a hobby that yields results sometimes superior—but often comparable or inferior—to cheaper, more convenient, commercially produced barbecue.

> *Jon:* Let me ask you the obvious.
> *Brian:* What's that?
> *Jon:* Why do you do this?
> *Brian:* It's fun.
> *Jon:* What makes it fun?
> *Brian:* I like to cook. I'm a fairly decent indoor cook *[laughing]*. What makes *anything* fun? It's an activity that one derives pleasure from even though it can be aggravating at times. And I like the cooking part of it. I like the competition part of it. And I also like the *friendly* competition part of it. There's not a team here that if you needed something and they had it, they'd be happy to loan it to you whatever it is. And there's a certain type of competitive camaraderie that exists among all the teams whether you know 'em or not. It's not a cutthroat kind of thing at all. And it's an opportunity to socialize too with people who share your interests in the activity.

I found Brian's response to this question fascinating, not just because of what he said but also because of what he struggled to say. In a separate interview, when I asked Brian how he joined the team, I got over fourteen minutes of tape answering that question—no probes, no follow-ups, just Brian talking. Here it takes multiple prompts before he finally gets to what seems to me to be the heart of competition barbecue's appeal for him—the friendly competition and social aspects of the activity. His insight is reinforced by my observation that Brian—more than any other team member—spends hours visiting other teams' sites, invites them over to the Swine by Design site, and seems to know many of the competitors and judges, despite joining the world of competitive barbecue only about halfway into Swine by Design's existence.

Hugh, when asked the same question, responds in a way that, I was surprised, shared many aspects of Brian's response, with some additional reasons:

> It's fun. Enjoyable. It's fun to sit back. Get away from your house. Get away from your normal responsibilities. Have a couple beers. Have a

couple cigars. Sit around and BS with people. Now we know so many people. You know you go to a competition, everybody's known you a long time. I have three kids at home. So it's really nice to get away with some of your best friends and just kind of hang out. Plus it's fun to win. You know, if we weren't winning, I don't know if we'd all be doing this.

Ken, another occasional Swine by Design team member, echoes those thoughts as they talk together in response to my question during the overnight shift: "It's the outdoors. Sitting around. Feeling the chill of a summer night. Getting hopped up on espresso. Listening to tunes. Drinking Jack. Tending fire. It's primitive. It's nature. It's companionship. It's conversation. It's fun. It's guy stuff, you know?"

Guy Stuff

As I am thinking about Ken's summative comment, it occurs to me that the competitive barbecue scene—the outdoors, the music, the meat, the coffee and whiskey, the fire, the friendships, the discussions, and, I would add, the competition—is about not only "guy stuff" as a popular cultural stereotype but also a performance of masculinity in a self-conscious, affirmative way. Examples of complex feelings, thoughts, and actions concerning maleness, masculinities, and identities abound in my field log—an exploration of which yields a sense of how closely interlocked these ideas of men and barbecue truly are. To say that the members of Swine by Design cook "like men" may seem absurd. After all, there is no definitive way that men do things with food. But in working with Swine by Design, one gets the sense that their cooking and food habits in the team environment in general differ widely from how they do things during their daily home lives away from competitive barbecue.

One particularly telling aspect to this distinction involves what the team actually eats over the two days of the competition. The answer surprised me. When I embarked on this project I anticipated returning from my fieldwork well fed on barbecue staples: chicken, pulled pork, and ribs, of course, but also the sides that I love as much as the meat—coleslaw, beans, cornbread, potato salad, hush puppies, and so on. Not such a taxing research project! I was surprised, then, after a full day at my first observation, that actual meals were never made. All of Swine by Design's food-preparation energy is focused on the competition, and meals during the two days of competition are afterthoughts at best and more likely not thought of at all. Meat is always tasted after someone, typically Andrew, determines that the official submission process has finished and everything else is leftover. But the tasting is just that—a taste. The team scrutinizes their submission for smokiness, moistness, color, tenderness, and meat flavor—some talking through each point, like Brian, and others popping a bit in their mouth and walking off to consider it in quietude like Ed. Cam says that after inhaling smoke for two days and feeling smoke roasted yourself from the heat, the last thing you want to do is sit down to a thick rack of ribs.

When there *is* food to eat, it is typically snacks like salsa and chips that Brian brings to the competitions or food bartered for with another team. Cam brought a salmon that he smoked at home for the team to taste one morning, and after the team had their fill, he bartered with Zeke for eggs Benedict. At another competition the wives of the neighboring (male) team members boiled crabs and corn, and after they had eaten and entertained their guests, they invited Swine by Design to partake. On another weekend, Swine by Design hosted a barbecue for the team's sponsors the evening before the judging but did not cook anything for the party on site. Hugh brought all the food from home, including barbecued ribs and pulled pork, and heated it on site in electric pots and portable burners, avoiding using the competition cooker. This stood out to me as a stark contrast to another neighboring team, a family, where the mother of the family brought potato salad, coleslaw, rolls, cornbread, and cobbler to the competition and her husband cooked some extra barbecued chickens and ribs so that they could sit down to a family meal at the end of the first day.

Much in the same way that firehouse cooks (Deutsch 2004) seem to use words or actions to "masculinize" certain food behaviors—especially those considered more domestic or feminine such as preparing vegetables, cleaning, or serving others—so does the barbecue team consciously and deliberately work to make masculine similar types of cooking behaviors, or else exaggerate and parody the effeminate features of such activities. Of the few roles that Swine by Design explicitly brands as feminine, that of "garnish fag" is the most glaring. The moniker is ingrained enough in the workings of the group that Ed—bearing supermarket bags full of lettuce, parsley, bell peppers, and curly kale—announced to the team, "I'm garnish fag this weekend, guys," and Brian said the same thing when his turn in the season came. Produce for garnish is the only food in the competition that is neither meat nor sauce, and it does stand out as a departure from the rest of the cooking activity. For blind-box submissions, meats may be garnished with lettuce leaves, parsley, or cilantro, and it is the garnish fag's duty to clean these ingredients and keep them fresh for judging, no easy task in the summer heat. Garnishing for on-site judging is much more elaborate. Though the food itself is not actually garnished on site, the judge inspects the cooker, at that point cooling to about two hundred degrees, which he or she opens to find not only picture-perfect pink meat but also a cornucopia of crisp produce—curly kale and colorful bell peppers—adroitly arranged by the team member responsible for garnishing just seconds before the judge's arrival, in order to keep it looking fresh in the smoky heat. The garnish is then freshened for subsequent judges.

But the mocking of the garnish fag's role does not occur in name alone. At KCBS competitions, where there is no on-site judging, the presentation and garnishing of the food in Styrofoam containers does not begin until the music is cued, blaring show tunes, which this season was most often the cast recording of *My Fair Lady*. Ed was careful to announce, after suspecting my interest in this practice, "For the record, this is my wife's CD." Furthermore, the Swine by Design manual, which Andrew wrote and which is the bible of the team, containing elaborate and exacting recipes, photographs of plate presentations, equipment checklists, Gantt charts of cooking times, and diagrams of site setups, also includes instructions for garnishing. After step-by-step recommendations for cleaning the greens, keeping them fresh, and placing the meat in relation to the garniture comes the admonition to "serve with a limp wrist."

Throughout this discussion I have not mentioned Deirdre's role in all of this. I saw Deirdre in a variety of roles throughout the season—in two competitions as a team member; in one as a blind judge, which, interestingly, is not illegal or explicitly identified as a conflict of interest by one sanctioning body; and entirely absent for two others. The main reason I have not addressed her much in the sense of qualifying the above discussion about the performance of masculinities on site is simply that I do not see her as changing things much. Deirdre is not tasked with roles more or less "womanly" than others, with two major exceptions. Once, during her first competition, she decided to polish the trophies in advance of the on-site judging—which the team typically does not do—and Brian commented that it was good to have a "woman's touch" for that. At the same competition, Hugh asked Deirdre to serve the drinks to the judges—a particularly domestic role that is significant,

I think, in its public-performance aspect. Working with the team day to day, she ices drinks, skins ribs, adds wood to the fire, and acts as "one of the guys." During the judging, however, her position as a woman on the team is highlighted to the point that although she is the newest member of the team, and most of the team members are asked to leave the site after shaking the judges' hands, she is asked to play a more active role in the performance of the on-site judging process.

The Performance of Barbecue

Athleticism

Competition barbecue is hardly a sport in the conventional sense. There is a lot of sitting around, drinking beer and sports drinks, talking, and listening to music. There are also very occasional strenuous physical activities such as icing drinks with fifty-pound bags of ice, carrying six ten-pound pork shoulders from the meat truck, or stooping at an odd angle to get the fire going. It may seem ridiculous to think that a competition devoted to sedentary activity and consumption of fatty meats—where competition seeds become available because of coronaries rather than injury—is anything but loafing. But in many ways, sport and athleticism are important aspects to the performance of competition barbecue. My barbecue log begins, "I'm writing this on Tuesday because Monday I was dead to the world. My muscles were aching, my nose and throat were bathed in phlegm, the back of my neck and legs were enflamed with sunburn, and I had a headache so crippling I could barely stay standing. Rough weekend, huh? Was I hiking a remote mountain trail? Kayaking through rapids? Playing in a rugby tournament? No. I was doing qualitative research at the Barbecue Battle."

Now admittedly I may not be the most robust of field researchers, but the point itself is important. Competition barbecue involves two full days of sun, smoke, heat, and physical activity—which, however light, is more than I did in two days of writing a field log in addition to waking hourly overnight to check the meat and fire for smaller teams without distinct shifts. It can be exhausting to the uninitiated. By the end of the season I came home without needing to recover, but I also knew better how to pace myself during my observations—keeping better hydrated, in the shade, with my head farther from the constant plume of smoke.

Even a casual observation reassures me that others at these competitions find them deserving of the marker of a sport. Many teams, like Swine by Design, have uniforms. In fact, Swine by Design has two sets of uniforms—a practice T-shirt, which they wear for cooking during the weekend, and a "game time" golf shirt for judging and awards ceremonies. Consistent with the team's style, Swine by Design uniforms are somewhat understated, with simply the team logo in the place of an alligator or other emblem, but other teams' uniforms are much more elaborate. Many of the teams have "Pit Crew" emblazoned across their shirts, identifying them as a barbecue-pit team member in a direct analogy to that other famous sport with pits, auto racing. Such teams are often the more entrepreneurial ones that sell T-shirts without the "Pit Crew" designation to fans and visitors.

Like an organized sport, these competitions are held in conspicuous, spectator-oriented places. The logical place to hold a competition for outdoor cookery might be a field or parking lot adjacent to a building, which could potentially provide water, electricity, restrooms, and shelter for the cooks. What we see instead are competitions held as major tourist attractions for downtown rejuvenation activities, sponsored by the chamber of commerce in small towns, or held as fund-raisers for firehouses and other nonprofit organizations. Though competition cooks do not typically offer tastes of their food, and indeed at some competitions are forbidden by local public health departments from doing so, these competitions are spectator events. Yet, for the most part, there is not much to see. Of the thirty-six or more hours of a competition, the time when a spectator can see team members preparing meat might be only two or three hours in the aggregate. During the remaining time, meats cook slowly in a closed cooker. As a consequence, the actual "event" for the spectators often consists of commercially vended barbecue and other foods, live music, a beer garden at some competitions, the awards ceremony, and slight glimpses of other teams in action. The teams, unable to show much "action," sometimes sell sauces, rubs, or memorabilia if allowed, and decorate their site to differentiate themselves from their competition.

The spectators' presence at the competitions does much to change the dynamic of the team from one of pure recreation and competitive spirit to one of crowd pleasing. Many teams, like Swine by Design, use creative team names, signage, trophies, elaborate rigs, and memorabilia to draw interest in their site. Others, especially small teams with less time to spare, tend to discourage tourist traffic by maintaining a relatively low profile through a more utilitarian design and minimal signage.

Some members of Swine by Design, like Frank and James, are happy to stand atop the rig and people watch, not looking to engage with the crowd. Others, like Brian, are game for conversation and explaining the Swine by Design process, even spending downtime in front of the rig on the main fairway, inviting questions and comments from the public. Still others surely share the attitude of Hugh, who says the answers to all of my questions really come down to one thing: "Barbecue chicks. Groupies. That's the answer to everything. That's why we do it. That's why our wives don't like it. That's why we spend the money. That's it. It all comes down to barbecue chicks."

While Hugh might truly believe that "barbecue chicks" are the raison d'être of Swine by Design, my observations do not reinforce his comment. At no point in any of the competitions were the Swine by Design members visibly admired by groupies of any persuasion, beyond general inquiries such as "What's cooking?" or "What kind of wood do you use?" But Hugh's comment is too emphatic to be dismissed. What Hugh sees, I think, is the masculine team-sport element of mild-mannered architects suiting up for the game to become admired as heroes, wanted by women and envied by men. In the same way that a group of men in public is unremarkable, but the same group of men in firefighter uniforms or football uniforms takes on another aura entirely, so does the competition team of Swine by Design represent a set of ideals and mythologies separate from and not necessarily representative of the individual players.

Showmanship
"Night Help? Rover's Hind Leg East? Pan Handle Smokers? Smokin Jokin? Aunt Jean's Barbecue? Barbecue Country? Fuhgeddaboutit? Mad Max? Fire Starters? Smoke Encounters of the Third Swine? Ribs by Andy? Smitty's Bar-B-Q? JDC's Soon-to-be Famous Shotgun House Rib Rub? Roland Porkers?" This roll call preceding Swine by Design's first competition of the season introduces a dichotomy that runs as an undercurrent throughout the competition barbecue world. There is levity, a considerable amount of self-parody, and a high social value placed on the "sport" of competition barbecue, as reflected by the team names. At the same time these teams are investing huge amounts of time, money, and energy into the competition and want to win for prize money, esteem, and entry into national forums. At the conclusion

of a cook's meeting later in the season, a contest organizer summarized this dichotomy: "All you new teams, if you have any questions, there's a lot of teams here that have done this competition before. Ask 'em. There's not a team here that won't help you out. I strongly recommend, however, that you *not* accept any unsolicited cooking advice." Zeke reinforced this statement from the back of the tent, yelling, "Hey, I hear the judges like things really black and charred this year."

The other important dichotomy that shows itself repeatedly in competition barbecue is the different way that the team has to behave as a competitor versus a public spectacle. With the exception of extroverted Brian, Swine by Design is not a showy team, preferring to let their considerable mass of trophies speak for them. They often cover the front entrance to their site with the banners of their corporate sponsors rather than encouraging spectators to approach. Members of other teams often stand to the front of their site, hawking merchandise, answering questions, and generally being crowd pleasers. Swine by Design has much less tolerance for this. For example, Andrew nearly lost his composure once while trying to restart some dying coals with an electric fan when a woman walking by said, "You should use water to put that fire out." Andrew commented through clenched teeth that he wanted to get the fire going, providing a mini-lecture on the physics of fire.

The team seems to be in a difficult situation. They need the public's support, for cash prizes garnered from admission fees, for permits and street closings to accommodate the competitions, and for drawing corporate sponsors. But the team is really there to compete rather than to entertain. This issue increases the tension at some competitions more than others. At one competition in a major city, a seven-dollar admission fee is charged to the general public, and while many visitors assume it includes all-you-can-eat samples from the teams, the health department has threatened disqualification and fines to any team giving samples, as only licensed caterers are allowed to distribute food in that locality. The paying visitors, however, did not understand the seriousness and gravity of the order. Nor did the homeless people congregating along the fence behind the sites, begging for food as pounds and pounds of leftover meat went to waste. Brian told me that after the awards were announced, and there was no risk of disqualification, he tried to feed anyone who asked, but that it would be a shame if slipping someone a rib had resulted in the team being disqualified.

Design and Gadgetry

Another important aspect in the performance of competition barbecue for Swine by Design is the role of design in their cooking. As James mentions, Swine by Design differentiates itself from most of the competition by being composed of white-collar, largely design professionals. But does their professional orientation actually influence their barbecue or team dynamics as their name suggests? Hugh is quick to dismiss this line of thinking:

> No. It's a gimmick. It makes us stand out as different. Gives the judges something for the judges to remember us by at MIM competitions. Because you get points for showmanship. And the design thing lets us do that without being too tacky. But the meat is the same. At KCBS it doesn't matter who you are. It doesn't matter what you have for a rig. But at Memphis in May I think there's three or four blind judges and then three on-site judges and of the seven categories in the scoring, three of them are really due to the presentation. If you have a good look I would like to think it gives us a little bit of credibility. And that we're just not a bunch of people that decided to come in and cook something.

Though Hugh identifies the team's design orientation as a constructive gimmick but not necessarily influential to the way they operate, much of what I learned through observation questions this idea. While the team realistically does not "design" its barbecue, much of what they do seems informed by their perspectives as design professionals.

All competition barbecue teams need to be organized. They are competing sometimes hundreds of miles from their homes, have a ten-minute window of time in which to submit their entries for foods that take hours or even days to prepare, and are often operating in locations without access to supplies. Indeed, that is one reason the teams, despite being competitors, support each other so much. Everyone forgets *something* sometime—paper towels, plastic baggies, garbage bags, brushes, knives, and dishes move graciously from rig to rig. Other teams I spoke with use checklists, sticky notes, and timers to keep them organized and on schedule, but Swine by Design seems to take organization to a new level. In the week before a competition the team's lead organizer for that particular contest distributes a large spreadsheet file to the team by e-mail. The heart of the file is a Gantt chart with a bar for each member of the team and a timeline from competition commencement to finish. Each team member is assigned a shift, with tasks listed at various times throughout each shift: "3:00 Start cooker, 5:00 Start shoulders, 8:00 Rotate shoulders, 5:00 Foil shoulders," and so on. From this chart team members know days in advance who they will be working with, what they will be expected to do, and who will be working the other shifts. Another page of the file itemizes the pieces of equipment each team member is expected to bring, and still another shows the schematic floor plan of the site setup, drawn to scale using architectural tools. A master copy of these spreadsheets is kept in a fat Swine by Design binder, which also contains recipes, instructions, photographs, logistical information such as directions, parking permits, hotel reservation numbers, and nearly every other imaginable bit of information.

But despite the team's obsessive organization, things sometimes still go wrong. Brian recounts one incident:

> *Brian:* Whoever put the recipes together misinterpreted one of the— several of the ingredients. I don't know whether it was a little t, big t, tablespoon, teaspoon thing or what. But it was something of that nature. And we didn't do worth a damn. After it was all done we were all packed up and we were ready to leave. We had everything all folded up. And we were so shell shocked that we opened up one of the boxes and started going through stuff trying to, one, decompress and, two, debrief. Try to see if we couldn't sort out what happened. And we got back to the rub that we used. And it was the saltiest crap that ever was. And our stuff is *not* salty. It's got a modicum of salt in it, of course. Like every rub does. But it was just awful. And we went, this has got to be it. Everybody's tasting this the same way. And it was *disgusting*. We were probably lucky to get the poor placement we did. So that was a lesson learned.
> *Deirdre:* So the lesson there is to taste your food.
> *Brian:* You're right. Therein lies the rub, so to speak. You're right.

The lesson to taste did not seem to have been learned during my time with Swine by Design, however. My field log explores numerous discussions that deal with the tension between what the spreadsheet says and the team members' intuition, observation, or sense about the matter. In every instance, these discussions were philosophical and theory based, and never were they settled by tasting the meat in question. Here is an example from the log:

> There is a discussion about when to foil the ribs, done about halfway through the cooking process to keep things moist and not overly smoky. The meat is done earlier than anticipated this year. Zeke says the same is true for him. There is some tension between what Andrew's spreadsheet says to do and what people's instinct says to do. From a culinary perspective, you almost never cook to the appropriate time; you always consider internal temperature and tenderness for long-cooked items. That is to say, cooking something for X hours at X degrees isn't a sure bet of a good end product. Food, as an agricultural product, varies widely, despite agribusiness's efforts to curb this. Each pig is different. Shoulders could have been smaller than normal, the temperature between 230 and 250 could have spent more time on one end of the large range than the other, the mix of wood could have altered the cooking time, as could the amount of time the meat spent in marinade and brine. The "correct" answer, from a culinary perspective, is to take the meat's temperature and pull and taste some for tenderness and use the cooking time only as a guide.

Here's what I recorded on tape as a note to myself:

> The ribs are on the schedule to be foiled at seven a.m. They had thought that they were getting spare ribs instead of loin ribs—which did Andrew plan for? Cam says that loin ribs take less time to cook than spare ribs do. What I think is interesting is that no one is checking the ribs themselves to further the debate; they're just having a sort of philosophical discussion about which finish first and why.

Gadgetry also plays an important role in the mythology of a competition barbecue team. Just as the team emphasizes organization and thought over the sensory considerations of the food itself, they seem to adopt a similar deference to the equipment. A neighboring team had a police light on a timer so that every forty-five minutes, no matter where on the grounds they were, someone was reminded to baste the meat. Swine by Design's new addition in gadgetry was a set of digital thermometers that wirelessly transmit temperature data to a remote location. They are further enhanced by high- and low-range alarms for when the cooker or meat reach a certain temperature. Andrew tells

Frank, "With this baby I can be asleep in the hotel room and be woken up when the meat's done." I find his comment and the introduction of this new tool interesting for two reasons. First, Andrew seldom leaves the site, and the thermometers are simply used to transmit from the cooker to the rig a few feet away. He seems to value the *potential* convenience of the tool. Second, the idea of technology allowing for greater ease and leisure becomes ridiculous when it is being used for what is already strictly a leisure activity. The team spends hours as it is standing, sitting, talking, drinking, and checking thermometers. Were the last part not necessary, they could *really* be doing the rest anywhere. That is to say, if every logical convenience were incorporated, the team would be doing exactly what Andrew jokingly suggested—they would buy barbecue and submit it for judging—saving them time, money, and energy. However, such an approach would undoubtedly be much less fulfilling than the ritualized routine that makes the Swine by Design experience such an important part of each of its members' lives.

Conclusion

Embedding oneself with a competition barbecue team is a constructive way to learn how to cook good barbecue, and also to explore this rich world. The answer to the initial question presented at the beginning of this chapter, "Why not just buy some good barbecue and call it a day?" has less to do with barbecue and more to do with larger themes explored in the chapter and the study as a whole—performing gender, performing barbecue, performing sport—and can't be removed from the larger dynamic of family and profession. Mastering something—anything—in a competitive environment, on a team with a shared goal, can be a rewarding experience, and barbecue is no exception.

In exploring this world, the earnestness by which the team pursues their goal is clear. This is serious, expensive, hot, dirty work, but nonetheless it seems uniquely rewarding. A season after the conclusion of this study, Swine by Design dissolved. Andrew, who towed the rig, moved away, and the team sold the rig to another team. Some of the team members joined former competitors, and others dropped out altogether. Some focused their skills on their home cooking, and one dreams of opening a bar and barbecue restaurant. In many ways, the team members fell victim to their own *why* question—the question of why they would want to spend hundreds of dollars and hours competing in barbecue each season went from being laughed off early in my fieldwork to being ruminated on later as team members developed professionally and experienced increasing family pressures. Swine by Design left the circuit as a good-not-great, fun-yet-serious team.

It is with deep gratitude to the pseudonymous Swine by Design that I write about their world. My preconceptions of spending a portion of my dissertation fieldwork gorging on barbecue, learning the secrets of the masters, and gaining a deep understanding of why and how men cook for leisure in this setting were instantly shattered by the heat, hard work, and seriousness of the topic, the setting, and the team members. I shouldn't have been surprised. When the subject at hand is as complex as good barbecue, a good barbecue team can hardly be less so.

References
Abarca, Meredith. 2007. "Charlas Culinarias: Mexican Women Speak from Their Public Kitchens." *Food and Foodways: History and Culture of Human Nourishment* 15, no. 3–4: 183–212.
Bogdan, R. C., and S. K. Biklen. 1998. *Qualitative Research for Education: An Introduction to Theory and Methods*. Boston: Allyn and Bacon.
Deutsch, Jonathan. 2004. "'Eat Me Up': Spoken Voice and Food Voice in an Urban Firehouse." *Food, Culture and Society: An International Journal of Multidisciplinary Research* 1, no. 1: 27–36.
Elie, Lolis Eric. 1996. *Smokestack Lightning: Adventures in the Heart of Barbecue Country*. Berkeley: Ten Speed Press.
Ely, Margot, Margaret Anzul, Teri Freidman, Diane Garner, and Ann McCormack-Steinmetz. 1991. *Doing Qualitative Research: Circles within Circles*. London: Falmer Press.
Ely, Margot, Ruth Vinz, Maryann Downing, and Margaret Anzul. 1997. *On Writing Qualitative Research: Living by Words*. Philadelphia: Falmer.
Lofland, J., and L. H. Lofland. 1995. *Analyzing Social Settings: A Guide to Qualitative Observation and Analysis*. New York: Wadsworth.

9

Barbecue as Slow Food

Angela Knipple and Paul Knipple

The Slow Food Movement began in Italy in 1986 and reached new heights with the Slow Food Nation event in San Francisco in 2008—where celebrities, chefs, and members from all over the United States and around the world came together to celebrate the principles and progress of the movement. Long before any movement defined it, however, Slow Food was plentiful in the Mid-South in the form of barbecue. But what is Slow Food, and how does barbecue fit the definition? And, most important, if the Slow Food Movement is flourishing, why is barbecue at risk of no longer being Slow Food?

There is a difference between lowercase "slow food" and the "Slow Food" that defines a movement. Lowercase "slow food" brings to mind a pot of greens simmering on the stove for hours. It references those foods that have been part of our heritage in the South for centuries and that take time to prepare. Barbecue, with its hours of low heat and intense smoke, is perhaps the world's finest slow food and can easily be called one of the signature foods of the Mid-South. The term "Slow Food" (uppercase) was coined in reaction to the global encroachment of fast food. The movement was born on Rome's beautiful Spanish Steps, which were built in the early eighteenth century to connect Spain's embassy to the pope in the Piazza di Spagna to the church of Trinita dei Monti on the hill above. The construction of the Spanish Steps was fraught with Italian and papal politics; however, since their completion, they have become a gathering place for the people of Rome and a site for protests of civil issues. They have also been the scene of much art, serving as the home of English poet John Keats at the time of his death in 1821 and appearing in movies like *Roman Holiday* (1953) and *The Talented Mr. Ripley* (1999).

In 1986, however, a considerably less artistic venture came to Rome.

It was in that year that the first McDonald's came to Italy, setting up in no less historic a space than the Piazza di Spagna itself. The contrast between the history and art of the Spanish Steps and the cookie-cutter American fast food of McDonald's inspired feelings of anger and loss that were too great for one man to ignore. Italian journalist Carlo Petrini led a group of friends in protest against the McDonald's. Under Petrini's leadership, this group set up protests on the Spanish Steps to express their concern that the ancient heritage of Italian cuisine was at risk if a McDonald's could be welcomed in the heart of Rome. From this group, Petrini formed Agricola, a wine and food society. Over the next three years, the society grew, becoming more than just a group of concerned Italians. In 1989, the Slow Food Manifesto was signed by delegates from fifteen countries, and an international movement officially began.

For an organization whose manifesto calls for "qualified supporters who can help turn this (slow) motion into an international movement" (Slow Food International 1989), Slow Food International has moved and grown in anything but slow motion. In just twenty years, the organization has reached a membership of over eighty-five thousand people in 132 countries (Slow Food International 2008). To support the mission of the organization, Slow Food International has started a publishing house to produce its own books and magazines. And, in an effort to have greater effect on world culinary culture, the University of Gastronomic Sciences opened in Bra, Italy, in 2004 to teach students from around the world ways to link farms to chefs and lovers of good food.

How, though, could an international organization, particularly such a high-minded one, possibly mesh with good old down-home Southern barbecue? Consider the Slow Food Manifesto, which begins with a condemnation of the frenetic pace of modern life and the dangers that living at such speeds presents. The manifesto goes on to propose a solution:

> A firm defense of quiet material pleasure is the only way to oppose the universal folly of *Fast Life*.
> May suitable doses of guaranteed sensual pleasure and slow, long-lasting enjoyment preserve us from the contagion of the multitude who mistake frenzy for efficiency.
> Our defense should begin at the table with *Slow Food*. Let us

rediscover the flavors and savors of regional cooking and banish the degrading effects of *Fast Food*. (Slow Food International 1989)

If one is to "rediscover the flavors and savors of regional cooking," surely there can be no finer flavors or savors than that of barbecue in the Mid-South. While Petrini likely thinks first of his home in the Piedmont region of northern Italy, his 2005 book *Slow Food Nation: Why Our Food Should Be Good, Clean, and Fair* demonstrates his awareness of the great variety of food traditions around the world. Moreover, in this book, Petrini moves beyond Slow Food as the name of a movement and defines what Slow Food is—good, clean, and fair food. The definition of Slow Food is summarized in the philosophy of Slow Food International: "Slow Food is good, clean, and fair food. We believe that the food we eat should taste good; that it should be produced in a clean way that does not harm the environment, animal welfare or our health; and that food producers should receive fair compensation for their work" (Slow Food International 2009).

Given this definition of Slow Food, is barbecue a Slow Food? As we have said, barbecue is certainly a "slow food." The time it takes to cook a pork shoulder or a whole hog is not insignificant. A good pitmaster will be at the restaurant or in the backyard hours before anyone else is awake. And the time to cook that shoulder or hog is nothing compared to the time taken to perfect the art that is barbecue. That time, too, pales in comparison to the generations through which the knowledge and lore of barbecue have passed. Determined dedication and mastery of the culturally mediated knowledge and skills it takes to produce good barbecue are what make a true pitmaster.

Barbecue as "Good" Food

We all know that barbecue tastes good, but there's more to being a "good" food than just flavor. In the context of Slow Food, to truly be considered a good food, a food must be delicious, but it must also build community, celebrate culture, and promote regional diversity (Petrini 2007, 96–97). So what is it that makes barbecue a good food? First, let us consider flavor. The "recipe" for barbecue is simplicity itself—meat, spices, and smoke. Yet the subtleties of combining these three items and the nuances of flavor and texture they create are remarkably complex.

By cooking slowly, pork stays moist and rich. The fat within the pork melts slowly to create a barrier that keeps the juices of the meat inside ("Barbecue Science" 2008). Over the hours of cooking, the flavors of the spices from rubs and marinades penetrate the meat to enhance the natural sweetness of pork with something new. And while smoke may seem an unusual ingredient, the flavor of the smoke is an indelible part of the barbecue experience. The pride of the pitmaster in producing a perfect pink smoke ring when his pork is sliced speaks volumes of the importance of smoke as more than just a cooking method. The simplicity of ingredients also means that traditional barbecue has few or no additives or preservatives. While some cooks may use factory-produced sauces to marinade or baste barbecue, great pitmasters make their own sauces and spice blends, which in turn means that they do not usually add artificial ingredients to their barbecue.

Barbecue also builds community and celebrates the culture of the Mid-South. People come together to support and enjoy barbecue produced by their favorite pitmasters. In small towns across the Mid-South, communities come together to declare their barbecue the best in the region. While the origins of barbecue in the South remain shrouded in mystery, one of the most likely theories is that the technique of roasting meat slowly over coals came to the South with Spaniards, who learned from the indigenous people of the West Indies (Dove, n.d.). Historically, barbecue has been a prevalent food in the South since well before the Civil War. In those days, the slaughter of a pig brought rural communities together, and the barbecue that followed the slaughter was a celebration (Lovegren 2003, 36–44).

In later years, barbecue has come to celebrate culture in the Mid-South through the handing down of recipes and techniques, often within families. Barbecue is also often shared by a family on special occasions. While the availability of commercially produced barbecue has turned it into a plausible everyday food, it still retains the indefinable sense of being something more than that. This is in part because barbecue is truly an artisanal product and pitmasters are skilled artisans whose contribution of skill is the most substantial component of the finished product. As an artisanal product, no two batches of barbecue are exactly the same (International Trade Centre, n.d.). The knowledge of a great pitmaster is an inexpressible thing, something that he or she has spent years acquiring and perfecting. While anyone can read a barbecue recipe or even watch videos of techniques, nothing replaces the knowledge gained through hands-on practice and the stories passed down through the oral tradition of barbecue from a pitmaster of one generation to the pitmasters of the next.

There is no doubt that barbecue celebrates regional diversity. While every pitmaster has personal methods, the general barbecue styles throughout the Mid-South show great diversity even within the region, from the dry spice rubs on ribs in Memphis to the sweet sauce flavors of sandwiches in Tipton County, Tennessee, to the vinegary whole-hog barbecue of Lexington, Tennessee. The cuts of meat used and the flavor profile of the seasonings create styles that are truly unique, all within a two-hour drive of one another.

Barbecue as "Clean" Food

It is not hard to establish that barbecue is a "good" food, but is barbecue a "clean" food? In the context of Slow Food, a clean food should be nutritious, have a positive impact on the ecosystem, and promote biodiversity (Petrini 2007, 114). Let us first take a look at the nutritional aspects of barbecue. Does it harm our health? As Alexander Woollcott once said, "Everything I like is either illegal, immoral, or fattening." There is no getting around the fact that barbecue can be fattening, but, taken in moderation, its palliative effects on the taste buds and the soul are worth the risk of detrimental effects on our waistlines. While it might be a stretch to say that pork is health food, it is worth noting that while its protein content is comparable to that of beef, its fat is mostly mono-unsaturated, as opposed to the saturated fat of beef. This means the fat in pork is more likely to be burned by the body for fuel instead of stored as fat. Also, while the cholesterol content of pork is higher than that of beef, the LDL cholesterol content (the bad cholesterol) is lower (National Pork Board 2009).

What, then, of the moral component, of the impact of barbecue on the environment and the animals harvested to make our meals? Because the Slow Food Movement seeks to preserve regional food traditions, let us consider the traditional barbecue of earlier days in the Mid-South. While most pigs were not specifically raised for barbecue, they would have been raised in a pasture, or at least a reasonably sized pen. Growth hormones were unheard of, and antibiotics for food animals were rare (Carlson and Fangman 2000). The pigs would have been allowed to forage for their food, resulting in less need for industrially produced feed. Also, the pigs would have been fed table scraps, thus eliminating food waste on the farm. All in all, the pigs would have lived a decent life and would even have had a positive effect on the environment as their manure went back to the earth in quantities that were healthy for the pasture as fertilizer. In modern terms, these farms would have been successful examples of sustainable agriculture. They produced healthy food for local people. They enhanced the environment and did not deplete natural resources. They integrated natural biological cycles and changed methods based on the seasons. They were economically viable and enhanced the lives of the farmers and the community around them (U.S. Department of Agriculture 2009; Fertel, Chapter 6, this volume).

Also, to be considered a clean food according to Slow Food standards, barbecue must support biodiversity. Biodiversity is a relatively new word, having been first used in scientific publications as recently as 1980. In the strictest sense, biodiversity can be defined as the total variety present in nature, at the level of the gene, the population, or the species. The word is now commonly used to refer to conservation values and may be properly understood as simply a new word for ideas that have been written about since the days of Aristotle. In terms of barbecue, what we're actually talking about is agricultural biodiversity, specifically the use of multiple breeds of pigs. In the early days of barbecue, a lack of biodiversity was not a concern. Many different breeds of pigs mingled on farms without the breeding manipulation of the late twentieth century that resulted in more uniform genetics and the three low-fat, high-protein breeds of hogs that are so commercially prevalent today. In the past, a farmer might raise multiple breeds of pigs simply because he liked their temperament, their appearance, or the flavor of the meat they produced (Faith 2007). These pigs were what are now considered heritage breeds, currently maintained only through specialty farmers. While Southern barbecue is not generally known for using any specific breed of pig over another, all pitmasters agree that the quality of the meat is a large factor in the flavor and texture of the final product. Heritage breeds tend to produce more flavorful meat with greater marbling of fat throughout. This marbling is actually a trait that has been deliberately bred out of modern pigs (*Bon Appétit* 2009). In the context of barbecue, more marbling means that there is more internal fat to slowly break down and produce juicier, more flavorful barbecue.

In addition to the quality of life of these animals, the quality of their deaths should also be considered. Pigs on traditional farms were not loaded into multitier trucks to be shipped hours before being unloaded at a loud and unfamiliar slaughterhouse. Instead, they were typically slaughtered on an as-needed basis at the same farm where they had spent their lives. While the topic of slaughter is never pleasant, it is easy to see that an on-farm slaughtering would be less stressful for the animal than the modern slaughterhouse method.

Beyond the methods of raising the pigs, cooking the meat has the potential to harm the environment as well. Here, it is harder to say that the impact has been negligible. It is obvious that barbecue smoke enters the atmosphere. Because barbecue smoke is not likely to be a significant threat, we choose to focus on the benefits—deliciously scented, pure wood smoke curling away from a pit is far more attractive than a monolithic smokestack belching a black cloud. Does the black carbon produced by barbecue pits contribute to global warming? Yes, but only as a miniscule percentage. Because barbecue is produced in small, localized areas like the Mid-South, the black carbon produced is an extremely small portion of the overall black carbon production of the United States. The black carbon produced by cooking in general in the United States is insignificant when compared to that produced by the everyday cooking fires in both rural Asia and other developing countries (Rosenthal 2009). Even the impact of those cooking fires pales in comparison to the amount of black carbon produced by crop burning and deforestation, which are estimated to be responsible for 42 percent of the total black carbon produced in the world (House Committee 2007). Put in this context, it is perhaps more accurate to say that the smoke from barbecue pits contributes primarily to happiness and hunger pangs.

The fuel for cooking barbecue is the final concern. As with smoke, the way in which wood for fuel is gathered has the potential to harm the environment. In earlier days, burning wood in a barbecue pit was just another use for the firewood used to heat homes and cookstoves every day. Since those uses for firewood have dwindled in modern times, it is important now to consider the source of the wood used for barbecue pits. Sustainable and responsible forestry techniques not only provide wood for commercial use but also encourage the health of forests (Responsible Forestry, n.d.). Barbecue as an industry has the opportunity to participate in sustainability by sourcing locally and sustainably produced wood. For some pitmasters, this means working with sawmills to take sawdust and leftover wood to use in the pits. For others, it means working with local factories to take seconds of products like ax or shovel handles. Finally, traditional use of locally grown hogs and locally harvested firewood would have meant minimal dependence on fossil fuels for transport. Based on the lives the animals led and the sustainability of fuel used for cooking barbecue, it is safe to say that traditional barbecue was "clean." Of course, this is not necessarily the case with barbecue in the modern age, but some of the older restaurants in the Mid-South still source some of their materials locally today.

Barbecue as "Fair" Food

Was and is traditional barbecue "fair"? According to Slow Food International, in order to be considered fair a food's producers must receive fair compensation for their work and the food must be accessible to the community (Petrini 2007, 135–36). Have barbecue producers traditionally received fair compensation for their work? More than just fair, barbecue has often been a boon to its producers. An individual with the knowledge and skills to make delicious barbecue can make a good living. Further, barbecue has traditionally been an economic equalizer. No formal education is required to become a pitmaster. While the chemical and physical processes that make barbecue delicious are interesting to learn, a pitmaster does not have to formally understand them in order to produce great meat. The techniques of barbecue are not taught in culinary schools. Instead, a family member or friend may teach the secret art of barbecue, or those secrets may be discovered with practice and patience.

Once the preparation of barbecue has been perfected, all that remains is to figure out how to sell it. To a great extent, barbecue within a community sells itself. The scents of wood smoke and cooking pork are unmistakable, and after hours of smelling them, locals are often unable to resist. In earlier days, the skills needed to run a small business selling such a high-demand product were minimal—basic math and perhaps a way with people. For someone trying to get ahead selling barbecue, the initial investment was minimal as well. The only infrastructure required was a hole in the backyard and a hand-lettered sign in the front yard. With the beginnings of financial success, a pit might be built from cinder blocks, stones, or a barrel drum. Some of the best barbecue stories start with simply a pitmaster and a single pit—the barbecue then gathered enough fans that the venture grew, almost organically, into a business. To this day, some of the finest barbecue is still sold on weekends under tents along country roads or from portable pits set up along busy streets in large cities. The barbecue is there until it sells out, and then it's gone until it reappears another weekend. Eventually, these itinerant pitmasters may set up a more permanent location. Great barbecue places are often found in converted gas stations or seedy strip malls. Some stay in their original location, regardless of their success, but others move to newer locations, specially built for barbecue.

Another aspect of being a fair food is accessibility. Barbecue has always been relatively accessible economically, but the role of race in Southern society also must be considered. Barbecue and access to barbecue provide an interesting lens with which to view race relations in the South. In the antebellum South, slaves would have eaten barbecue, and they would have cooked it for their owners on plantations. There would have been no sense of community, though, no shared table. One less-than-scholarly work does provide a glimpse into special occasions in the plantation life of the Old South. In *Gone with the Wind*, Margaret Mitchell writes about a barbecue at the Wilkes plantation: "Over behind the barns there was always another barbecue pit, where the house servants and the coachmen and maids of the guests had their own feast of hoecakes and yams and chitterlings, that dish of hog entrails so dear to negro hearts, and, in season, watermelons enough to satiate" (Mitchell 1936, 107). This image of all people, both black and white, being contented in their separate positions in the antebellum South has been widely refuted, but it still has a powerful hold on the imagination. Despite the abolition of slavery, it took another hundred years before African Americans in most of the South were able to sit down with their white neighbors to enjoy barbecue.

During the civil rights era, the most visible food—at both ends of the desegregation spectrum—was fried chicken. In Atlanta, determined segregationist, restaurant owner, and governor of the state of Georgia Lester Maddox used newspaper ads featuring talking chicken cartoons to advertise his restaurant and to comment on political matters. Ultimately, Maddox sold his restaurant, famous for its skillet-fried chicken, rather than desegregate (*New Georgia Encyclopedia* 2004). In Montgomery, Alabama, Georgia Gilmore was fired from her job as a cafeteria worker for her organizing activities during the Montgomery bus boycott. She then turned her home into a secret restaurant where leaders of the civil rights movement met to plan and to enjoy her fried chicken (Nelson, Silva, and York 2005). Barbecue also played a part in the civil rights movement. Prior to the Civil Rights Act of 1964, restaurants were not required to desegregate. When Memphis pitmaster James Willis told his story to Brian Fisher of the Southern Foodways Alliance, he remembered how his family was not welcome to come into the restaurant where he prepared barbecue. In fact, because he is African American, he was not welcome to go into the dining room himself (Fisher 2002). Barbecue has even made it to the Supreme Court on several occasions. For example, Ollie McClung of Birmingham, Alabama, took his opposition to desegregating his restaurant into legal channels, fearing the impact of integration on his profits. When the Supreme Court ruled against him, he abided by the decision and was surprised to see that his profits were secure, and that the integration process was peaceful and smooth (*Time* 1964).

Not all barbecue was segregated before the Civil Rights Act. As Jason Sheehan (2006) of the *Denver Post* poetically puts it, "I believe that barbecue drives culture, not the other way around. Some of the first blows struck for equality and civil rights in the Deep South were made not in the courtrooms or schools or on buses, but in the barbecue shacks. There were dining rooms, backyards and roadhouse juke joints in the South that were integrated long before any other public places." In the Mid-South, barbecue was a unifying force in at least one town in the Mississippi Delta. Abe's Barbecue in Clarksdale, Mississippi, was founded by Lebanese immigrant Abraham Davis in 1924. His son Pat feels that his father's experiences as an immigrant in a small town in Mississippi gave him a unique perspective on the struggles of African Americans to gain civil rights. Abe refused to participate in segregation forty years before the Civil Rights Act made desegregation into law. Abe's was a well-known stop for African American activists during the harshest days of the civil rights movement, with both Abe and Pat making sure that all customers felt welcome and could enjoy great barbecue no matter the color of their skin (Drash 2009).

Today, although racial tensions have not been entirely erased, a good barbecue place is one of the finest examples of common ground in existence. People of every description gather to enjoy spicy ribs and juicy sandwiches. On a typical day, office workers in business suits, laborers in work boots, and doctors in scrubs can all fill a restaurant together. That barbecue was not always accessible to everyone is more an indictment of Southern society than of barbecue. As equality has permeated to some extent into contemporary Southern society, equal access to barbecue has as well. Barbecue is as "fair" as society allows it to be, and as society itself becomes more fair, so does barbecue.

Based on the three Slow Food criteria of "good, clean, and fair," barbecue, as it has been traditionally prepared, has for the most part been a Slow Food. Not just good, barbecue was, and is, darned good. Gathered firewood would have done minimal harm to the environment through time. Pasture-raised hogs have traditionally lived a good and sanitary life. Pitmasters have been more than fairly paid—they have often been afforded the opportunity to become entrepreneurs and earn a living wage while achieving notoriety and status in their local communities.

Barbecue as an Endangered Slow Food

Why, then, is barbecue's status as a Slow Food threatened? To a certain extent, barbecue is a victim of its own success. Barbecue is good food, so good that demand for it has grown far beyond the weekend picnic or the small roadside stand. To meet these demands, barbecue restaurants have turned to technology.

Technology runs on the idea that faster is better, and the industrial food system has taken that tenet to heart. Barbecue goes against that logic, and yet, barbecue has been affected by technology. Customers want barbecue to be ready when they order it, so pitmasters have had to find ways to hold their barbecue at a ready-to-eat temperature for hours. Customers also expect barbecue from a restaurant to taste the same every time. This requirement for consistency is nothing new in the restaurant business, but it does make it harder for pitmasters to work in the traditional way since smoke can taste noticeably different according to which trees are used, even among trees of the same species.

Technology has also tackled another problem of barbecue pits—the danger of fire. By getting rid of the open pit and live coals, a barbecue restaurant is much less likely to be damaged by fire. Many restaurateurs see an additional cost benefit. The artisan's skill in cooking meat is important, of course, but the word "pitmaster" derives from the ability to control the fires of the pit. In the early days of barbecue, one of the pitmaster's primary responsibilities was the overnight tending of the fire. Thanks to temperature-controlled gas or electric cookers, pitmasters are no longer required to be at the restaurant all night and, therefore, don't have to be paid for that time. This economic benefit comes at a high cost. Pitmasters are vanishing as they are no longer required to practice the art of managing fire. The generation of cooks in more modern barbecue restaurants has no need to learn the skills that the pitmasters of old brought to barbecue preparation. As skilled pitmasters retire, in many cases, they are replaced by unskilled laborers instead of artisans who learned from the knowledge of those who came before them.

Advancements in transportation and preservation mean that a successful barbecue restaurant has the ability to feed people all over the world. Obtaining barbecue can be as easy as a trip to the store or a visit from a courier. Once a restaurant is producing barbecue in quantities to be sold in supermarket freezer cases, regional diversity is at risk. Taking Mid-South barbecue to this extreme is detrimental to the celebration of unique regional varieties of barbecue. This is true not only in the Mid-South, where dominant providers threaten smaller businesses, but in other regions as well, where "carpetbagging" barbecue may unduly influence other styles. Today there is a great variety of barbecue and demand for that variety; nonetheless, commercialization of barbecue increases the potential for homogenization.

The tremendous demand for pork for barbecue means that barbecue as a Slow Food is endangered by the same forces that inspired Carlo Petrini to begin the Slow Food Movement in the first place. The industrialization of the food system since World War II has severely affected not only barbecue but virtually every aspect of our culinary traditions. Freshness has been sacrificed for convenience. Quality has been sacrificed for cost. It is practically impossible to find "good, clean, and fair" food as a product of the industrial food system. To give the industrial food system some credit, this situation was not the stated goal of its development. Instead, food system industrialization was intended to cement the ability of producers to deliver a safe and reliable food source. Industrial agriculture strives to make land as productive as possible (Philpott 2007). Economies of scale, however, have introduced new health, safety, and environmental concerns that were never part of our food system prior to industrialization.

Today, 80 percent of all pork produced in the United States is raised in the industrial food system in confined animal feed operations (CAFOs) (DeVore 2003). In December 2006, Jeff Tietz published a disturbing article in *Rolling Stone* magazine detailing the lives of both pigs and workers at CAFOs belonging to the world's largest pork producer. The pigs at these CAFOs live in conditions that can only be called horrible. They are crowded into pens far too small to allow them to move freely. They never see sunlight or nestle into hay. If it were not for the exhaust fans running constantly in the buildings, they would die from breathing the toxic fumes that rise from the pools of waste beneath the slatted floors they stand on. The same fumes make working with the hogs in these confined conditions very dangerous. Waste flows out into open lagoons where it collects, emitting toxic gases into the surrounding air. Tietz's article recounts stories of workers being overcome by those gases, falling into the lagoons, and drowning.

Open lagoons are not only a danger to the employees of the CAFOs. Such operations can flood in heavy rains and pollute local streams and rivers. Pig manure can be a good fertilizer for pastures, but only if the manure is in the right quantities and of the right quality. One detriment to the quality of this manure is the quality of the feed being given to the pigs in CAFOs. This feed is high in nitrogen and phosphorus, which often makes hog manure unsuitable to use as a fertilizer even without the other chemicals that are present. Bacteria level is another concern. While all manure contains some level of bacteria, CAFO pigs are sometimes fed the remains of other pigs, increasing the bacteria in their manure significantly. This manure, then, cannot even be used to fertilize hay which will be fed to other animals (Tietz 2006). An additional concern is that pigs in CAFOs are more susceptible to disease because the stress of crowded conditions lowers their immune systems. That same crowding means that disease can spread through a CAFO very quickly. Therefore, preventative antibiotics are introduced to these pigs in their feed, vaccines are systemic, and insecticides are a necessity. All these medicines and chemicals eventually make their way into the waste in the lagoons.

CAFOs are not examples of sustainable farming. The goal of CAFO farming is to produce as much pork as quickly and cheaply as possible. The concern of CAFOs is not for the animals but for profit margins. CAFOs are also less concerned about the quality of the meat that they produce. The pigs raised in CAFOs are not the breeds of pigs that were raised on the small farms of the past. Instead, CAFO pigs have been specially bred to produce larger quantities of meat with less fat around the meat and less marbling throughout it. While this allows the pork producers to claim health benefits for pork, it does not enhance the flavor. Also, the quality of meat is adversely affected by the stress levels of the animal. Stress causes increased production of lactic acid while the animal is alive. When the animal dies, this excess lactic acid causes a fast drop in the pH of the meat, which in turn causes the meat to be what the industry calls PSE—"pale, soft, and exudative" (Purdue University Animal Sciences, n.d.). In the context of barbecue, PSE meat doesn't hold its texture as well. It tends to dry out faster on thinner cuts of meat like ribs and to become mushy on thicker cuts like shoulders.

Can a pitmaster produce "clean" barbecue using meat from pigs raised in CAFOs? The answer is a definitive "no." And yet, in most areas, pitmasters have little other meat, if any, to choose from. If it is available, pork from sustainably raised heritage-breed pigs is priced at a premium. It is often too expensive for pitmasters to use given the slim profit margins of barbecue.

Finally, consider fairness. Today, barbecue is readily available to everyone. Business opportunities, however, are more limited. The food safety regulations that began to be drafted in the late 1800s have made it more difficult for talented pitmasters to become business owners. While these regulations are in the interest of the health and safety of diners, they are also expensive and difficult for many potential business owners to navigate. As fewer pitmasters become small business owners, the traditional skills of the artisan are not used. Again, with the pitmaster removed from the business, these skills are in danger of being lost (Fisher 2002).

Saving Slow Barbecue

How can we preserve barbecue as a Slow Food? How do we protect one of our greatest cultural treasures in the Mid-South? One piece of wisdom says, "You can't have your cake and eat it too." A better piece of wisdom comes from the Slow Food Ark of Taste: "Eat it to save it" (Slow Food USA 2008). The Ark of Taste program was started in 1996 to promote biodiversity. The program has identified a list of animals, fruits, and vegetables that are at risk of extinction if farmers stop growing them. The best way to save these species is to increase consumer demand for them so that farmers will have a reason to continue growing them—eat it to save it.

This means a number of things when applied to barbecue. First, don't stop eating it because of CAFO pork. Pitmasters are currently forced by the market to do what is best from an economic perspective. To protect the skills of artisans, support barbecue places that have true pitmasters—men and women who still make barbecue in the slow traditional style. If nearby barbecue joints use heritage pork, support them. Until heritage barbecue is available at a restaurant near you, support heritage pork in your own home. Increased demand for clean pork can help turn the CAFO tide. It can also bring down costs, meaning that local pitmasters can better afford to choose clean pork. Supporting heritage pork means buying it and eating it. What better way to eat it than to make barbecue with it? Granted, as we have noted above, barbecue takes skill, but as we have also said, those skills can be acquired. Learning barbecue traditions and passing them on is another way to preserve them. And along with the satisfaction of making your own barbecue comes the even greater satisfaction of eating it.

While restaurants have increasingly trended toward technological solutions, for one weekend out of the year, a cloud of fragrant smoke billows once more over the bluffs of the Mississippi River in Memphis when the very hands-on pitmasters at the Memphis in May World Championship Barbecue Cooking Contest come to town. These pitmasters are only interested in preparing the best barbecue possible. They carefully select the best pork available. They would not dream of using anything except wood smoke to prepare their barbecue or of attempting to speed up the smoking process. And they use skills that they have learned and treasure, skills that they guard, skills that qualify them as artisans. The barbecue that wins is the best in the world—and it is, most assuredly, Slow Food.

References

"Barbecue Science." 2008. *www.bbqsuccess.com/barbecue-science/* (accessed February 10, 2008).

Bon Appétit. 2009. "Tips, Tools, and Techniques." May. *www.bonappetit.com/tipstools/ingredients/2009/05/heritage_pork*.

Carlson, Marcia S., and Thomas J. Fangman. 2000. "Swine Antibiotics and Feed Additives: Food Safety Considerations." University of Missouri Extension. January. *extension.missouri.edu/*.

DeVore, Brian. 2003. "Better Bacon: Sustainable Pork Producers Challenge the Meat Factories." *Sierra*, March–April.

Dove, Laura. n.d. "The History of Barbecue in the South." *BBQ: A Southern Cultural Icon*. *xroads.virginia.edu/~CLASS/MA95/dove/history.htm* (accessed January 19, 2010).

Drash, Wayne. 2009. "Barbecue, Bible and Abe Chase Racism from Mississippi Rib Joint." *CNN.com*, September 4.

Faith, Daniel P. 2007. "Biodiversity." *Stanford Encyclopedia of Philosophy*, December 4. *plato.stanford.edu/entries/biodiversity/*.

Fisher, Brian. 2002. "Interview with James Willis." BBQ Oral History Project and the Southern Foodways Alliance website, *www.southernfoodways.com* (accessed September 27, 2009).

House Committee on Oversight and Government Reform. 2007. *Testimony for the Hearing on Black Carbon and Climate Change*. October 18.

International Trade Centre. n.d. "Creative Industries: Definitions." *www.intracen.org/creativeindustries/Definitions.pdf* (accessed February 1, 2010).
Lovegren, Sylvia. 2003. "Barbecue." *American Heritage*, June.
Mitchell, Margaret. 1936. *Gone with the Wind*. New York: Scribner.
National Pork Board. 2009. "How Pork Compares to Other Meats." *www.porkandhealth.org/* (accessed February 5, 2009).
Nelson, Davia, Nikki Silva, and Jamie York. 2005. "The Club from Nowhere: Cooking for Civil Rights." *Morning Edition*, March 4. *www.npr.org/*.
New Georgia Encyclopedia. 2004. "Lester Maddox (1915–2003)." April 20. *www.georgiaencyclopedia.org*.
Petrini, Carlo. 2007. *Slow Food Nation: Why Our Food Should Be Good, Clean, and Fair*. Translated by Clara Furlan and Jonathan Hunt. New York: Rizzoli Ex Libris.
Philpott, Tom. 2007. "A Journey into the Heart of Industrial Agriculture." *Grist*, October 9. *www.grist.org/article/ednote*.
Purdue University Animal Sciences. n.d. "Effect of Stress on Meat Quality." *ag.ansc.purdue.edu/meat_quality/mqf_stress.html* (accessed February 10, 2010).
Responsible Forestry. n.d. "What Is Sustainable Forestry?" *responsibleforestry.com/what-is-sustainable-forestry/* (accessed February 10, 2010).
Rosenthal, Elisabeth. 2009. "Third-World Stove Soot Is Target in Climate Fight." *New York Times*, April 15.
Sheehan, Jason. 2006. "There Is No Such Thing as Too Much Barbecue." *This I Believe*, May 29. *www.npr.org/*.
Slow Food International. 1989. "The Slow Food Manifesto." *www.slowfood.com/* (accessed January 15, 2009).
———. 2008. "Slow Food Companion." *www.slowfood.com/* (accessed January 15, 2009).
———. 2009. "Our Philosophy." *www.slowfood.com/* (accessed February 25, 2009).
Slow Food USA. 2008. "Poppy Tooker on the Eat It to Save It Philosophy." October 10. *www.slowfoodusa.org/*.
Tietz, Jeff. 2006. "Boss Hog." *Rolling Stone*, December 14. *www.rollingstone.com/*.
Time. 1964. "The Supreme Court." December 25. *www.time.com/*.
U.S. Department of Agriculture. 2009. "Legal Definition of Sustainable Agriculture." March 18. *www.csrees.usda.gov/nea/ag_systems/in_focus/sustain_ag_if_legal.html*.

10

Southern Barbecue Sauce and Heirloom Tomatoes

JAMES R. VETETO

The Origins of Southern Barbecue Sauce

Barbecue sauce is a noteworthy and controversial topic to Southern minds. As he has with so many other topics related to Southern barbecue, John Shelton Reed (with help from his wife, Dale Volberg Reed) has made a thorough investigation into the historical origins of barbecue sauce across the region. Reed and Reed summarize the basics of barbecue sauce fixings in their 2008 book *Holy Smoke*:

> People have been using marinades to tenderize roasted meat, mops and finishing sauces to moisten it, and all three to enhance its flavor since time immemorial. These concoctions have almost always begun with a mildly acidic base of wine, vinegar, or lemon or other fruit juice, and then added something salty—salt, soy sauce, fermented fish sauce (the Romans' favorite)—and something spicy like red or black pepper, ginger, cinnamon, or cloves. Optional ingredients have included sweeteners, garlic or something in the onion line, and maybe some butter, lard, or oil to replace the fat lost in cooking and to help the sauce adhere. The tomato was a relatively late addition, and of course it's still controversial in North Carolina, but put *all* this stuff in, and you've got something like the commercial sauces that line supermarket shelves today. (24)

Modern barbecue sauces have precedents that stretch back into antiquity. A medieval table sauce for meat from around 1430 contained vinegar, the sour juice of unripe grapes, and spices including powdered black pepper, ginger, and cinnamon. By the 1700s sauce makers started calling their tomato-free concoctions "ketchup," and often used a variety of ingredients including vinegar, white wine, lemon peel, pepper, cloves, ginger, mace, nutmeg, anchovies, and shallots. English cookbooks from the 1780s and 1790s include variations on how to barbecue pork by roasting it beside a fire and collecting the drippings, basting the pork with red wine all the while. The wine and juices from the dripping pan were taken for sauce stock, and combined with lemon, sweet herbs, anchovies, butter, and other ingredients. The resulting sauce was boiled, strained, and served hot. In eighteenth-century colonial America, Virginians and Carolinians were cooking whole hogs and basting them with saltwater and butter, and this is likely the type of simple meat moisturizer that George Washington was fond of using on his barbecue. An 1824 cookbook reported that barbecue pork was being served with something more akin to gravy than the barbecue sauces we know today. Ingredients included water, red wine, garlic, salt, pepper, mushroom ketchup, and butter, all of which were thickened with flour (Reed and Reed 2008).

True vinegar and pepper sauces may have originated in the West Indies, where chili peppers were encountered by early European colonists. In 1698 it was reported that a feast was put on by natives who were cooking pigs that had been brought over from Europe and had naturalized. A mop of lemon juice, salt, and chili peppers was used, and the pork was served with a table sauce consisting of the same ingredients available in hot or mild strengths. The taste for peppers may have been brought to Southeastern American shores by Creoles or slaves from the West Indies islands and combined with vinegar as a replacement for hard-to-find lemon juice. By 1767 Thomas Jefferson was growing cayenne peppers at Monticello, and by 1812 he was also growing "Bull Nose" and "Major" pepper varieties. He also made vinegar from grapes by the forty-gallon batch, and mentioned steeping peppers in vinegar for use as a meat seasoning in his journals. Jefferson's concoctions may have been among the early predecessors of the style of barbecue sauce that is still found in eastern North Carolina today. The basic mix of peppers, lemon juice or vinegar, and butter or lard caught on quickly in early America and by 1830 was widespread among the Southern states (Reed and Reed 2008; Moss, Chapter 2, this volume). Of course, even then, special ingredients such as apple cider vinegar, whiskey, and "secret herbs" were being added to barbecue sauces and "dips," beginning a long tradition of trade secrets protected by Southern barbecue saucerers that continues unabated today.

Current Sauce Geographies

By the early twentieth century, the relative uniformity of Southern barbecue sauces began to change as the restaurant business gained momentum and regional styles of preparing and serving barbecue took on a more particular and unique character (Moss, Chapter 2, this volume; Egerton 1987). Saucerers at barbecue restaurants began perfecting their own secret concoctions. This tradition had its origins in the colonial period but reached new heights as commercially oriented barbecue joints began to pop up across the land. Recipes were handed down from master to apprentice and either memorized by a select few or locked down in secret and safe places. Hand-me-down stories and mythologies began to swirl around the sauces, such as the one about the traveler in Hot Springs, Arkansas, who paid his monthlong hotel bill with a barbecue sauce recipe that catalyzed the McClard's Bar-B-Q dynasty (McClard's 2009), or the secret sauce used at the St. Patrick's Irish Picnic in McEwen, Tennessee, rumored variously to have originated in Ireland or developed locally in the 1920s (Bradley-Shurtz, Chapter 5, this volume).

Moving from east to west across the American South puts you in touch with a kaleidoscope of barbecue sauce geographies, distinct but not entirely unique, overlapping with each other like the waves of human migration and ethnicity that have helped shape their development. On the east coast of North Carolina, where minimalism is the motto and goal, minced whole-hog barbecue is served with a vinegar-based sauce that is only lightly seasoned with pepper flakes and a few other secret ingredients, some as risqué as scotch or moonshine. The idea is to let the meat do the talking and to use the sauce sparingly as an understated complement. This Coastal Plain style of barbecue is available to lesser degrees in South Carolina and Georgia, where it is served, as in North Carolina, with a mixed-meat-and-vegetable concoction called Brunswick stew. Eastern-style North Carolina barbecue is apparently a descendant of the original Southern barbecue that was developed in the Tidewater area of Virginia, but is for all intents and purposes extinct there today (Moss, Chapter 2, this volume). If you travel westward into the Carolina Piedmont things start to get a little more interesting, at least to my mind. Tomato is added to the vinegar in small amounts, and locals call the sauce "dip," an apparent carryover from a more ancient way of labeling sauces, "dipney" (Reed and Reed 2008). Other "secret ingredients" start popping up in increasing numbers, making the sauce options more varied. Down about Charlotte and moving into north and central South Carolina, and sporadically in Georgia, a mustard-based barbecue sauce becomes the regional specialty. Henry's Smokehouse in Greenville, South Carolina, features a classic, dark yellow, tangy mustard-based sauce with red and black flecks of pepper mixed in, available in hot or mild degrees of spiciness. Outside of the mustard-based region, barbecue sauces in South Carolina and Georgia are a mishmash of styles—generally tending toward very vinegary tomato-based sauces, with a more frequent use of tomato and sugar than in the Carolina Piedmont.

Getting into the Appalachian Mountains of western North Carolina and East Tennessee, one notices perhaps the first clear break from the Eastern and Piedmont traditions altogether. Although you certainly do find sauces in the mountains akin to the Piedmont dip, it is also the first area where you consistently encounter a thick tomato-and-molasses-based barbecue sauce in the geography of traditional Southern barbecue. (Of course these days, with the trend toward chain restaurants and barbecue mobility, you are likely to encounter any style of barbecue in any region more frequently.) Perhaps the most famous and quintessential example of this style can be found at Ridgewood Barbecue in Bluff City, Tennessee, where a barbecue platter consists of thinly sliced pieces of smoked ham drizzled in a dark red, sticky-sweet sauce with home-cut french fries piled in a poetic mess on top (Veteto and Maclin 2009).

In areas of Alabama it has been firmly documented that there are barbecue sauces that are mayonnaise based, but I have never stumbled across any establishments that served it. The closest I came was at Shemwell's Barbecue in Cairo, in far southern Illinois on the banks of the Mississippi River, where the barbecue was served grilled between two pieces of butter-slathered bread like a grilled cheese sandwich and the sliced pork was covered in a spicy white sauce. The sauce appeared to be a mayonnaise-based concoction with tomato and mustard mixed in minimally (the waitress wouldn't even give me a clue as to the ingredients), which to my surprise and delight was tasty. Shemwell's sauce seemed akin to what other writers have penned about Alabama mayonnaise-based sauces.

Heading west of Nashville, Tennessee, will land you in West Tennessee, where the barbecue is cooked whole-hog, slaw is served on the sandwiches, and the density of barbecue joints greatly increases. For a rural area there is a ridiculously high number of barbecue joints. In the urban heart of the Barbecue Belt, Memphis, the smoked pork is shoulder instead of whole-hog and is available at a hundred or so restaurants around the city. Memphis is also host to the most famous barbecue competition in the world, Memphis in May, held annually on the banks of the Mississippi River just off Beale Street (Veteto and Maclin 2009). By this point in our hypothetical barbecue sauce journey, we have reached the Mid-South. Beyond it in Texas and Kansas City, one finds barbecue sauces that increase decisively in their levels of sweetness and beef, rather than pork, as the dominant meat of choice. But those areas are topics for another time and another author. My particular subject matter is Mid-South barbecue, and my muse is her sauces. Let's take a closer look.

Mid-South Barbecue Sauce

As we argued in the introduction to this volume, the quintessential Mid-South barbecue sauce is a seamless blending of four key ingredients that I like to call the "Big Four": tomato, vinegar, spicy pepper, and sweetener of choice. In order to test my theory of Mid-South barbecue sauciness, I interviewed Phillip McClard, the third-generation sauce maker at McClard's Bar-B-Q in Hot Springs, Arkansas—home to perhaps the most famous barbecue sauce in all of the Mid-South. When I told him my theory of the perfect Mid-South barbecue sauce (which I freely admit is heavily influenced by having grown up eating at McClard's since about age three), Phillip confirmed my general suspicions, without giving up the particulars of his own famous secret family recipe:

> *Phillip:* I'm not too crazy about the real vinegar stuff either. I mean we do put vinegar in ours, we do, but . . . every bit of that [tomato, vinegar, pepper, sugar] goes into ours. Plus some more stuff. But yeah, every bit that what you said goes in there. And don't forget water *[laughs]*, put a lot of water.
> *Me:* You guys are kind of somewhat in between those flavors with a little more heat than some.
> *Phillip:* Yeah. And sometimes I'll stub my toe and put a little too

much of something in a bucket, you know, that happens when you're in here at three thirty or four o' clock in the morning and your mind ain't working real good like it should, you might forget or you might put a little bit too much of something and it might be a little hotter sometimes than other times. That's just like if you made anything at home, you know if you made something at home sometimes it'll vary, it's all gonna vary sometimes.

Southern food writer John Egerton has found McClard's sauce to be "a nicely balanced blend of thickness, hotness, sweetness, and tartness" (1987, 153). In other words, the perfect Mid-South barbecue sauce.

Although McClard's sauce is representative of an ideal blending of the four key ingredients to Mid-South sauces, there is significant variation throughout the region. Each variation typically highlights one of the other three ingredients (excepting tomato, which is nearly ubiquitous): sweetener, spice (various peppers), or vinegar. At Stubby's Bar-B-Que and Purity Bar-B-Q in Hot Springs, you get a sweeter tomato-based sauce, and at Mickey's Bar-B-Q you get a fairly balanced Mid-South sauce that is a darker brick red than McClard's bright pink. Over in Conway, Arkansas, at Hog Pen BBQ they serve a red sauce containing molasses that is on the sweet side but not overbearingly so. It tends more toward a sauce style typical of Kansas City or Texas. Down in the Timberlands of South Arkansas, sauces are on the sweeter side and brick red to orange in color, indicative of the region's closer proximity to the Texas border (Nolan, Chapter 4, this volume). Interstate Bar-B-Q in Memphis is known for its secret sauce that is close to the consistency of tomato paste with some heat to it, and Charlie Vergos's Rendezvous, although more famous for its dry-rub ribs, has a darkish red sauce for its pulled-pork sandwiches that fits pretty squarely in the middle of the Big Four with a hint of mustard.

Though my sauce theory for the Mid-South in my experience is generally true, it must also be said that there are some outliers. Scott's-Parker's Barbecue in Lexington, Tennessee, has a vinegary sauce that is light on tomato with a slight bit of heat in the aftertaste. Such sauces are fairly common in rural West Tennessee. They are more akin to the vinegar-based dips that you encounter in Lexington, North Carolina, 545 miles to the east, than they are to the tomato-based sauces of Memphis, 111 miles to the west, and the rest of the Mid-South. At Sim's Bar-B-Que in Little Rock, Arkansas, they prepare their chopped-

McClard's sauce painting. Photo by James Veteto.

pork sandwich on two slices of white bread doused with a tangy, bright yellow mustard-based sauce, the only one of its kind that I know of other than Old Hickory's mustard-based sauce down in South Arkansas (Nolan, Chapter 4, this volume). Some barbecue restaurants in the Mid-South, however, flirt dangerously with mustard as a key ingredient without going all the way. Craig's Barbecue in De Valls Bluff, Arkansas, en route between Little Rock and Memphis, features a mixed tomato-and-mustard-based sauce, available in hot, medium, or mild. Craig's secret blend also contains a variety of other unique ingredients, including pork fat drippings and green peppers.

As seen in the examples above, Mid-South barbecue sauces can vary greatly in flavor, color, texture, and ingredients. Despite all of this variation and the occasional outlier, I'll stake my reputation on a theory that places the bulk of the region's sauces somewhere in between the Big Four, with tendencies toward one or the other. My own family's secret sauce fits squarely within that definition, attempting to achieve the perfect balance midway between all four elements. Perhaps this unique character of our barbecue sauces is another reason why they call this region the Mid-South.

I would like to close this section with a poem that I wrote about my family's barbecue sauce, and I suggest that barbecue sauces in general are a worthy subject of the poetic senses. Though I have seen some fine poetry celebrating the virtues of Southern barbecue in general (e.g., York 2004; Applewhite 2004; Marion 2004), I am not aware of any that focus on sauce in particular. Poetry, of course, can touch us in ways that prose and other rational pursuits cannot and can convey a deep sense of meaning and satisfaction to those who enjoy it. The same, I would argue, can be said of a properly prepared Mid-South barbecue sauce.

Colonel Neff's Sauce

It all started
when my grandparents were buzzed on booze
one evening at cocktail hour
over fifty years ago.

"We can make a better sauce than you can buy at the store."

I think it was that old-timey, self-sufficing attitude
of the World War II generation
that done it.

Now four generations later
my little son and I choke together
as the air is hot with skillet roasted peppers
and my wife slowly mixes it up in the kitchen.

I think back to fishin'
blackberry pies, homegrown tomatoes
and evening boat rides.

Big huge family meals
fried apples
potato salad
rice pilaf
coleslaw
butter-slabbed corn on the cob
and banana split ice cream sundaes.

Smell of gardenias in the air
hot, muggy summer evenings
chirp of crickets in the grass
chasing lightning bugs through the dusk

and oh that lip-smackin' sauce!

The perfect blend
of tomato, vinegar, sweet, and spice
nothing like it.

People been bugging me for years for the recipe,
offering me all manner of family secrets in exchange.

But I just can't do it
—I'm not usually like this—
but this is our thing,
a family thing.

And as I choke on air
and smell the tang
and my taste buds wake in joyful anticipation
this bright, Southern mountain morning

I think of my grandparents
somewhere better
sitting at a better table, at cocktail hour
sipping martinis and bourbon
then fixing dinner

smokin' them ribs over hot coals
with that super tangy barbecue sauce that's still in demand

      down here

four generations later.

What Is Old Is New Again: Southern Heirloom Tomatoes

While in the main I agree with Reed and Reed's (2008) contention that regional barbecue traditions should be left alone by both the rise of fast-food industries and the more recent developments in foodie-based Slow Food and sustainability movements, I can't help but temper my agreement with two main exceptions—Southern heirloom tomatoes (in subregions that use tomato-based products in their sauces) and Southern heritage animal breeds. Although both of these are time-honored traditions throughout the American South, they have been rendered almost extinct in their contemporary usage by both more modern and traditional barbecue restaurants alike. I think this should change, and for several good reasons. In this section I will introduce some of the main varieties of Southern heirloom tomatoes that I am most familiar with and give suggestions for incorporating them back into our barbecue sauce traditions moving forward.

I have been both a gardener and a committed conservationist of Southern heirloom vegetable varieties since 1996. I served as the coordinator for the Southern Seed Legacy Project at the University of Georgia from 2005 to 2008 (I now direct the project at its new home at the University of North Texas) and have conducted thesis and dissertation research on the heirloom vegetable and fruit heritage of the southern Appalachian and Ozark Mountains over the past seven years. Along the way, as both a farmer and researcher, I have encountered an amazing variety of flavors, colors, shapes, sizes, and growing characteristics in Southern heirloom tomato varieties. This tremendous variety in Southern tomatoes has the potential to affect the flavor of barbecue sauces in numerous ways. Probably the most tangible is the sweetness and acidity factor. I have found generally that mountain people in the South like pink or yellow tomato varieties, which tend to be sweeter and therefore less acidic in flavor, while lowland Southerners prefer a more acidic tomato, generally red in color. That's not to say that mountaineers don't grow red tomatoes or that lowlanders don't grow pink or yellow tomatoes. My own preference is for sweet, meaty pink tomatoes, particularly of the Rose or Brandywine variety, and they are what I use in my own family's barbecue sauce recipe.

I will focus here mainly on mountain heirloom varieties and their characteristics because they are what I am most familiar with, but I encourage all Southerners to seek out Southern heirloom tomato varieties that may still be available in their own localities (mainly through elderly seed savers) and to incorporate them into their barbecue sauce recipes. Given the current economic climate, this is probably only feasible for home gardeners and sauce makers and maybe a few "gourmet" barbecue restaurateurs, but if we join together and keep these treasured heirlooms in circulation in our culinary traditions it can only be hoped that they will once again be eaten by a majority of Southerners in the future. In fact, programs like the Renewing America's Food Traditions (RAFT) alliance are working hard to make sure that heirloom foods are being incorporated back into American markets (Nabhan 2008). And I can assure you, a barbecue sauce made with heirloom tomato paste is a different, and better, animal than one that is made with ketchup. That is one secret of my family's sauce that I am proud to share, in the hope that it stimulates others to help preserve our region's last remaining heirloom tomatoes before they are lost to history. Let me introduce you below to a few of my favorite heirloom tomato varieties that I have collected, swapped for, and become otherwise acquainted with throughout the years.

Red Oxheart. This tomato has a unique shape thought to look like an ox heart. It used to be the main canning tomato in Ashe County, North Carolina, and is still mainly used for that purpose. It is great for making tomato sauce, barbecue sauce, and salsa. It also makes good juice because it stays uniform and does not separate in the can. It is easy to de-seed and doesn't fall apart in boiling water because it is very meaty. Red Oxheart is a late ripening tomato.

Beefheart. This large tomato is red on the top half and purple on the bottom half and has a very good taste to it. The bottom half of the tomato tapers to a point, which makes it have a heart shape. It is a long tomato that is greater in length than it is in width. It is a very rough-looking tomato (especially on the blossom end) that will catface. It has been passed down in the Bradford family of Bald Mountain, North Carolina, for over a hundred years and is rumored to have originated with German settlers in the area. Beefheart is a very good sauce tomato.

Brandywine. A very big pink tomato that is sweeter than regular red varieties. Among other things, it makes a good green tomato cake, which you bake in the fall once the cooler weather sets in and makes the green tomatoes sweeter. Southern families eat the green top of the tomato fried as well. It has been grown by families in the Green Valley Community of Ashe County, North Carolina, for at least a hundred years, and it is speculated by locals that it was brought in by German settlers.

Brandywine is a regular taste-test winner at tomato competitions for its sweet and full flavor and was a commercial variety introduced in Philadelphia by the seed firm of Johnson and Stokes in 1889 (Weaver 1997). A rumor among the seed-saving community has Brandywine originating in Amish communities, and it is hard to know where Johnson and Stokes got the original seed stock that they improved upon. In any case, it has been grown long enough in North Carolina and other areas to have adapted to local conditions and qualify as a Southern heirloom. I grow another type of tomato, Rose, that is similar in taste and texture to Pink Brandywine for inclusion in my own family's barbecue sauce recipe.

Cow Tits. A red tomato that looks like a roma but is more square. It hangs off the vine like a cow teat and ripens from the bottom up, which makes it look like it has a nipple when it is first ripening. It is meaty and good for sauce, canning, and salsa and produces earlier than Red Oxheart for canning. It has been grown for generations in the North Carolina mountains.

Mister Stripey. This is a big knotty yellow tomato with a red core and stripes running through it. It is a sweeter variety. Troy McCoury of Burnsville, North Carolina, obtained it thirty-five years ago from Selman Hensley and has being growing it ever since. He introduced it to the H.P.S. seed company, and they made it commercially available. It originally came to North Carolina from Virginia and probably before that came from Pennsylvania, likely having Amish origins. It is very similar to other Southern tomato varieties such as German Johnson, Hillbilly, Pineapple, Georgia Streak, Stripey, Candystripe, and Old German, but they each have slight variations and preferences among Southern gardeners. Mister Stripey is good for sweeter sauces and makes them yellow in color. It is also grown in the Arkansas Ozarks.

The five varieties described above are just a small number of the many heirloom tomatoes that are still being grown in the American South today. They are mostly being grown by home gardeners of the elderly generation who grew up in farming families. Many of these seed savers are in their last few years of being able to maintain a garden and have no one left in their families to pass their seeds on to. If we can reincorporate some of this agricultural biodiversity back into regional culinary dishes such as barbecue sauces, we will be engaging in delicious acts of what Gary Paul Nabhan has called "eater-based conservation" (2008, 2). Heirloom tomatoes are of interest not only because of their fine culinary qualities but also because they are infused with important familial and Southern cultural histories (Nazarea 2005). When we use them in our lives and keep the seeds and stories going, we are actively keeping these important cultural memories alive.

References

Applewhite, James. 2004. "Barbecue Service." In *Cornbread Nation 2: The United States of Barbecue*, edited by Lolis Eric Elie, 14–15. Chapel Hill: University of North Carolina Press.

Egerton, John. 1987. *Southern Food: At Home, on the Road, in History*. Repr., Chapel Hill: University of North Carolina Press, 1993.

Marion, J. Daniel. 2004. "Song for Wood's Barbeque Shack in McKenzie, Tennessee." In *Cornbread Nation 2: The United States of Barbecue*, edited by Lolis Eric Elie, 133. Chapel Hill: University of North Carolina Press.

McClard's Bar-B-Q. 2009. "Our History." McClard's Bar-B-Q website. *www.mcclards.com/mcclards-bbq-history.htm* (accessed October 1, 2009).

Nabhan, Gary Paul, ed. 2008. *Renewing America's Food Traditions: Saving and Savoring the Continent's Most Endangered Foods*. White River Junction, VT: Chelsea Green.

Nazarea, Virginia D. 2005. *Heirloom Seeds and Their Keepers*. Tucson: University of Arizona Press.

Reed, John Shelton, and Dale Volberg Reed. 2008. *Holy Smoke: The Big Book of North Carolina Barbecue*. Chapel Hill: University of North Carolina Press.

Veteto, James R., and Edward M. Maclin. 2009. "Introduction to Tennessee Barbecue." Southern Barbecue Trail, Southern Foodways Alliance. *www.southernbbqtrail.com/* (accessed March 11, 2010).

Weaver, William W. 1997. *Heirloom Vegetable Gardening: A Master Gardener's Guide to Planting, Seed Saving, and Cultural History*. New York: Henry Holt.

York, Jake A. 2004. "To the Unconverted." In *Cornbread Nation 2: The United States of Barbecue*, edited by Lolis Eric Elie, 141–42. Chapel Hill: University of North Carolina Press.

11

Mid-South Barbecue in the Digital Age and Sustainable Future Directions

EDWARD M. MACLIN AND JAMES R. VETETO

This final chapter echoes themes from earlier in the book—stories of locality, identity, and tradition embodied in the consumption of smoked pork barbecue. Here we argue that barbecue is not just a local experience. As a food and a practice, barbecue is inherently *social*. By social, we do not just mean that barbecue structures human relationships (although neither of us has ever met anyone who routinely makes and eats barbecue as a solo venture). Barbecue is social in that it brings together a heterogeneous association of people, technology, and materials (Latour 2005). Of course, this has always been the case. Even when barbecue was restricted to farmers or hunters smoking meat for immediate family and friends there was a network at play—one involving wood, meat, butchering tools, indirect heating technology, the cooks, and the lucky eaters. In such an assemblage, the technologies used have a profound effect on both the structure of the event and the experience of those present. Increasingly, these networks of people, technology, and materials are widely distributed across both virtual and physical spaces in ways that change the barbecue experience for everyone involved. To illustrate, we offer three barbecue vignettes, followed by a look at how technology shapes experience as barbecue enters the digital age. To conclude, we will look at some promising trends toward the sustainable local production of Southern heritage barbecue.

Craig's Barbecue, De Valls Bluff, Arkansas

On a Tuesday at high noon in June 2009, Maclin arrived in De Valls Bluff, Arkansas, to meet Veteto for lunch and discussion of the present volume. De Valls Bluff marked the approximate midpoint between Maclin's location in Tennessee and Veteto's in Arkansas, about an hour and a half drive for each of us. It is also the site of Craig's Barbecue—known for their ribs and sliced barbecue pork. Driving with the windows down along old Highway 70, the smell of wood smoke let us both know that we were close. Craig's is a small white clapboard building from the 1940s with red trim and two entrances, a legacy of the restaurant's segregated past. As Maclin pulled into the parking lot with his nine-month-old daughter, the scent of smoke and the crunch of white gravel under his tires awoke memories of his own childhood. Once inside, they found a table near the door (one of only a few in the restaurant), and when Veteto arrived the conversation turned almost immediately to barbecue—the spiciness of the sauce, sliced versus chopped pork, wet versus dry ribs—intertwined with discussion of the history of this restaurant.

Craig's is a sit-down restaurant, but not in the sense of fine linens and hors d'oeuvres. In fact, the walls of the establishment can only be described as worn and perhaps a little dirty, but not in an unsanitary way. The short menu is at the back of the room above a counter just outside of the kitchen. There is no cash register in sight, and every once in a while an African American waitress emerges from the kitchen to take orders and money, deliver food to hungry customers, or bring back change from beyond. By listening closely when the kitchen door flips open or while visiting the bathroom, one can usually hear the gentle beats and inspired singing of soul or gospel music. While we were there as many people ordered food to go as stayed to eat inside. A woman took our order at the table, rather than having us order at the counter as is common at many fast-food restaurants. And make no mistake—though the food arrived on paper plates rendered translucent by the grease, this was no fast food. Veteto quickly cautioned Maclin that, unlike in West Tennessee, when you ordered pulled pork at Craig's they served it chopped. We decided to order sandwiches and share a plate of ribs. The sliced pork was rich and smoky, if different from our beloved West Tennessee–style pulled fare, and the ribs were falling-off-the-bone tender. Maclin's daughter had some of her first barbecue at Craig's (a rib bone) while sitting in her car seat and enjoying the sights, sounds, and smells.

What she couldn't appreciate, at her tender age, was the setting of Craig's within the cultural and ecological landscape of De Valls Bluff, Arkansas. De Valls Bluff is a small town of under one thousand people, located about an hour east of Little Rock along the White River. The area is rich in agricultural land and dark river-rich soil, and driving to town from the interstate one passes hay fields, rice farms, and small-to-medium-sized houses, many with vegetable gardens. A first impression of the population (and the clientele of Craig's) is that it is diverse but not wealthy and definitively rural. The buildings in De Valls Bluff along the highway are tinged with age, well used, giving the feeling of a community that is older and active but not undergoing major new growth. Craig's itself is an older building, and contributes to a feeling that tradition is important here. Our perceptions are not based on deep ethnographic insight—we have only been through town a few times specifically to eat at Craig's—but on observations coupled with our experiences in other such small Southern towns. Our perceptions were likely also colored by the purpose of our trip—to find good barbecue and to discuss the details of the present volume. We will return to perception, tradition, and culinary journeys momentarily.

Charlie Vergos's Rendezvous, Memphis

A year and a half earlier, in the spring of 2008, we had co-chaired a session on Mid-South barbecue at the annual meeting of the Society for Applied Anthropology in Memphis, Tennessee. For a pair of academics, beginning a discussion of barbecue at a professional conference requires a certain amount of preparation and a larger amount of chutzpah—especially when that session is held in the back dining room of Memphis's historic Rendezvous. Holding the session at the Rendezvous served two purposes. First, it provided an enveloping sensory experience for attendees. The setting of the restaurant drove home our points far more effectively than a PowerPoint slide ever could hope to. Second, the Rendezvous is itself a contradiction—it is perhaps the most famous Memphis barbecue landmark, steeped in local lore, but it is also an explicitly large-scale commercial venture that overshadows locality.

On the day of our session we were shown into a back room where our server, "Robert Junior," would be bringing food for the group. Robert

Junior has worked at the Rendezvous for over twenty-four years—and is the son of "Robert Senior," another employee who has been serving ribs at the restaurant for over forty-five years. Catered group dinners at the Rendezvous begin with appetizers of smoked sausage and cheddar cheese sprinkled with a special mixture of paprika, salt, and herbs and served on paper plates. While the restaurant does serve pulled-pork barbecue, it is certainly not their most popular item. The specialty of the house is "dry rub" ribs: the rib meat is succulent, but is cooked with a dry rub rather than a wet sauce. Rendezvous ribs have legendary status as something like the Platonic ideal of dry ribs and can be ordered as a half rack or full rack. Following the presentations and discussions, one attendee remarked that it was "the most delicious conference session" he had ever attended.

The Rendezvous is located in downtown Memphis just a few blocks from the blues clubs on Beale Street. The restaurant is down a flight of stairs in an alley off Second Street, and newcomers often wonder whether they have arrived at the right location, or have found a service entrance by mistake. The restaurant opened in 1948 in the basement of Charlie Vergos's diner. The interior is windowless with aged dark walls and furniture, throwing emphasis onto the tables with red and white checkered tablecloths. Highway and street signs across the walls convey a sense of locality—the idea that this is the center of the barbecue universe, and all other points should be measured from here. While waiting for a table (and there is often a wait) you can look through glass cases full of artifacts from Memphis of the 1940s. The Vergos family includes restaurant founder Charlie, who was a former head of the Memphis Convention and Visitors' Bureau, and his son John, who served for eight years on the Memphis City Council. The restaurant is linked to charities and events throughout the city, including the Memphis Zoo, the Dixon Gallery and Gardens, and the Make-a-Wish Foundation. The restaurant is a favorite among locals, but also among tourists and traveling business people.

Bozo's Bar-B-Q, Mason, Tennessee

The town of Mason, Tennessee, is located about an hour east of Memphis along U.S. Highway 70—once a major thoroughfare before the interstates were built, now a road weaving much of rural Tennessee together in a mosaic of farmland, small towns, and speed traps. In 1923

Thomas Jefferson "Bozo" Williams opened Bozo's Hot Pit Bar-B-Q across the street from its current location (the restaurant moved in the early 1950s). Bozo's was owned for many years by the Williams family, and despite recent changes in ownership it remains a barbecue landmark. During the 1980s, Bozo's was engaged in a decadelong trademark battle with Bozo the Clown. The restaurant ultimately won, but only after the case went to the U.S. Supreme Court—one of the findings being that the restaurant's fame made it an interstate venture. Maclin's grandparents lived near Bozo's when he was growing up, and often found that "we live near Bozo's" was enough to satisfy queries about the location of their rural home—more helpful than naming the town itself, since so few people had heard of Mason.

Mason itself bears some resemblance to De Valls Bluff. It is a community surrounded with agricultural land, with a population of around a thousand, and it is about an hour from the banks of the Mississippi River. Mason was a railway stop during the 1800s and early 1900s, but the bustling downtown—once busy with local markets and a thriving music scene—has deteriorated. The town's major intersection has been dominated by the same two gas stations (or variants of them) since the 1980s. At the same time, the town's borders have expanded to encompass new residents, and the forty-mile-an-hour speed limit signs (which only strangers ignore) have moved outward as new housing developments to the north of town have sprouted. Though many of the buildings seem old or in a state of slight disrepair, the flow of traffic through town and to the handful of shops, gas stations, and restaurants shows that Mason retains a vibrant energy.

Maclin entered Bozo's on a March afternoon in 2008 with his new wife, along with Veteto and his parents, to offer them a taste of his favorite local barbecue. Bozo's is a pale brick building, stained in parts by years of smoke. The parking lot is usually full near lunchtime and in the early evenings. Entering the front door, Maclin was struck by the smell—not just the scent of barbecue, but the smell of the foyer itself, which flooded his mind with childhood memories. The restaurant's entryway and dining counter, and part of the large sign in front of the building, were featured in the 2005 film *Walk the Line* about the life of Johnny Cash. The walls are covered with a pale reddish wood paneling that, combined with the wooden chairs, Formica tabletops with metal edging, green barstools at the serving counter, black and white tiled floor, and red and white gingham curtains, maintain the 1950s look of the interior. The windowsills and numerous shelves are decorated with assorted statues of pigs—many standing on two legs and wearing clothing. One wall features a handful of photographs of the founder, Bozo Williams, and his family as well as the restaurant in earlier years. Two photos depict an incident in the 1950s when "the Mexicans crashed into Bozo's" and show a car firmly embedded in the restaurant's entrance.

Our whole entourage had pork sandwiches that day. The "white pig" is pulled white meat topped with coleslaw and served with sauce on the side. Eating in the restaurant, Maclin was reminded of his grandmother—one of the world's slowest eaters, who prided herself on eating everything on her plate. She could clean a rib bone to the point that forensic detectives would have had trouble finding any meat, and her dinner plates probably didn't need to be washed since she was so thorough. At Bozo's, the Maclins always knew that they needed to pace themselves so that they would not be bored while waiting for Grandmaw to finish. Grandfather Maclin always had to make the rounds, shaking hands with other customers whom he knew from farm bureau meetings, the county commission, or church, or because they were cousins many times removed. The waitstaff knew the Maclin family by name, partly because they had eaten in the restaurant once a week or more for decades and partly because Mason just isn't that big. With time and changes in ownership, some things have changed—you can't get a sixteen-ounce Coke in a glass bottle anymore, and the french fries are different—but the barbecue tastes the same as Maclin remembers from growing up. The Veteto family paid it high compliment by comparing the sauce to McClard's from Hot Springs, Arkansas, and to their own homemade sauce. When we left, it was with an agreement to come back if we were ever all together in the area again.

Local Histories and Historic Localities

The three vignettes above show three very different restaurants in three communities, but with a few similar threads. All three restaurants rely to some extent on the history embodied in their physical space. Whether it is the basement entryway at the Rendezvous, the 1950s decor at Bozo's, or the dual entrances at Craig's, the restaurants are all situated firmly in time and local contingency. These restaurants have historically been rooted in their local communities. At the same time, though, each of these restaurants sits within a larger context that enables its current (and historical) operation. While the local history of each restaurant is wrapped up in family and community, the "historic localities" of each site are more far flung.

At Bozo's, a key factor in the U.S. Supreme Court case over the Bozo's trademark—between Bozo's the restaurant and Bozo the Clown—was that the restaurant was able to demonstrate that they served an interstate customer base (Margolick 1991). A similar argument was made in the case of Ollie's Barbecue in Alabama: because Ollie's meat came from across state lines, their business counted as interstate commerce and as such was subject to federal regulation. The resulting Supreme Court case (*Katzenbach v. McClung*) was a key decision in upholding the Civil Rights Act of 1964 (Weiner 2003). In the same way, the networks of actors at play historically at Craig's and the Rendezvous stretch across multiple levels of scale—city, state, regional, and national. In fact, given the scale of changes in population distribution, farming practices, and changes in food distribution and refrigeration technologies, change in the structure of the networks surrounding these restaurants should be properly regarded as the norm rather than a novelty.

Looking at farming practices, for example, from the 1970s onward there was a dramatic shift in hog farming away from open lots and toward contained farms modeled after modern large-scale poultry operations (Thu and Durrenberger 1998). These shifts had profound environmental, economic, and social effects within farming communities. Among these, the efficiencies of large-scale operations contributed to a drop in hog prices and a loss of jobs among independent owner-operators (Ikerd 1998). Changes in hog production also led to a shift toward lean meat that was supposedly being demanded by consumers (Thu and Durrenberger 1998). Lean meat is produced through management practices such as early weaning and age-specific feeding, as well as through genetic changes made possible in part by artificial insemination—all of which are more easily achievable under mass production (Rhodes 1995). The result of these shifts has been an increase in vertical integration, with giant firms now operating multiple hog operations, food processing plants, and retail operations (Barkema, Drabenstott, and Welch 1991). Such technological changes affect multiple actors within the barbecue complex—not least of all the pigs themselves. While changes in hog production have certainly affected the owners and operators of barbecue restaurants, these shifts have remained largely invisible to the end consumer.

Technology and Taste

During the 1980s, the Rendezvous entered into a relationship with another Memphis-based company—Federal Express. The new service, which began as a novelty, allowed customers across the country to order food by phone and receive their ribs by next-day airmail. In 1987, the service was seeing as many as fifty to sixty orders a day (Alva 1987). By 1989, the flying ribs were bringing in $100,000 a year (Greene 1989). Orders by phone attracted such high-profile customers as Bill Cosby and Frank Sinatra (Robbins 1988).

Charlie Vergos's Rendezvous was the first in a long line of other Memphis-based barbecue restaurants that now offer online ordering, including Corky's, Neely's, and Cozy Corner. In addition to maintaining their own websites, barbecue restaurants increasingly are embedded in new virtual communities. The Rendezvous, Bozo's, and Craig's, as well as Corky's, Neely's, Cozy Corner, and other Mid-South restaurants, now have active fan pages on social networking sites like Facebook. A recent search of the microblogging site Twitter revealed numerous posts from people—both inside and outside Memphis—enjoying Rendezvous ribs. Of the three restaurants featured at the beginning of this chapter, Craig's has perhaps the least web presence. Craig's has no official homepage, but is mentioned frequently on road-food websites and has a Facebook group with fans from Arkansas, Mississippi, Oklahoma, Tennessee, and Missouri. All of the restaurants are also mentioned in various weblogs, such as this entry on Craig's from *BBQ Quest*:

> I was driving back from vacation in the Ozarks and decided to hit this place. It is on the old Highway 70 between Memphis and Little Rock. . . .
> It had rained hard for about two days here. Things inside were a bit soggy. But potential health code violations have never kept me from good BBQ. I got the dinner plate hot. You can get mild, medium, or hot. Apparently you can get extra hot too but I didn't know that until after I ate. I like a spicy BBQ as long as it isn't so hot to interfere with actually enjoying the food. The hot sauce is a thick, spicy, orange sauce that would hold up well on most any meat. I got the pork. It was tender, and thick sliced but still soft enough to chew through on a sandwich without stopping to cut it up.
> . . . There were a lot of drive-up customers from out of town. One

guy was returning from Oklahoma where he had moved after growing up. The place has been around since the '40s. It's nice to see such longevity when it is earned from the consumers. (Pena 2009)

Online communities form new localities not dependent on geographic limits. These communities may allow former residents to remain in contact with the people, places, and food of their past. They may also allow new members from other regions to participate in the barbecue process—to take some claim on various local barbecues as their own. However, no change happens in isolation; the sensual appeal of the restaurant-in-context shifts along with that context. Technologically mediated changes in the experience of barbecue come in at least three varieties: context changes, shifts in perception, and transformation into spectacle.

What is the difference between a plate of ribs at a table in the back of Charlie Vergos's Rendezvous and a plate of the same ribs in an apartment in New York City? The context in which a meal is consumed includes simultaneous factors such as table settings, ambiance, and side dishes, as well as nonsimultaneous factors including recent meals, time of day, and season (Cardello 1995). The context in which a plate of ribs is consumed is not trivial; it affects assessments of food quality. More than that, if external environmental factors contribute to beliefs about barbecue—about tradition, taste, and authenticity—then those factors may be considered to be part of cognition itself (Clark and Chalmers 1998). This is not to say that the flavor of barbecue-by-air is quantitatively different because the context is different, only that it will be a different experience.

Similarly, prior expectations may influence perceptions of the barbecue experience (Cardello 1995). A virtual barbecue explorer may have read multiple reviews of menu items, seen photographs, looked at maps, and talked to others in chat rooms before ever setting foot in Bozo's or Craig's. A recent search revealed conflicting opinions about Bozo's. Consider this example, from the blog of "Fred," a neurosurgeon living in Switzerland:

> As a kid traveling with my parents, we always timed a trip to or from Memphis to coincide with lunch or supper [at Bozo's]. The place was always crowded, and the BBQ was wonderful.
> ... I am here to tell you that Bozo's BBQ is still going strong, has

great southern style food and hospitality, even sold me a Bozo's ball cap. Next time you are in Mason, Tennessee, drop by. (Fred 2006)

Now contrast that with the following post, from *Chowhound*:

> On the advice and recommendation of a handful of travel guides, folks around town, and a soul or two on this board we ventured to Bozo's Hot Pit Barbecue last night to sample the food there. Sadly, I was a little disappointed.
>
> The food—the side items, especially—are all uniformly good. Unfortunately, the meat that they serve falls under the category of "roast pork," i.e. there was no smoke flavoring anywhere in the meat; no telltale pink coloring, no real depth of flavor. Likewise, the ribs appeared to have been cooked in an oven. Don't get me wrong, I'm a big fan of roast pork, and the ribs had a flavorful spice blend rubbed into them and were falling-off-the-bone tender. But I expected more from a place one friend of a friend had described as "better than any barbecue place in Memphis." (Cooper 2002)

In fairness to Bozo's, we have both been there quite recently and found the food to be excellent, but Web pages have a tendency to linger, and preconceptions that are established online can play a large role in how a restaurant is perceived. Expectations related to food are accompanied by a host of stereotypes and essentialisms about small Southern communities. During our visit to Craig's, we brought with us not only our appetites but also years of experience in small Mid-South towns—experience that may have given us insight into De Valls Bluff or misled us, but nonetheless influenced our dining experience.

Changes in experience are not only a result of the mental states of the eater. As barbecue spreads across the Internet, changes in both the product and its packaging occur. The evocation of tradition and locality that is found in physical restaurants is made explicit within restaurant websites. The Rendezvous site (*www.hogsfly.com*), for example, includes a section on history as well as references to the longevity of the staff and links between the restaurant and the city at large. The new connections between people and meat forged on the Internet have the potential to reshape the barbecue landscape by allowing comparisons that might not have been made before. How do Rendezvous ribs compare to ribs in Kansas City? You can order some and find out. Which restaurant has the best barbecue in West Tennessee? You can print a list of candidates, complete with satellite-generated maps pinpointing their exact location and reviews by dozens of self-proclaimed barbecue experts.

In 1999, the rights to the Bozo's trademark were bought by Isaac Tigrett (Jennings 2007). Tigrett, perhaps best known as the developer of the House of Blues and Hard Rock Cafe chains, had a new franchising idea involving Bozo's Bar-B-Q. Tigrett originated the concept, then marketed it as a just-add-cash project—for an initial investment of only $10 million! The project website (*www.bozosbar-b-q.com*) consists of a five-minute-long presentation laying out the design. The viewer is first asked to select their region: either the U.S. market or the Mid-East/Asia market. The choice results in one of two possible presentations that appear to be almost identical, except that in the Mid-East/Asia market, all references to pigs or pork have been replaced with references to lamb, and drawings of pigs have been replaced with similar drawings of lambs. The presentation lays out a range of possibilities for a Bozo's franchise, including drive-in restaurants, large-market restaurants with stages for concerts, and even an amusement park. The theme is barbecue-meets-carnival-sideshow—with large hanging banners of a Devil Child, Alligator-Skin Girl, and Tattooed Lady. The familiar Bozo's sign is mirrored in fictional signs advertising a catfish restaurant, a concert venue, elephant rides, and the world's largest ball of string. Words flash across the screen as the Beatles' "Sgt. Pepper's Lonely Hearts Club Band" plays: "Pig [or lamb] Power!" and "The pork [or lamb] shall rise again!" The Confederate flag is mimicked: blue diagonal crossbars on a red field are studded with white pigs (or lambs) rather than stars. The staging is pure spectacle, in which "everything that was directly lived has receded into a representation" (Debord 2002). Within this spectacle, the idea of Bozo's becomes more important than its actual physical form. If the promotion were to take hold, the spectacle of Bozo's would in fact become its reality. As of our publication date, no franchises have been opened and the original Bozo's Bar-B-Q remains untouched.

Where mass consumerism and virtual space converge, the barbecue landscape morphs into a form of hyperreality. In this space, the real-life heat of the pit is replaced with the warm glow of a computer monitor, the experience of the pitmaster is replaced with the collected wisdom of the blogosphere, and the staged images of food become the ideal to which reality must aspire. In the hyperreal world, actual reality becomes unthinkable, as local diversity is shunned for its illusionary double (Eco 1990).

Luckily, reality has not given way completely to the virtual. Technology has, though, changed the way that we experience barbecue. From the raising of pigs to the prevalence of online reviews and discussion groups, and from next-day air to restaurant websites, the networks of people, materials, and technology that make up "barbecue" have shifted. This process is ongoing. The use of telephones and automobiles allowed interstate traffic to reach Bozo's in the 1960s, whereas in the 1920s both people and word of mouth traveled more slowly. The future of barbecue will be shaped by technological change in ways that are difficult to predict. Denver food critic Jason Sheehan has said, "I believe that barbecue drives culture, not the other way around" (Sheehan 2006). Here Sheehan has restated an old anthropological question: does culture drive behavior, or does behavior drive culture? We will not attempt to answer that question here; we will simply say that technology, barbecue, and culture will continue to influence each other and change together into the foreseeable future. Let us all hope that something of the spirit of traditional Mid-South barbecue will continue to live on despite technological and cultural change, and despite the mixed results of "progress," for it is an institution worth preserving.

Barbecue Futures?

We hope we have been able to demonstrate throughout the present volume, and specifically in this concluding chapter, that barbecue as a Southern food culture and institution has been undergoing the same massive changes that have enveloped most of the world over the past hundred years in a process that has usually been labeled under the catch-all term "globalization." As we have also seen, some of the changes in the modern era have been good and some bad. While overnight barbecue arriving at the front door and virtual barbecue communities are positive developments for some, they certainly will not satisfy the yearning shared by those of us who have grown up eating at small barbecue joints characterized by the sweet smoky scent of hickory wood; the jumble of plates and cutlery clanging in the kitchen; smiling waitresses asking, "Whatta y'all have?"; sweet tea that will rot your teeth; the colorful decor of wood paneling and old signs; and the friendly faces of people from all walks of life. There is nothing like it to those who know it.

That being said, it is obvious that technocultural change has shifted the ground under our collective smoked pork, as we know it. As John Shelton Reed and Dale Volberg Reed (2008) have described for North

Carolina barbecue and Rien Fertel (Chapter 6, this volume) has for West Tennessee, the processes of modernization have made it all the more difficult for traditional barbecue restaurants to survive. Economies of scale have made quality whole hogs increasingly impossible to find. The spread of fast-food barbecue joints with electric smokers—and the backing of corporate capital—has left those few who still engage in the long, gritty process of preparing traditional barbecue in a struggle to adapt, compete, and survive. It is much the same story that anthropologists have documented among traditional cultures and processes worldwide as they face the pressures of an increasingly globalized world. It may be that we are witnessing the swan song of barbecue as we have traditionally known it, but we as anthropologists and participants in the culture of Mid-South barbecue do not necessarily think so. We will conclude this volume with a story of hope for the future of Mid-South barbecue and that of Southern barbecue in general.

Angela Knipple and Paul Knipple (Chapter 9, this volume) have argued convincingly that barbecue is appropriately conceived as a "Slow Food" as defined by the international and U.S. chapters of the Slow Food Movement. This designation has the potential for several outcomes of varying degrees of desirability for different segments of the population. One outcome, all too familiar to Slow Food circles, is that Southern barbecue will be transformed into a nouveau specialty food to be enjoyed only by the economically privileged at effete and expensive dinner gatherings. Here we are talking about things like pumpkin-plum barbecue sauce on pork garnished with cilantro and served with wine. Now, we don't have a problem with such foods in general—and they may be extremely delicious and satisfying—but they do not meet our expectations of what Southern barbecue properly *is* (which, we admit, is a topic of much dispute even among traditionalists). For us, Southern barbecue has always been a proletariat-based food that has migrated upward to other social classes like hickory smoke billowing forth from metal stovepipes. We hope this will remain the case.

Finally, let's cut briefly to the Georgia Piedmont for a look at another possible outcome. In the fall of 2009 Veteto attended a "Field of Greens" festival and fund-raiser for organic farmers affected by recent floods at Whippoorwill Hollow Farm, located near Conyers, Georgia, about thirty minutes out of Atlanta. Slow Food Atlanta was one of the organizers of the event. For fifteen dollars you got all the food, beer, and music you could eat, drink, and listen to. About noon, twenty or so local restaurants put out delicious samples of food that ranged from the simple to the sublime. Some of the most notable were stone-milled grits, pulled pork, and roast duck on sourdough bread topped with local goat cheese. Veteto washed it all down with a smooth oatmeal porter brewed with rainwater collected nearby at a local restaurant and brewery.

He would have been satisfied with such fare alone, as it was far fresher, fancier, and more local than he was used to. Then around three o'clock he noticed that a crowd had started to gather on a hill near the beer taps. He clambered uphill to investigate. The crowd included a person of just about every ethnicity, social class, age group, and occupation to be found in rural Georgia. Indian software designers mingled with down-home Georgia farmers and local punk artists. Veteto joined the crowd and witnessed what he is convinced is one delectable and very real future for Southern barbecue. As chefs from three local restaurants chopped away at different tables on pork shoulders, the crowd was given the specifics of the event. It turns out that three different Southern heritage pigs raised by three local sustainable farmers had been prepared by the participating restaurants. They had brought in judges for the event and a whole lot of extra pork to share around. Each was made in a distinct manner, but all were vaguely recognizable as being along a continuum in the Georgia-Carolina style. It certainly wasn't Mid-South barbecue, but Veteto was glad for it, since he wasn't in the Mid-South.

Among the crowds, he didn't get the chance to catch up with the farmers to find out what specific breeds of heritage hogs were being used, but there are many that are still available in these contemporary times, along with others that have sadly gone extinct. The Mulefoot Hog, for example, is a critically endangered black variety. Only 150 purebred individuals remain of the breed that was once known as the highest-quality "ham hog" to roam the forests and the farms of the Southern states. It was historically nicknamed "Ozark Hog" in the South and is almost certainly descended from the Spanish *preta negra* hogs that were first shipped to the Americas in the 1500s (Nabhan 2008). There is also the Guinea Hog, another black variety of pig once common to Appalachia. It was originally brought to the region by West African slaves; the African Guinea stock then picked up genes from the British Isles swine that were already there. Thomas Jefferson grew related varieties at Monticello. They were traditionally fed and fattened on mast provided by Appalachian forests, and the meat was known to be breaded in

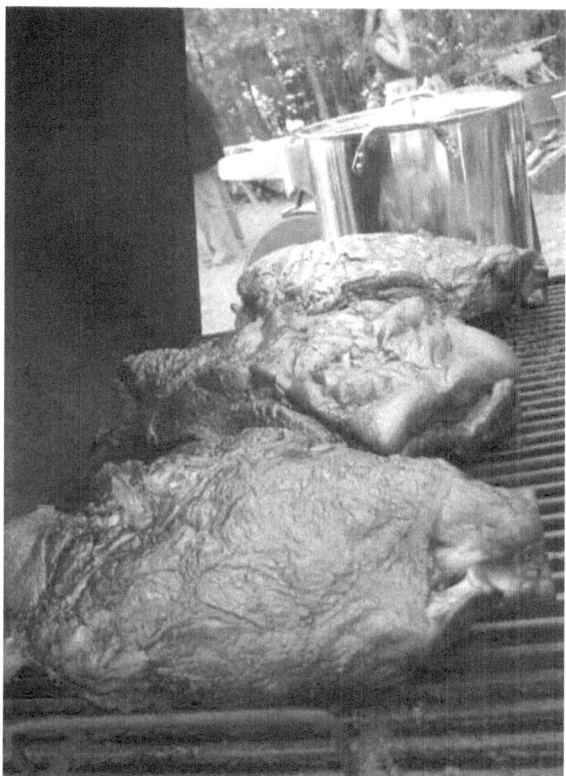

**Locally grown pork, smoked and almost ready to pull.
Photo by Jessie Fly.**

biscuit dough and ashes and served along with various barbecue sauces (Nabhan 2008). Another breed is the black and white Ossabaw Island Hog, which arrived on the southeast coast of America just nine years after Ponce de León's first visit to Florida in 1513. It may in fact be the most closely related, genetically, of living animals to the Iberico hogs in Spain when America was first being explored by the Spaniards. Gary Paul Nabhan describes its meat thusly: "With dark purple to rosy red pork, an intense but nuanced aroma, and a lustrous texture, the meat of the Ossabaw Island hog still arouses the same sense of pleasure that it did more than four centuries ago, when homesick Spaniards roasted it on the barrier islands off of the Georgia coast" (2008, 172).

Some may be cranky and say, "That heritage stuff ain't the barbecue I grew up with. I do just fine with my corporate hogs." That may be the case, but heritage breeds are probably those that our grandparents grew up with and most definitely those that our great-grandparents did. And we are lucky that there are organizations and initiatives such as the American Livestock Breeds Conservancy (*www.albc-usa.org*) and Renewing America's Food Traditions (*www.albc-usa.org/RAFT/*) that are dedicated to conserving heritage hogs among farmers and getting them back out into the marketplace.

Others may argue that change is inevitable and good, and that barbecue is no different than other modern pursuits. It is undeniable that change is the only constant. The Southern hogs that were brought to this country by the Spanish and English and by African slaves have obviously withstood a lot of cultural and political change over the past four hundred years. Our country is no longer ruled by the Spanish or English, and it no longer practices slavery, but yet those hogs have *endured*. And so has traditional barbecue, despite the moves toward hyper-commercialization and technological solutions by an overly aggressive modern capitalist system. Perhaps it is time for some of us to put on the brakes, cherish what is good, and help bring heirloom foodstuffs back into our everyday lives and culinary traditions. That would be a big change for most of us in America, and in our opinion, a change in a positive direction. Current anthropological scholarship is much concerned with moving beyond mere critique and into potential "imaginaries." In the best of that tradition, we *imagine* that reincorporating heirloom foods and sustainable farming practices back into barbecue traditions is a noteworthy direction worth exploring for the Mid-South and beyond. Indeed, as can be seen throughout this volume, it is a path that is already being explored by many daring and curious souls, and particularly among those with a taste for good Mid-South barbecue.

References

Alva, Marilyn. 1987. "Ribs by Air; Memphis Restaurant Jets Pork Ribs Nationwide." *Nation's Restaurant News*.

Barkema, Alan, Mark Drabenstott, and Kelly Welch. 1991. "The Quiet Revolution in the US Food Market." *Economic Review*, May–June: 25–37.

Cardello, Armand. 1995. "Food Quality: Relativity, Context and Consumer Expectations." *Food Quality and Preference* 6, no. 3: 163.

Clark, Andy, and David Chalmers. 1998. "The Extended Mind." *Analysis* 58:10–23.

Cooper, Randal. 2002. "Bozo's Barbecue—Tennessee: With a Note about Gus's." *Chowhound*, May 12. chowhound.chow.com/.

Debord, Guy. 2002. *The Society of the Spectacle*. Translated by Ken Knabb. Published online at Bureau of Public Secrets, *www.bopsecrets.org/SI/debord/* (accessed February 10, 2010).

Eco, Umberto. 1990. *Travels in Hyperreality*. Orlando: Houghton Mifflin Harcourt.

Fred (pseud.). 2006. "Bozo's BBQ." *Fred's Thoughts and History*, October 25. *fredmishmash.blogspot.com/2006/10/bozos-bbq.html*.

Greene, Bob. 1989. "Dining by Overnight Mail Becoming the Latest Food Fad." *Free-Lance Star* 105, 76.

Ikerd, John E. 1998. "Sustainable Agriculture, Rural Economic Development, and Large-Scale Swine Production." In *Pigs, Profits, and Rural Communities*, 157–69.

Jennings, Lisa. 2007. "From Indian Ashram, HRC Vet Tigrett Seeks Bozo's Sale." *Nation's Restaurant News*, November 4. *www.nrn.com/article/indian-ashram-hrc-vet-tigrett-seeks-bozo%E2%80%99s-sale*.

Latour, Bruno. 2005. *Reassembling the Social: An Introduction to Actor-Network-Theory*. Clarendon Lectures in Management Studies. Oxford: Oxford University Press.

Margolick, David. 1991. "In Court, a Bitter Duel for the Right to Be a Bozo." *New York Times*, August 2.

Nabhan, Gary Paul, ed. 2008. *Renewing America's Food Traditions: Saving and Savoring the Continent's Most Endangered Foods*. White River Junction, VT: Chelsea Green.

Pena, Erik. 2009. "Craig's BBQ—De Vall's Bluff, AR." *BBQ Quest*, August 6. *thanatos70.blogspot.com/*.

Reed, John Shelton, and Dale Volberg Reed. 2008. *Holy Smoke: The Big Book of North Carolina Barbecue*. Chapel Hill: University of North Carolina Press.

Rhodes, V. James. 1995. "The Industrialization of Hog Production." *Review of Agricultural Economics* 17, no. 2: 107–18.

Robbins, William. 1988. "Memphis Journal: Where Barbecue Lovers Go Simply Hog Wild." *New York Times*, January 11.

Sheehan, Jason. 2006. "There Is No Such Thing as Too Much Barbecue." *This I Believe*, May 29. *www.npr.org/*.

Thu, Kendall M., and E. Paul Durrenberger. 1998. *Pigs, Profits, and Rural Communities*. Albany: State University of New York Press.

Weiner, Mark S. 2003. "The Semiotics of Civil Rights in Consumer Society: Race, Law, and Food." *International Journal for the Semiotics of Law* 16, no. 4: 395–405.

CONTRIBUTORS

Kristen Bradley-Shurtz is currently a PhD student in the department of English with a concentration in folklore studies at the University of Louisiana at Lafayette. She holds an MA in folk studies from Western Kentucky University. Though she has varied research interests, her primary interest in folklore led her close to home with a study (in this volume) of the barbecue traditions of St. Patrick's Church and School in McEwen, Tennessee. Kristen is a proud graduate of St. Patrick's School and has been pleased to find that extraordinary traditions do exist in our own backyards.

Jonathan Deutsch, PhD, is a classically trained chef and associate professor of tourism and hospitality at Kingsborough Community College, City University of New York and Public Health, CUNY Graduate Center. He is the author (with Rachel Saks) of *Jewish American Food Culture* (Greenwood, 2008; Bison Books, 2010) and editor (with Annie Hauck-Lawson) of *Gastropolis: Food and New York City* (Columbia University Press, 2009).

John T. Edge is director of the Southern Foodways Alliance, an institute of the Center for the Study of Southern Culture at the University of Mississippi. Edge is also a contributing editor at *Gourmet*. He writes a monthly column, "United Tastes," for the *New York Times* and is a longtime columnist for the *Oxford American*. His work for *Saveur* and other magazines has been featured in six editions of *Best Food Writing*. Edge is the author of six books, including the James Beard Foundation Award–nominated cookbook *A Gracious Plenty: Recipes and Recollections from the American South* (2002), and has also edited seven books, including the foodways volume of the *New Encyclopedia of Southern Culture* (2007).

Rien T. Fertel is a PhD candidate in the Tulane University history department. His dissertation, in progress, examines the intersections of culture, race, class, and consumerism in late nineteenth-century New Orleans. He wrote his master's thesis at the New School for Social Research in New York on the commodification and codification of food and local identities in early Creole cookbooks.

Angela Knipple comes from a long line of barbecue lovers. Her first barbecue memories are of sharing barbecue sandwiches with her grandfather at Bozo's in Mason, Tennessee, but these days she gets excited about watching her son learn the craft of the pit from her father. She is a member of Slow Food Memphis and enjoys cooking, eating, and sharing the food of the South through her writing.

Paul Knipple began his love affair with pork at an early age with his first plate of barbecue spaghetti at Bill's Barbecue in Memphis and a beans and bacon dish, the first recipe he mastered. Paul lives in Memphis with his wife, Angela, and their son, Patric. He is a member of Slow Food Memphis and a certified Memphis in May barbecue judge.

Edward M. Maclin is a PhD candidate in the anthropology department at the University of Georgia. In addition to barbecue and other food studies, his interests include political ecology, network research, and the anthropology of organizations. He has worked for the past two decades as an environmental educator and researcher, including ten years managing the historic Children's Garden at the Brooklyn Botanic Garden in New York. He holds a master's degree in botany from the University of Tennessee. When he is not researching institutional culture, he can often be found writing, reading, or standing behind a hot smoker.

Robert F. Moss is a food historian and freelance writer living in Charleston, South Carolina, where he is a regular contributor of restaurant reviews and culinary features for the *Charleston City Paper*. His latest book, *Barbecue: The History of an American Institution*, was published by the University of Alabama Press in 2010.

Gary Paul Nabhan, PhD, is currently research social scientist at the Southwest Center and adjunct professor of geography at the University of Arizona. He is the author of two dozen books on various scientific and literary subjects, which have won numerous national and international awards and have been translated and published in five languages and countries. He has published well over fifty refereed journal articles in prestigious publications such as *Nature, American Anthropologist*, and *Conservation Biology*. His natural history essays have been published in various venues including *Orion, Audubon*, and *Sierra*. He is the founder of the Renewing America's Food Traditions (RAFT) alliance and editor of the book *Renewing America's Food Traditions: Saving and Savoring the Continent's Most Endangered Foods* (Chelsea Green, 2008).

Justin M. Nolan, PhD, is associate professor of anthropology at the University of Arkansas. A native of South Arkansas, Nolan's work examines social ecology and cultural conservation in different regions of the American South. Nolan's publications have examined foodways in the Mississippi Delta and Piney Hills, folk medicine in the Ozarks, wild-plant restoration in the Cherokee Nation, and the recent revival of traditional hunting and fishing technologies in the rural Timberlands of Arkansas and Louisiana. His book *Wild Harvest in the Heartland: Ethnobotany in Missouri's Little Dixie* was published by Rowman and Littlefield in 2007.

James R. Veteto, PhD, is assistant professor of anthropology at the University of North Texas (UNT). He grew up eating barbecue between the hometowns of his mother's family in Hot Springs, Arkansas, and his father's family in Lexington, Tennessee, and learned the art of smoking meat from his grandpa, Jim Neff. He is director of the Southern Seed Legacy Project and the Laboratory of Environmental Anthropology at UNT. Veteto's research interests include food and culture, environmental anthropology, ethnoecology, and agricultural anthropology. He has conducted research on the comparative mountain agrobiodiversity and culinary traditions of southern Appalachia, the Ozarks, and the Sierra Madre Occidental of Northwest Mexico. His work has been published in various popular and academic journals, including *Agriculture and Human Values* and *Culture and Agriculture*, and he is coeditor of the book *Environmental Anthropology Engaging Ecotopia: Bioregionalism, Permaculture, and Ecovillages for the Sustainable Future*, under contract with Berghahn Books.

INDEX

Page numbers in boldface refer to illustrations. The letter "t" indicates a table.

Abarca, Meredith, 118
Abe's Barbecue (Clarksdale, Miss.), 37, 160
Adams, Carol J., 113, 114
advertising, barbecue, 110, 113–14, 126, 191
African Americans, viii, 35, 43–49, 52, 56, 93, 132, 182
   and barbecue history, ix, 30–31, 48–49, 71–72, 93, 159–60
   and the Delta, 58
   in El Dorado, AR, 52
   and Memphis, 34–35, 39
   as pitmasters, 17, 71–72, 93
   and politics, 33–34, 159–60
   and socioeconomics, 93
   in Southern history, 17, 33–35, 52, 159–60
   See also civil rights movement
Agrarian Connections Farm (Grove Creek Farm), xi, 107
agriculture, industrial, 99–100, 110, 113, 156–57, 187
   and confined animal feed operations (CAFOs), 19, 162–64
agriculture, sustainable, 19, 112, 157–58, 163–64, 176, 181–82, 194, 196
agriculture, traditional
   conservation of, xi, 107, 193–94, 196
   endangered, 99–100, 110, 187
   history of, 30, 45, 67, 90, 92, 93–94, 155–57
   and plantations, 30, 159
agrobiodiversity. *See* biodiversity

alcohol
   and barbecue sauce, viii, 169
   and barbecue traditions, 62, 174–75
   beer, 8, 36, 38, 124, 125, 130, 137, 138, 142, 143, 193–94
   and church barbecues, 8
   and fundraisers, 8
   moonshine, viii, 62, 169
   and pitmasters, 44
   and plantation barbecues, 30
   and Prohibition, 37
   and temperance barbecues, 29–30
   toasts, 26–27, 29
   whiskey, viii, 8, 27, 29, 139, 168
Alva, Marilyn, 188
American Annual Register, 29
American Indians, vii, 1, 3–4, 25, 54
American Livestock Breeds Conservancy, 196
Anderson, Eugene N., 54
anthropology
   barbecue and, 3
   cognitive, 17
   cultural, 1, 3, 5, 19–20, 62, 192–93, 196
   of food, 3, 5, 13–14, 51–52, 54, 60–62, 85
   of food and memory, 10–11, 52, 54, 60–61, 85–86
   gendered, 9–10
   public, 15–16
Appalachian-style barbecue, 26, 136, 170, 176, 194–95
Applewhite, James, 174

Arkansas Intelligencer, 28, 32
Arkansas Star, 28
Arkansas-style barbecue
    Craig's, 18, 44, 111, 173, 182–83, 186, 187–90
    family, 11
    McClard's, 11–12, 16, 36–37, 169, 171–73, **173**, 186
    and race, 43–63
    sandwiches, 8
    sauces, 171–73
    sauce tomatoes, 57t, 178
    and social networking, 188
    whole-hog, 84
    See also Piney Woods region
Association of Religious Data Archives, 69
Auchmutey, Jim, 5
automobiles, 36–37, 76, 192

babricot, vii
barbacoa, vii, 1, 25
barbecue
    as art, 77–80
    as "booty call," 17, 44
    and car culture, 36
    and Catholicism, 69–70
    and civic life, 30
    as "clean" food, 155–58, 162–64
    and coercion, 30–31
    as cultural construct, 3–4
    and dancing, 26, 44, 67
    as "fair" food, 158–61, 162–64
    and fundraising, 8, 81, 193–94
    as "good" food, 153–55, 162–64
    homogenization of, 110–12, 162
    industrialization of, 162 (*see also* agriculture, industrial)
    as invented tradition, 3
    modernization of, 192–93
    and Muslims, 95
    and organic food, 112, 193
    as performance, 142–49
    persistence of, 1, 99–102
    and power, 112–13
    and railroad construction, 32–33
    and religion, ix, 2, 7–9, 65–81, 90
    as religion, 7, 9
    and savagery, 3–4, 10, 139
    and sexuality, 114
    as Slow Food (movement), 153 (*see also* Slow Food)
    as slow food (traditional), 153 (*see also* slow food)
    as social institution, 25
    as sport, 84, 101, 142–44
    and temperance movement, 29–30
    and violence, 16, 26, 29–30, 31–33
    and Zen, viii, 108
barbecue (word), vii–ix, 1, 85
barbecue, commercial, 188, 191–92
    business practices, 94–95, 110–14, 169, 188
    change in, 3, 13–14, 110–14, 161–64, 188, 191–92
    and competition barbecue, 119
    future of, 13–14, 188
    history of, 13–14, 34–40, 92, 188
    problems with, 161–64
    rise of, 34–40, 92, 161–64
    and women, 10
    See also barbecue, professional; barbecue, traditional
barbecue, competition, 10, 18, 40, 84, 117–50
    Kansas City Barbecue Society (KCBS), 124, 126, 141, 146
    Memphis in May (MIM) World Championship Barbecue Cooking Contest, 40, 117–50, 165, 171, 183–84
barbecue, cooking methods
    in competition, 121–22, 125–26
    historic, 25, 28–29, 34, 86
    pits, 28–29, 35, 45–47, 72–74, 77–81
    racks, vii, 38
    slow-smoking, vii, 1, 35–36, 38, 54, 77
    and technology, 19, 100, 114, 148–49, 161, 181, 192
    transmission of, 86–90
    whole-hog, 83–84, 86, **87**, **89**, **91**, 96

barbecue, geography of, 2–6, 8, 19, 26–27, 34, 60, 155, 169–74. *See also* barbecue traditions, geographic
barbecue, history of, 25–40, 167–79
  beginnings, vii–ix, 4, 18
  European origins, 4
  German origins, 4
  Native American origins, vii–ix, 3–4, 25
  origin myths, 85–86, 154
  regionalization of, 33, 34–35, 99–101, 169–70
  spread of, 26–27, 34–40
  whole-hog, 26, 84–102
barbecue, mobile, 60–61, 158–59
barbecue, and online communities, 188–191
barbecue, origin myths, 85–86, 154
barbecue, professional, 84, 98. *See also* barbecue, commercial; barbecue, traditional
barbecue, regional variation in, 2, 5, 8, 16, 33–35, 51–62, 112–13, 169–71. *See also* whole-hog barbecue
barbecue, Southern, 3, 5–6, 10–11, 13, 83, 156, 181, 192–96
barbecue, theft of, 30, 47–48
barbecue, traditional, 3–5, 10, 25–35, 59–61, 77–81, 155–60, 181, 193. *See also* barbecue, commercial; barbecue, professional; whole-hog barbecue
barbecue, whole-hog. *See* whole-hog barbecue
Barbecue Belt, 171
barbecue blogs, 188–91
barbecue dishes
  beef brisket, 3, 5, 55–59, 57t, 68
  beef ribs, 58
  chicken (*see* chicken, barbecue)
  chitterlings, 159
  ribs, 57t: dry, viii, 5, 38, 60, 125, 155, 172, 182–84; wet, 5, 182
  sandwiches: pork shoulder, 5, 25, 40, 46–47, 111, 155, 172, 182; rib, 36
  See also side dishes
barbecue Eucharist, 9

barbecue flavorings
  dip, 5, 8, 168, 170, 172
  dry rub, viii, 5, 38, 60, 125, 155, 172, 182–84
  sauce, vii–viii, 5, 7, 8, 80–81, 154, 167–79 (*see also* barbecue sauce; chicken: barbecue sauce for; *and under* barbecue traditions, geographic; family; Piney Woods region)
barbecue landscapes, 16, 113–14
  change in, 3, 114
barbecue pit. *See under* barbecue, cooking methods
barbecue pitmasters. *See* pitmasters
barbecue restaurants
  franchises, 39, 77
  history of, 12–13, 16
  McDonaldized, 110
  roadside stands, 36
  See also barbecue, commercial; barbecue, professional; barbecue, traditional; *and individual restaurants*
barbecue restaurants, owners of
  Halsell, Ernest, 37
  Pickard, Devin, 5, 12
barbecue sauce, vii–viii, 5, 7, 8, 80–81, 154, 167–79
  Abe's, 37
  "Big Four" ingredients, 19, 57t, 171, 172, 173 (*see also* sauce ingredients)
  Bozo's, 186
  Brummett's, 56
  "Colonel Neff's Sauce" (poem), 174–75
  competition, 124, 126, 129, 143
  Craig's, 188
  historic, vii–viii, 5, 29, 34, 167–68
  homemade, 186
  ingredients (*see* sauce ingredients)
  Jones's, 45, 47
  Kansas City, 172
  Leonard's, 35
  McClard's, **11**, 11–12, 16, 36–37, 169, 171–73, **173**, 186

barbecue sauce *(continued)*
   mustard-based, 57t, 58–59
   Old Hickory Sauce, 58–59, 173
   origins, vii–ix
   Piney Woods, 60
   and poetry, 172
   recipe change over time, 88
   regional variation and variants, 5, 8, 60, 154–55
   and secrecy, 12, 17, 37, 61, 71–72, 97–98, 108, 168–69, 173, 175, 177
   Siler's, 88, **89**
   St. Patrick's Barbecue, 70–73, 77, 79, 80, 81
   Texas, 172
   See also barbecue sauce geographies; chicken: barbecue sauce for; *and under* barbecue traditions, geographic; family; Piney Woods region
barbecue sauce geographies, 169–70, 171–74
barbecue serving modes
   chipped, 8
   chopped, 8, 35, 37, 47, 58, 172, 182, 194
   ground, 8
   minced, 8, 129, 169
   pulled, 8, 35, 44, 57t, 58, 75, 107, 111–12, 114, 129, 139, 186, 194
   shaven, 8
   shredded, 8, 129
   sliced, 8, 37, 58, 170, 182, 188
barbecue smoke ring, 108, 128, 154
barbecue smokers, 7, **55**, 107–8, 117, 121–22, 131. *See also* electric barbecue cookers; gas barbecue smokers; Hickory Creek Bar-B-Q Cookers
barbecue technology, 19, 100, 114, 148–49, 161, 181, 192
barbecue traditions
   and change, 16, 99–102, 189–92
   and innovation, 13–14, 80, 100–101, 161, 189–92
   and persistence, 99–102
   See also barbecue traditions, geographic; *individual barbecue styles*
barbecue traditions, geographic
   Alabama, 8, 60, 109, 170, 187
   American Indian, vii–viii, 4, 54, 154, 168
   Appalachian, 16, 26, 170, 176–78, 194
   Argentina, vii
   Arizona, ix
   Arkansas (*see* Arkansas-style barbecue)
   and barbecue sauce, 3, 5, 8, 19, 34, 60, 155, 169–74
   Beale Street, 35, 40, 171, 184
   California, 34
   Chicago, ix
   European, vii, 4
   Georgia, ix, 2, 8, 26, 107, 169–70, 193–95
   German, vii, 4
   Hispanic, vii
   Illinois, 170
   Irish, Scots Irish, 54, 65–81
   Kansas City, MO, ix, 8, 34, 38, 171–72
   Kentucky, 2, 26, 70
   Louisiana, 2–3, 51–63
   Memphis (*see* Memphis-style barbecue)
   Mexico, vii
   Mississippi, ix, 2, 27, 30, 32, 37, 160
   New England, 25
   North Carolina (*see* Carolina barbecue; "Eastern-style" barbecue)
   Pacific Northwest, vii
   Piney Woods (*see* Piney Woods region)
   South Carolina, 8, 16, 25–26, 40, 60, 84, 168–70
   Spanish, 3, 154, 195
   Tennessee, ix, 2, 5, 8, 17, 26–27, 29–30, 33, 40, 65–81
   Texas (*see* Texas-style barbecue)

Virginia, 16, 25–26, 30, 39, 168–69
West Tennessee (*see* West Tennessee–style barbecue)
barbecuity, 102
barbeculture, 85, 97
Barkema, Alan, 187
barter, 35, 140
Bass, S. Jonathan, 90
Bauer, Karl Jack, 31
beef, 26, 27–28, 30–31, 37, 55–59, 62, 115n1, 155. *See also* beef brisket
beef brisket, 3, 5, 55–59, 68
beef ribs, 58
B. E. Scott's Barbecue (Lexington, Tenn.), 86, 89. *See also* Scott's-Parker's Barbecue (Lexington, Tenn.)
Bill's Bar-B-Q (Memphis, Tenn.), 84, 87, 96, 99. *See also* Thomas and Webb pit house (Memphis, Tenn.)
biodiversity, 155–56, 164, 176–79, 201
bio-power, 113. *See also* agriculture, industrial
blues (musical style), 35, 40, 59
Bobby's Bar-B-Q (Henderson, Tenn.), 88. *See also* Siler's Old Time BBQ (Henderson, Tenn.)
Bogdan, Robert, 118
Bon Appétit, 156
Bower, Anne L., 51
Bozo's Bar-B-Q (Mason, Tenn.), 109–11, 184–87, 189–92
and U.S. Supreme Court, 187
Brewster, Zachary W., 112
Brown, Linda Keller, 14, 51, 54
Buddy's Barbecue (Knoxville, Tenn.), 110

CAFOs (Confined Animal Feed Operations), 19, 162–64
Cairo, Ill. (Alexander County), 170
Caldwell, Melissa L., 19, 108, 112
Calhoun's Barbecue (Knoxville, Tenn.), 110

campaign barbecues, 27–28. *See also* politics
capitalism, 94, 99–100, 109, 113–14, 196
Capone, Al, 37
car culture, 36–37, 76, 192
Cardello, Armand, 189
Carib, vii–viii
Carlson, Marcia S., 155
Carney, George O., 62
Carolina barbecue
Appalachian Mountains and, 170
history of, 4–5, 39
Holy Smoke (Reed and Reed), 4–7, 9, 25, 60, 103n3, 167–68, 170, 176, 192–93
and modernization, 192–93
regional variation in, 60, 169–70, 194
sauces, 8, 168–69, 172
sauce tomatoes, 177–78
South Carolina, 8, 16, 25–26, 40, 60, 84, 168–70
whole-hog, 84
See also "Eastern-style" barbecue
Cash, Johnny, 185
Cash, W. J., 83
cattle, vi, viii. *See also* beef; beef brisket
celebrations, barbecue and
Christmas, 30
church, 29, 33–34, 65–81, 90, 114
Emancipation Day, 34
family, 9, 11, 30, 84, 90–91, 107–8, 114, 154
Fourth of July, 10, 26–27, 30–31, 34, 84, 90, 94
Memorial Day, 10
seed swaps, xi, 107
war (homecoming and send-off), 31–33
weddings, 107, 115
Centerville, Tenn. (Hickman County), 12–13
change, technocultural, 13–14, 80, 100–101, 161, 189–92
charlas culinarias interview technique, 118

Charleston, S.C. (Charleston County), 40
Charlie Vergos's Rendezvous (Memphis, Tenn.), 16, 38, 172, 183–84, 186–87, 188–90
chicken, barbecue, 28, 57t, 67, **78**, 107, 124
  barbecue sauce for, 73, 77, 79, 125
  barbecuing techniques for, 77–81, 125–26
chili (dish), 38, 57t, 59, 62
chitterlings, 159
Civil Rights Act, 159–60, 187
civil rights movement, 43, 48, 159–60, 187. See also desegregation; race; segregation
Civil War, 31, 32–33, 66, 109
Clarksdale, Miss. (Coahoma County), 37, 160
class (socioeconomic)
  divisions, 5, 49, 55, 132–33, 135, 193–94
  stratification, 44, 111
Clifford, James, 15
Clinton, Bill, 37
coa. See *barbacoa*
coleslaw. See slaw
community
  food and, 68–81, 90–93, 153–54, 158–59, 186–87
  food communities, virtual, 114
  online, 189
  rivalry, 6
  values, 9
"Community Study, A" (Humphreys County, Tenn., Archives), 66
competition barbecue. See barbecue, competition
Confederacy, 6, 71. See also Civil War
conservation, 19, 62, 156, 176
  cultural, 19, 62
  "eater-based," 19, 164, 178
consumerism, 191
Conway, Ark. (Faulkner County), 172
Cooper, Randal, 190
Corky's Barbecue, 18, 110, 115, 188
Cosby, Bill, 188

Counihan, Carole, 4–5, 9, 10
Cozy Corner (Memphis, Tenn.), 10, 188
Craig's Barbecue (De Valls Bluff, Ark.), 18, 44, 111, 173, 182–83, 186, 187–90
Crockett, Davy, 12–13
Crosby, Bing, 35
cultural identity. *See* ethnicity; identity formation; *and under* Piney Woods region; Southern culture
Cultural Politics of Food and Eating, The (Watson and Caldwell), 19, 108, 112
culture
  of competition barbecue, 117–50
  and food traditions, 51, 83–84
  and gender, 76, 114
  Piney Woods, 53–55, 62
  regional, 5, 53–55, 61–62, 154
  restaurant, 92
  Southern, 53, 60, 83–84, 111, 154, 192–93
  West Tennessee, 84–85, 94, 99, 108
  See also anthropology
Curt's Smokehouse (Lexington, Tenn.), 85, 89, 96

Daily Times News, 39
Debord, Guy, 191
deforestation, 157
Delta-style barbecue, 3, 40, 56, 160–61
Denver Post, 160
desegregation, 43–44, 110, 159–60. *See also* segregation
desire, commodification of, 113
Deutsch, Jonathan, 76, 114, 140
De Valls Bluff, Ark. (Prairie County), 18, 44, 111, 173, 182–83, 186, 187–90
DeVore, Brian, 162
"dip," 5, 8, 168, 170, 172
diversity
  agricultural, 19 (*see also* biodiversity)
  racial, 6, 61
  regional, 2, 6, 16, 19, 110, 153–55, 191
domination, 114
Douglas, Mary, 54
Drabenstott, Mark, 187

Drash, Wayne, 160
drinking. *See* alcohol
dual audience approach, 15
   and the academic-popular divide, 15
Dubois, Christine M., 5, 7
Dupre, Daniel, 109
Durrenberger, E. Paul, 110, 113, 187

"Eastern-style" barbecue, 5, 58–59, 169–70
eating, ritual aspects of, 7, 13, 61
Eco, Umberto, 191
economics, 48–49, 101–2, 110–13, 155–56, 158–61, 164–65, 176–77, 187
economies of scale, 99, 162, 187, 193
Edge, John T., 43–49, 103
Egerton, John, 2, 7, 44, 83, 90, 169, 172
elections. *See* campaign barbecues
electric barbecue cookers, 13, 18, 39, 100–102, 107, 121, 161, 193
Elie, Lolis Eric, 9–10, 15, 35–36, 39, 83
Ely, Margot, 118
Engelhardt, Elizabeth S. D., 15
environment, the
   environmental degradation, 157–58, 162–64, 187
   global warming, 157
   sustainability, 155–58, 176, 181, 194, 196
ethnicity, 4–7, 51, 54, 60, 62, 111–12, 169, 194
ethnography, 14–15, 52, 56, 118. *See also* oral history
ethnohistory, 14
Eurocentrism, 1, 4
Evans, Amy, 10, 37, 103

Faith, Daniel P., 156
family
   authors' families, xi, 2, 10–11, 52, 81, 107, 174–75, 186
   barbecue sauces, 11, 19, 167–79, 178–79
   barbecue traditions, 54, 178–79, 181
   in competition barbecue, 120–21, 123, 126, 133–37, 140, 149–50
   outings, 76–80, 84, 90, 154
   pitmasters' families, 11–13, 37, 38, 44–48, 77–80, 90–94, 185–86
   values, 113
Fangman, Thomas J., 155
fast food, 16, 39–40, 99–102, 110–13, 151–53, 176, 182, 193
Fayette Insider, 109
feasting, 15, 25, 29, 91, 109
Federal Express, 188
Ferris, Marcie Cohen, 35
field methods, 14–15, 118
Field of Greens fundraiser, 193
Fisher, Brian, 35, 38, 159–60, 164
flag, Confederate, 6, 191. *See also* Confederacy
flour, 57t, 168
Food and Culture (Counihan and Van Esterik), 4–5, 9, 54
food and memory, 10–13, 52, 54, 60–61, 85–90. *See also under* anthropology
food pornography, 18, 113–14, 191
food sharing, 51, 62
foodways, 14, 54, 61–62, 76
food writers and food writing, 2, 7, 14–15, 132, 172
Foucault, Michel, 113

game species, wild. *See* wild game
gas barbecue smokers, 39, 121, 161
gender
   and barbecue consumption, 114
   and barbecue landscapes, 108, 113–14, 144, 149
   in barbecue practices, 9–10, 77, 75–77, 90, 117–18, 132–42
   and food, 9–10, 114
   of pitmasters, 9–10, 75–77, 90
   in Southern culture, 27, 114
geography. *See* barbecue, geography of
Girardelli, Davide, 111
Glenmary Catholic Missions, 69
goat, viii, 28, 37, 67, 194
Gone with the Wind, 159

Good, James K., 52
"Great Barbecue, the," 109–10
Greene, Bob, 188
Greenville, S.C. (Greenville County), 170
Grimes, Alexia, 69
Grove Creek Farm. *See* Agrarian Connections Farm
Guinness Book of World Records, 17, 65, 67, 81n1
Guthman, Julie, 116

Harrison, William Henry, 28
Hays, Dennis, 88–89, 97
Hays Meat Company, 85, 88–89, 97
    Norwood, Crystal and Derek, 85, 88–89, 93, 97, 102
Hays Smokehouse (Lexington, Tenn.), 88
health, 101, 112, 114, 143–45, 153, 155–56, 162–64, 188
Hedgepeth, William, 102
Henderson, Tenn. (Chester County), 84, 86, 88, 89–90, 94, 96–97
Henry's Smokehouse (Greenville, S.C.), 170
heritage animal breeds, 19, 114, 156, 164–65, 176, 194–96. *See also* whole-hog barbecue; *and under* hogs, heritage breeds
Herndon, Dallas T., 32
Hickory Creek Bar-B-Q Cookers, 100
Higginson, Thomas Wentworth, 30
Hilliard, Sam Bowers, 92
History of Tennessee from the Earliest Times to the Present, A (Goodspeed), 26
Hitt, Jack, 71
Hobsbawm, Eric, 4
Hog Pen BBQ (Conway, Ark.), 172
hog production, **46**, **47**
    change in, 110, 113, 187
    future of, 181, 187, 192–96
    general, 113
    quality of death, 156–57
    quality of life, 156
    See also barbecue, commercial; slow food

hogs, **46**, **47**
    heritage, 19, 114, 156, 164–65, 176, 194–96 (*see also* hogs, heritage breeds)
    See also hog production; whole-hog barbecue
hogs, heritage breeds
    conservation of, 196
    Guinea Hog, 194
    Mulefoot Hog, 194
    Ossabaw Island, 195
    Ozark Hog, 194
    preta negra, 194
holidays, barbecue and. *See* celebrations, barbecue and
Holtzman, Jon D., 10
Holy Smoke (Reed and Reed), 4–7, 9, 25, 60, 103, 167–68, 170, 176, 192–93
homestead barbecuing, 10, 108. *See also* celebrations, barbecue and
Honeyman, Mark, 112
Horner, W. B. R., 27
Hot Springs, Ark. (Garland County), **11**, 11–12, 16, 36–37, 169, 171–73, 186
House Committee on Oversight and Government Reform, 157
Hughes, Louis, 30–31
Humphrey, Theodore C., 54, 61
hyperreality, 191

identity formation, 5–9, 13, 54–55, 60–61, 85, 96–98, 181
Ikerd, John E., 187
"imaginaries," and barbecue traditions, 196
immigrants, viii–ix, 4, 37, 49, 160
Ingold, Tim, 15
interdisciplinary research, 14, 15, 20
International Trade Centre, 154
Interstate Bar-B-Q (Memphis, Tenn.), 172
interstate commerce, 185, 187
interview techniques
    charlas culinarias, 118
    ethnographic methodology, 118
    interviewee selection, 84
    semistructured, 56

Invention of Tradition, The (Hobsbawm and Ranger), 4
"invisible barbecue," 109–10

Jacks Creek, Tenn. (Chester County), 84, 87, 96
Jacks Creek Bar-B-Que (Jacks Creek, Tenn.), 84–85, 87, 96
Jackson Gazette, 27
Jefferson, Thomas, 27, 168, 194
Jeff's (Memphis, Tenn.), 36
Jelly-Roll, 52
Jennings, Lisa, 191
Jim Crow, 44
Jim's Rib Shack (Memphis, Tenn.), 36
Joe's After Hours (Memphis, Tenn.), 36
Johnny Mills's (Memphis, Tenn.), 35
Johnson, Greg, 36, 37, 86
Jonas, Susan, 94
Jones, Michael Owen, 79
Jones Bar-B-Q Diner (Marianna, Ark.), 16, 43–49
Joyner's Jacks Creek (Jacks Creek, Tenn.), 96. *See also* Jacks Creek Bar-B-Que (Jacks Creek, Tenn.)

Kansas City Barbecue Society, 124, 126, 141, 146
Kansas City–style barbecue, 34
Kelly, Leslie, 3
Keogh, Pamela Clarke, 35
Kiple, Kenneth F., 26
Kliebenstein, James, 112
Knoxville, Tenn. (Knox County), 110

labor, 19, 39, 44, 85, 96, 98–101
lamb and sheep, 28, 30–31, 66, 124, 191
Lamphere, Louise, 15
Land of the Pines. *See* Piney Woods region
landscape, cultural, 183
landscape, ecological, 183
landscapes, barbecue. *See* barbecue landscapes
Lansky, Meyer, 37
Larson, Ben, 112
Latour, Bruno, 181

Lehman, John, 66
Leonard's Pit Barbecue (Memphis, Tenn.), 16, 35–36
Lévi-Strauss, Claude, 1, 19–20
Lexington, Tenn. (Henderson County), 85, 86–89, 95–96, 97, 103n2, 172
Lexington-Henderson barbecue corridor, 88
"Lexington-style" barbecue, 5
Lincoln, Abraham, 34
liquid smoke, 57t, 59
Little Pigs (Memphis, Tenn.), 38–39
Little Rock, Ark. (Pulaski County), 172
Liz's Bar-B-Q (Henderson, Tenn.), 84, **91**
Lofland, John, 118
Lofland, Lyn H., 118
Lovegren, Sylvia, 154
Love of the World Reproved, The (Cowper), 95
Luciano, Lucky, 37
Lukes, Steven, 112

Maclin, Edward M., 108, 170, 171, 182, 185–86
Macon, Uncle Dave, 67
Maddox, Lester, 159
Madison, James, 27
Mallinson, Christine, 112
Marcus, George E., 15
Margolick, David, 187
Marianna, Ark. (Lee County), 16, 43–49
Marion, J. Daniel, 174
marketing, barbecue, 110, 113–14, 126, 191
Marshall, Catherine, 15
Martel, Glenn, 52
Mason, Tenn. (Tipton County), 109–11, 184–87, 189–92
mass consumerism, 191
McClard's Bar-B-Q (Hot Springs, Ark.), 11–12, 16, 36–37, 169, 171–73, **173**, 186
McDonaldization, 110
McDonald's, 39, 152
McEwen, Tenn. (Humphreys County), 65–81, 169

meat
    marbling in, 123, 156, 163
    pink smoke ring on, 108, 128, 154
    See also individual types of meat
meat preservation, viii
Memphis, Tenn. (Shelby County). *See* Bill's Bar-B-Q; Charlie Vergos's Rendezvous; Cozy Corner; Interstate Bar-B-Q; Jeff's; Jim's Rib Shack; Joe's After Hours; Johnny Mills's; Leonard's Pit Barbecue; Little Pigs; Memphis-style barbecue; Miss Culpepper's; Payne's Bar-B-Q; Pig n' Whistle; Thomas and Webb pit house
Memphis Commercial Appeal, 40
Memphis Daily Avalanche, 32, 33
Memphis-style barbecue
    and Barbecue Belt, 170–71
    and family events, 107–8, 115
    history of, 33–40
    Memphis in May (MIM) World Championship Barbecue Cooking Contest, 40, 117–50, 165, 171, 183–84
    and race, 93, 111, 159–60
    restaurants (*see* barbecue restaurants; *and individual restaurants*)
    ribs: dry, viii, 5, 38, 60, 125, 155, 172, 182–84; wet, 5, 182
    and ritual, 7–8
    sandwiches: pulled pork, 5, 16, 35, 40; rib, 36
    and technology, 188
    vs. whole-hog traditions, 92–93
Mexican-American War, 31–32
Mickey's Bar-B-Q (Hot Springs, Ark.), 172
Mid-South, the (U.S. region)
    definition, 2–3
    history, 25–40, 169–71
migrants, 26, 66, 169
Mills, Johnny, 35
Mintz, Sidney, 3, 5, 7
Miss Culpepper's (Memphis, Tenn.), 36
Mitchell, Margaret, 159
Moglen, Eben, 109
Monroe, James, 27

Morison, Samuel Eliot, 28
Mussell, Kay, 14, 51, 54
mutton, 26, 34

Nabhan, Gary Paul, 177, 178, 194–95
Nashville Diocese, 67, 69
National Pork Board, 155
Native Americans, vii, 1, 3–4, 25, 54
Nazarea, Virginia D., xi, 179
Neely's Bar-B-Que, 188
Nelson, Davia, 159
networking, social, 19, 188
Neustadt, Kathy, 76
New Georgia Encyclopedia, 159
Newport, Ark. (Jackson County), 58–59, 173
News Democrat, 67–68, 71
Nissenson, Marilyn, 94
Nolan, Justin M., 62

Oldham, Paul, 67, 71, 72, 73
Old Hickory restaurant and barbecue sauce (Newport, Ark.), 58–59, 173
Old Timey Seed Swap, xi, 107
Ollie's Barbecue, 110, 187
oral history, 10, 14, 17–18, 84–85
Ornelas, Kriemhild Conee, 26
Oxford English Dictionary, 1

Papa KayJoe's Bar-B-Que (Centerville, Tenn.), 12–13
Parrington, Vernon, 109, 115
patriarchy, 53, 114
Payne's Bar-B-Q (Memphis, Tenn.), 10
Pearl, Minnie, 67
Pena, Erik, 189
Petrini, Carlo, 152–53, 155, 158, 162
Philpott, Tom, 162
Piazza di Spagna, 151–52
Piggly Wiggly (grocery), 38
Pig n' Whistle (Memphis, Tenn.), 36
pigs. *See* hogs
Piney Hills. *See* Piney Woods region
Piney Woods region, 51–62, **53**, 62n1
    as barbecue crossroads, 55, 56, 60
    barbecue sauce, 57–59, 60
    barbecue style, 54, 55, 57–59

belief systems, 54
culture, 53, 61
ethnicity, 54
and group identity, 53
social history, 53
Pioneers and Makers of Arkansas (Shinn), 42
pitmasters, viii, 153–55, 161, 164–65, 191
  Bannon, Theophilus "Spanky," 45–47
  Blankenship, Curt, 84–102
  Bradley, Cleve, 71–72, 79
  Brummett, Karl, 51–52, 55–56, 61–62
  Cathey, Bessie Louise, 40
  Davis, Abraham, 37, 160
  and gender, 10
  Hampton, Ronnie, 88
  Hays, Dennis, 88–89, 97
  Hilton, Jo, 96–97
  Hodge, Richard, 85–86, 90–91, 93, 97–98
  Hooper, Paul, 78
  Hooper, Scott, 78
  Hooper, Tommy, 72–80, **74,** 82n2
  Hooper, Wayne, 72–80, **78,** 82n2
  Jones, Hubert, 45
  Jones, James, 45–48
  Jones, Walter, 44
  Joyner, Joe, 84–85, 87–88, 91, 93–94, 96, 99–102
  Kinchen, Ike (and Liz), 84, **91,** 91–102
  Latham, Billy Frank, 18, 84–85, 87, 92–94, 99–102
  Mills, Johnny, 35
  Mrs. Softa, 10
  Norwood, Crystal and Derek, 85, 89, 93, 97, 102
  Parker, Ricky, 18, 85–89, **87,** 93–98, 101–2, 103n2
  of Piney Woods region, 59–60
  Ross, Phil, 78
  Scott, B. E. (Early), 86–89, 97, 103n2
  Sellers, Chad, 87–88
  Sells, Bobby, 88
  Siler, Chris, 84, 86, 88–89, **89,** 92–99, 101
  Sis Ward, 10
  Smith, Judy and Jerry, 79
  Soul Sister, 10
  Vergos, Charlie, 16, 38, 172, 183–84, 188–89
  Walsh, Frank, 70–72, 79
  Walsh, Mike, 70–72, 78–79
  Wells, Wayne, 78
  whole-hog, 83–102, **87, 89, 91**
  Willis, James, 35, 159
place, sense of, 6, 13, 90, 151, 160, 189
Pocius, Gerald, 79
politics, 16, 18–19, 27–28, 33, 90, 108–13, 115n2, 159–60
pork
  catfish, 7, 57t
  cooking methods (*see* barbecue, cooking methods)
  ham, 7
  middlin, 7
  organic, 112
  "other white meat, the," 113
  ribs, 7, 11, 35–37, 40, 56, 59
  sausage, 55, 57t, 58, 60–61, 184
  shoulder, 4, 11, 35, 66, 68, 72, 123–24; "Boston Butt," 7, 126; "picnic," 7
  skins, 45
  smoked, 11, 58
  tenderloin, 57t, 58
  ubiquity of, 60, 94–96
  ultralean, 113
  See also hogs, heritage breeds
Porky's (film), 114
poverty, 44, 49, 145
"progress," 52, 192
Prohibition. *See under* alcohol
Purdue University Animal Sciences, 163
Purity Bar-B-Que (Hot Springs, Ark.), 172

race, 4–9, 30, 33–34, 43–49, 112, 159, 182. *See also* African Americans; desegregation; segregation; slavery

RAFT (Renewing America's Food Traditions), 177, 196
Raichlen, Steven, 38
Ranger, Terence, 4
Ransom, Elizabeth, 111
Raw and the Cooked, The (Lévi-Strauss), 1
Reconstruction, 33
Reed, Dale Volberg. See *Holy Smoke*
Reed, John Shelton, 2, 4–6, 90, 92. See also *Holy Smoke* (Reed and Reed)
Rendezvous Ribs. See Charlie Vergos's Rendezvous
Rendezvous rub, 38, 172, 184
Renewing America's Food Traditions (RAFT), 177, 196
research, embedded, 149
Researches into the Early History of Mankind and the Development of Civilization (Tylor), 1
Responsible Forestry, 157
Rhodes, V. James, 110, 113, 187
Richard's Bar-B-Que (Bolivar, Tenn.), 84–85, 96
Ridgewood Barbecue, 170
ritual, ix, 7–9, 13, 61, 72, 84, 90–93, 95, 149
Ritzer, George, 110
Robbins, Michael M., 62
Robbins, William, 188
Rolling Stone (magazine), 162
Rose, Willie Lee Nichols, 30
Rosenthal, Elisabeth, 157
Rossman, Gretchen B., 15
Rustic Inn, 37

sauce ingredients
  "Big Four," 19, 171, 172, 173
  mustard, viii, 8, 46, 57t, 57–59, 170, 172–73
  and secrecy, 12, 61, 71–72, 97–98, 168–69, 173, 175, 177
  tomato (heirloom), 19, 176–79
scale, 34, 92, 99, 108–10, 113, 183, 197
Schäufele, 4

Scheper-Hughes, Nancy, 15
Schlosser, Eric, 112
Scott's-Parker's Barbecue (Lexington, Tenn.), 85, **87**, 89, 95–96, 97, 172. See also B. E. Scott's Barbecue (Lexington, Tenn.)
Securities and Exchange Commission, 39
seed savers, 177–78. See also seed swaps
seed swaps, xi, 107. See also Old Timey Seed Swap; Southern Seed Legacy
segregation, 35, 44, 159–60. See also civil rights movement
sense of place, 6, 13, 90, 151, 160, 189
Serematakis, C. Nadia, 10–11
Sheehan, Jason, 160, 192
sheep and lamb, 28, 30–31, 66, 124, 191
Shemwell's Barbecue (Cairo, Ill.), 170
Shinn, Josiah H., 27
side dishes, 8, 10, 30, 74–75, 139
  baked beans, 57, 57t, 114, 139
  barbecue spaghetti, 25
  beans, 57t, 58, 139
  Brunswick stew, 169
  cobbler, 30, 58, 140
  coleslaw (*see* slaw)
  corn bread, 30, 139
  ginger cake, 30
  hush puppies, 139
  potato salad, 58, 74–75, 139, 174
  sweet potato fries, 111
  sweet potato pies, 30
  tamales, 25, 37, 57t, 58
Siler's Old Time BBQ (Henderson, Tenn.), 84, 86, **89**, 89–90, 94, 96–97. See also Bobby's Bar-B-Q (Henderson, Tenn.)
Silva, Nikki, 159
Sim's Bar-B-Que (Little Rock, Ark.), 172
Sinatra, Frank, 188
slavery, 16–17, 29–31, 159, 168, 194, 196
slaw
  on barbecue sandwiches, 8, 25, 35, 57, 57t, 171, 186

as side dish, 58, 74–75, 115, 139, 140, 174
ubiquity of, 2, 57
slow food (traditional)
definition, 153
endangered, 161
Slow Food (movement), 18–19, 114, 151–66, 176, 193
Slow Food Ark of Taste Program, 164
Slow Food International, 152
Slow Food Manifesto, 152
Slow Food USA, 164
Smith, Stephen, 9
smoke ring, 108, 128, 154
social behavior, viii, ix, 51–52, 90–93, 111–12, 132, 138, 144–45
social media, 19, 120, 132–33, 188, 191
social networking, 19, 120, 132–33, 188
social relationships, 5, 26, 52, 54, 181, 187. *See also* gender; race; social behavior; Southern culture
Society for Applied Anthropology, xi, 183
sorghum, viii, 56, 57t, 84
South, the (U.S. region), 2, 25–40, 86, 169–71
Southern culture
of barbecue, 13, 83, 167, 181, 192–96
commodification of, 111
history, 53, 83, 169–71
identity, 60 (*see also* identity formation)
Southern Food (Egerton), 44, 90, 169, 172
Southern Foodways Alliance, 10, 13, 84, 103, 159
Southern politics, 2, 6, 9, 16, 27–28, 33, 48
Southern Seed Legacy, xi, 108, 176
seed swap, xi, 107
Spanish Steps, 151–52
Sperling's Best Places, 66
Staten, Vince, 36, 37, 86

Sticky Fingers (Charleston, S.C.), 40
St. Patrick's Church and School (McEwen, Tenn.), 65–81, **68**, **74**
St. Patrick's Irish Picnic, 17, 65–81, **68**, **74**, 169
Stubby's Bar-B-Que, 172
Supreme Court, U.S. *See* U.S. Supreme Court cases, barbecue
Sutton, David E., 7, 10, 51
swine. *See* hogs

Taino Indians (Caribbean), vi, viii, 25
Tall Pine Country. *See* Piney Woods region
tamales, 25, 37, 57, 58
Taylor, Joe Gray, 90
Telli, Andy, 66, 72
Tennessean (Nashville), 71
Tennessee barbecue
Appalachian Mountains and, 170
in barbecue geography, 5
and family histories, 2
history (*see* barbecue, history of)
in McEwen, Tenn., 65–82, 169
and online communities, 188–91
regional diversity of, 155
restaurants (*see* barbecue restaurants; *and individual restaurants*)
and ritual, 8
as social event, 107–8
and social networking, 188–91
See also Memphis-style barbecue; West Tennessee–style barbecue; whole-hog barbecue
Tennessee Register, 67
Texas-style barbecue, 2–3, 5, 8, 10, 34, 38, 59–60, 171–72
Thomas, Charles E., 52
Thomas and Webb pit house (Memphis, Tenn.), 87
Thu, Kendall M., 110, 113, 187
Tietz, Jeff, 162, 163
Tigrett, Isaac, 191
Timber Country. *See also* Piney Woods region; Timberlands
Timberlands, 3, 17, 52, 60, 61, 172. *See also* Piney Woods region

Time (magazine), 39, 160
tomatoes, heirloom
    Beefheart, 177
    Brandywine, 177
    Cow Tits, 178
    Mister Stripey, 178
    mountain, 176
    Red Oxheart, 177
traditions, consumable, 62
Trillin, Calvin, 40
Trolinger, Shannon, 65, 67, 69, 70, 72
Tylor, E. B., 1

University of Gastronomic Sciences, 152
University of Georgia, 176
U.S. Census, 66, 71, 93
U.S. Department of Agriculture, 156
U.S. Supreme Court cases, barbecue
    Bozo's trademark, 187
    Katzenbach v. McClung, 187
    Ollie's Barbecue, 110, 187

Van Esterik, Penny, 4–5, 9, 54
Veteto, James R., 62, 107, 108, 170, 171, 182, 185–86, 193–94
vinegar, 57t
    and food preservation, vii
    See also under barbecue traditions, geographic; sauce ingredients
Virginia, colony of, 25
Virginia "barbecue day," 26

Walk the Line (film), 185
Warnes, Andrew, 1, 3–4, 10, 14, 85
Washington, George, 27, 168
Watson, James L., 19, 108, 112
Weaver, William W., 178
Weiner, Mark S., 110, 187

Welch, Kelly, 187
West Tennessee–style barbecue
    and family events, 107–9
    and the Mid-South, 2
    pulled pork, 107, 182
    regional diversity in, 155
    and ritual, 8
    whole-hog, 83–102
Whippoorwill Hollow Farm, 193
Whitehead, Tony, 76
whole-hog barbecue, 5, 83–102, **87, 89, 91**
    endangered, 85, 99–101
    future of, 102, 192–96
    history, 26, 84–102
    origin story, 85–86
wild game, 28, 34, 46–47
Williams, Thomas Jefferson "Bozo," 185. *See also* Bozo's Bar-B-Q (Mason, Tenn.)
Willie King's, 36
wood
    alder, vii
    cherry, 121
    hickory, vii, 11, 28–29, 57, 57t, 59, 96, 108, 115, 121
    maple, 121
    mesquite, vii, 57t, 59
    oak, vii, 28, 45, 46, 57, 57t, 59, 108
    pecan, vii, 37
Wright, Wynne, 111
Writing Culture (Clifford and Marcus), 15

York, Jake A., 174
York, Jamie, 159
"yuppie chow," 112

www.ingramcontent.com/pod-product-compliance
Lightning Source LLC
Chambersburg PA
CBHW032052300426
44116CB00007B/701